Charles Hastings Collette

The Novelties of Romanism - In Three Parts

I. Development of Doctrines. II. Chronological Arrangement. III. Old and New Creeds Contrasted

Charles Hastings Collette

The Novelties of Romanism - In Three Parts
I. Development of Doctrines. II. Chronological Arrangement. III. Old and New Creeds Contrasted

ISBN/EAN: 9783337048303

Printed in Europe, USA, Canada, Australia, Japan

Cover: Foto ©Lupo / pixelio.de

More available books at **www.hansebooks.com**

THE NOVELTIES OF ROMANISM.

IN THREE PARTS:

I.—DEVELOPMENT OF DOCTRINES.
II.—CHRONOLOGICAL ARRANGEMENT.
III.—OLD AND NEW CREEDS CONTRASTED.

BY

CHARLES HASTINGS COLLETTE.

SECOND EDITION.
REVISED AND ENLARGED.

LONDON:
THE RELIGIOUS TRACT SOCIETY;
56, PATERNOSTER ROW, 65, ST. PAUL'S CHURCHYARD, AND
164, PICCADILLY: AND SOLD BY THE BOOKSELLERS.

"Hoc enim vel maximè, frater, laboramus, et laborare debemus, ut unitatem à DOMINO, *et per Apostolos* nobis successoribus traditam, quantum possumus, obtenere curemus," &c.

CYPRIAN, Epist. xlv., p. 91. Lipsiæ, 1838.

PREFACE.

The two leading claims made by the CHURCH of ROME are *Infallibility* and *Immutability*.

I. As to *Infallibility*: she claims to be guided in all her deliberations by the presiding presence of the HOLY GHOST. In what way this infallibility is proved to exist has never yet been made apparent; nor are the members of this Church agreed as to the locality or official organ of this Divine attribute. The claim is made, and that is sufficient. Her maxim is—

Roma locuta est: causa finita est.

II. As to *Immutability*: she claims to be absolutely unchangeable. She asserts that her doctrines and discipline have been the same always and everywhere. Her maxim and motto are—

Semper eadem!

While ascribing these two attributes to their Church, we cannot be surprised to find that the doctors of the Council of Trent professed to found all their decrees on alleged anterior fundamental truths, recognised as having existed from the introduction of Christianity. They declared that all the doctrines and practices which they, in that council, decided to be true and obligatory, were always the received doctrines and practices of the "Catholic church" in every age, without any variation from the time of Christ and his apostles, from whom each of such doctrines and practices originated; and that they were handed down by one unbroken tradition to the time of the assembly of this last (so-called) General Council of the Church. The assembled doctors professed to have simply *declared* what was of faith previous to that time. They do not pretend to have invented any new doctrine, but simply to have defined and declared what the doctrine of the Church was and always had been from the time of the apostles down to the meeting of the Council.[1]

---

[1] The following are a few of the sentences continually recurring in the proceedings of the Council of Trent:—

"Semper hæc fides in Ecclesia Dei fuit." Sess. xiii. c. 3.

"Ideo persuasum semper in Ecclesia Dei fuit, idque nunc denuo sancta hæc Synodus declarat." Sess. xiii. c. 4.

"Pro more in Catholica Ecclesia semper recepto." Sess. xiii. c. 5.

"Universa Ecclesia semper intelexit." Sess. xiv. c. 5.

"Persuasum semper in Ecclesia Dei fuit: et verissimum esse Synodus hæc confirmat." Sess. xv. c. 7.

"Sacræ literæ ostendunt et Catholicæ Ecclesiæ traditio semper docuit." Sess. xxiii. c. 1.

"Cum, Scripturæ testimonio, apostolica traditione, et patrum unanimi consensu, perspicuum sit:—dubitare nemo debet." Sess. xxiii. c. 3.

"Cum, igitur,—sancti patres nostri, Concilia, et universalis Ecclesiæ traditio, semper docuerunt:—sancta et universalis Synodus, prædictorum schismaticorum hæreses et errores,—exterminandos duxit." Sess. xxiv.

See also Sess. v. and Sess. xiii.

In perfect accordance with these views, thus decidedly enunciated by the Papal Church, a Roman Catholic bishop, at a public meeting at Warrington, on the occasion of the consecration of a burial ground, recently stated "that he was the representative in this country of no new system of religion, and the teacher of no new doctrines."

This public declaration suggested to the writer the compilation of the facts constituting the present volume, under the title of "NOVELTIES OF ROMANISM," as a reply to the broad and positive assertions thus confidently put forward by the Romish Church. These facts, he believes, are now for the first time brought together in such a manner as will enable the reader to trace the rise, progress, and final development of each successive *novelty* of that Church, in chronological order, divested of all controversial bias.

Part I. must not be considered otherwise than as furnishing a few plain proofs of the *novelties* of the doctrines treated. It was not the intention of the writer to attempt *a refutation* of the doctrines in question. That necessarily follows if they are proved to be of modern invention.

Part II., following the order of time, traces, through successive centuries, the chronological development of papal error, superstition, ecclesiastical arrogance, and priestly assumption.

Part III. presents the contrast between the simple scriptural creed of the primitive Church and that of Romanism, as fully developed and consolidated by the Council of Trent.

While the writer claims for his labour the merit of a compilation only, he may be permitted to hope that the reader will be thus furnished with a body of facts and trustworthy materials, which will be found useful in these times, should circumstances bring him into controversy with a Romanist.

CONTENTS.

	PAGE
INTRODUCTION	xvii

The objection of a Priest of Rome to argue with a Layman, because he is a Priest, considered. Title to Priestly Orders questioned. The doctrine of Intention. Cardinal Bellarmine's testimony as to the uncertainty of Priestly Orders, grounded on the doctrine of Intention. Bishop Caterino's opinion to the like effect. Orders not a Sacrament, and so admitted by Dominicus Soto. The Roman Catholic Priest cannot prove himself to be otherwise than a Layman.

PART I.

THE DEVELOPMENT OF DOCTRINES.

CHAPTER I.

SUPREMACY 1

Bellarmine's proposition that the Pope's Supremacy is proved by his titles, considered, 2. Prince of Priests—High Priest, 2. Universal Bishop, 3. Pelagius II. and Gregory I. reject the title, 3. Simon Vigorius on title "Universal Bishop," 5. Applied to Athanasius by Gregory Nazianzen, 5. Vicar of Christ, 6. Synods of Compiegne and Melun, 6. Dens on this title, 7. The title of Pope, 7. The restricted authority of the Bishop of Rome, even in Italy, 8. The Bishops of Milan, Aquilia, and Ravenna, independent of the Bishop of Rome, 8. "Mother and Mistress of all Churches," 8. Claims refuted by Ecclesiastical History, 9. Councils: Nice, Constantinople, Ephesus, Chalcedon, Constantinople II. and III., Nice II., 9—11. The Greek Church, 11.

CHAPTER II.

CANON OF SCRIPTURE... 13

Decree of Trent Council, 13. List of Apocryphal Books, 14. Trent declaration challenged, 14. List of Fathers and Doctors from the Apostles to the 16th century, in regular succession, who rejected the Apocrypha, 16—20.

CHAPTER III.

CANON OF SCRIPTURE (*continued*)....................................... 20

Authorities relied on by Romanists to prove the Apocrypha canonical, considered, 20. Council of Sardis—Council of Carthage, 21. Augustine, 24. Cajetan on the Sacred Canon, 25. Innocent I., 27. Isidore, 27. Gelasius, 28. Council of Toledo, 28. Council of Florence, 29. The Council of Trent shown to be the only authority, 29.

CHAPTER IV.

INTERPRETATION OF SCRIPTURE 30

The Interpretation of the Church and of the Fathers, the Doctrine of Rome, 31. This Doctrine invented in 1564, 31. The difficulties of the doctrine, 31, 32.

I. *The Interpretation of the Church.*—The startling statements of Cardinals Hosius and Cusanus, 35. What is the Church? 33. Bellarmine's several definitions: "The Representative Church," or Councils—"The Essential Church," including Laymen and Priests, have published no interpretation, 33. "The Consistorial Church," or "Court of Rome"—examples of interpretation examined and shown to be erroneous, 33. "The Virtual Church," *i.e.*, the Pope—examples given and admitted to be erroneous, 36. The Parish Priest, 37.

II. *Interpretation of Fathers*, their unanimous agreement required, 38. A "dead lock" as to the Scriptures, 38. Examples of leading texts on which Romanists rely, to prove peculiar doctrines on which Fathers either differed among themselves or modern Romanists differ from them, 39. And instances of interpretation given by Fathers expressly rejected by Romanists because they go against their modern doctrines, 40. Cornelius Mus on Relative value of Popes and Fathers, 42.

CHAPTER V.

TRANSUBSTANTIATION 43

Definition, 43. Pope Nicholas II., 44. Berengarius—Bellarmine, 45. Doctrine alleged to be founded on authority of Scripture, examined, 46.

CONTENTS.

On the alleged conversion of the substance of the elements, 46. Admission by Cardinals and Romish Doctors that it cannot be proved by Scripture, 47. Cajetan—Suarez—Bishop Fisher—Scotus—Alliaco, 47, 48—Augustine and Cajetan on the parallel between the two expressions "this is my body," and "the rock was Christ," 48. Rests on the authority of Pope Innocent III., 49. Observation on the Fourth Lateran Council, 49.

Proofs or admissions that the doctrine is modern: Scotus, Peter Lombard, Gelasius, Theodoret, Chrysostom, Ephrem, 50—52.

On the alleged "Real Presence," 53. The elements, symbols, figures, types, or images, 54. Clementine Liturgy, 54. Origen—Irenæus—Clement of Alexandria—Tertullian—Eusebius—Cyril of Jerusalem—Gregory Nazianzen—Marcarius—Ambrose—Jerome—Augustine—Theodoret—Gelasius, 55—57. The Greeks at the Council of Florence, 58.

CHAPTER VI.

INVOCATION OF SAINTS 59

The true question at issue stated, 59. Trent definition, 60. A religious worship—Delahogue—Veron, 60.

I. The theory pre-supposes that the person invocated must be in a beatific state—Bellarmine's explanation why saints were not invocated in Old Testament, 60. *Canonization.*—Pope said to be infallible in act of, 61. Decree of Alexander III., 61. Dens' reasoning why the Pope should be infallibly correct, 62. Not an Article of Faith, 62. Veron's opinion destroys the whole system, 63.

II. State of souls after death, speculation on, 65. Prayers for the Dead, 65. Led to the introduction of Saint Worship, 66. Romish difficulties: Luke xv. 10, 67—Eccles. ix. 5, 68. Romish doubts as to how Saints perceive our prayers, 68. Bellarmine—Biel—Veron, 69.

III. The alleged Antiquity of Doctrine, 69. Bellarmine—why prayers to Saints not mentioned in the Old Testament—Eckius admits not recognised in the New Testament—Veron's acknowledgment—alleged tradition examined, 70. When first used in Liturgies—Negative testimony from Fathers, 71. Positive testimony of Irenæus against the practice, 72. Delahogue and Perron's reasons why the doctrine is not found in the Fathers, 72, 73. First act of Angel Worship condemned by Council of Laodicea, 73. This Council strangely perverted by Merlin and Crabhe, 73. The Fathers included in their prayers for the Dead those now invoked by Romanists, 74. Controversies as to state of soul after death, 74. Those who held that Saints do not enjoy the Presence of God until Day of Judgment, 75. Augustine's testimony, 75. The points established, 76.

CONTENTS.

CHAPTER VII.

IMAGE WORSHIP 77

Trent doctrine, 77. Various opinions of Romish Doctors as to quality of worship, 78. Trent doctrine of Relative Worship, 78. Repudiated by Aquinas and others, 79. The doctrine of Relative Worship examined, 80. A Heathen argument condemned by Arnobius, Origen, Ambrose, and Augustine, 80. Introduction of Images in churches, opposed by Lactantius, 83. The testimony of Erasmus, Cornelius Agrippa and Agobard, 83, 84. A "Papal war" of opinions from A.D. 300 to Council of Trent, 1563, 84—87.

CHAPTER VIII.

IMAGE WORSHIP (*continued*) 88

On the Second Commandment, 88. On the translation "graven image," 88. On the word "adore," 90. On the division of the Commandments, 90. Omission of the Second Commandment from various Catechisms, 91—96.

CHAPTER IX.

PURGATORY 96

Importance of Doctrine, 96. Definition, 97. First Conciliar Decree (A.D. 1439), 98. Admission by Benedictine Editors of Ambrose's Works, that the doctrine could not have been admitted until 1439, 98. Dr. Wiseman admits doctrine not taught in Scripture, 99. His theory examined, 100. Veron's "Rule of Catholic Faith," 101.

The doctrine founded on Prayers for the Dead, and alleged evidence of Fathers, 101. First suggested by Origen, but his theory was condemned by a General Council and by Augustine, 104. Augustine's theory, 105. That of Gregory I., 105. Admission of Fisher, Bishop of Rochester, that the doctrine is of modern date, 106.

CHAPTER X.

PENANCE 106

One of Rome's Seven Sacraments, 106. The number seven first fixed by Council of Florence, 1439, 107—Cassander traces the adoption of this number to 1140, 107. The alleged effect of the Sacraments conferring grace, modern invention, 108.

Penance defined—The first integral part, Contrition and Attrition, 108. Forgiveness of sin granted without contrition, *i.e.*, true repentance, 110. The object of the teaching, 110. The Priest represents Christ, 110. The second integral part, Confession and Absolution, proved to be a modern invention, 112. Celestial Treasure of the Church, 114. Third integral part, Satisfaction—One man satisfying for another—The enormity of the doctrine, 114.

CHAPTER XI.

INDULGENCES 115

Alleged popular Protestant fallacies, 115. Pardon of Sin promised, proved to be so by Pope's Bulls, 117. Alleged to be only a remission of punishment due to the sin already forgiven in the Sacrament of Penance, 118. This position refuted, 118. Benefit alleged to depend on the disposition of the recipient, proved to be fallacious, 120. Sales denied, 122. Sales proved, 123. The theory of the "Celestial Treasure," 124. Contradictory opinions held by Romanists themselves, 125. Veron's theory of Indulgences, 125. Contradicted by Popes, 127.

Jubilee defined, 130. First Jubilee, 130. Various periods for granting Jubilees, altered by successive Popes from 100 years, to 6 years, 131. Immoral effects of, 132. Terms on which benefit of Jubilee may be gained, according to Dr. Wiseman, 133. These terms examined, and contradictory opinions of Romanists quoted, 134.

The fundamental principles on which Indulgences are based, challenged, 135. The alleged antiquity of the doctrine, challenged, 138. A pious fraud, 139.

CHAPTER XII.

TRADITION.. 139

Previously mentioned doctrines assumed to depend on Tradition, 140. The allegation of the Trent Council, and definition, 140. Importance of the doctrine, 141. Alleged to be of greater authority than Scripture, 141. Costerus, 141. The Trent allegation proved to be untrue, 141. Traditions founded on alleged matters of fact, 142. Various opinions expressed at Trent Council on, 143. Admissions by Romanists that they teach doctrines not revealed in Scripture, 144. Dr. Wiseman's definition of Tradition, 144. Reduced, nevertheless, to writing, 145. Difficulties attending the system, 146. Authority of the Fathers, 147. Remarkable admissions of the Fathers: Irenæus, Tertullian, Eusebius, Gregory of Nyssa, Cyril of Jerusalem, Theophilus of Alexandria, 148—150. The case stated on the ground of Tradition, 151.

PART II.

CHRONOLOGICAL ARRANGEMENT.

CHRIST is the foundation. The Doctrine of the Apostles, 155.
Original simplicity of worship, as testified by Justyn Martyr, 156.

A.D. 109—First innovation, mixing water with the wine at the Lord's Supper, 157.
,, 110—Offerings at the celebration of the Lord's Supper in course of time called Oblations, and then " Sacrifices," 158.
,, 113—Holy Water, Pagan origin and Heathen rise, 158 (see post, A.D. 852), and present abuse, 159. Customs considered at that time heretical, now orthodox in modern Roman Church, 160.
,, 140—Fast of Lent, 160.
,, 160—Annual commemorations of the departed, 161, not a religious worship, but which led to Prayers for the Dead, intercession of departed, and ultimately the Sacrifice of the Mass, 162.
,, 200—Offerings in memory of Martyrs, led to Offerings for the Dead, 162, and Prayers for the Dead, but had no reference to Purgatory, 163.
,, 240—First step to Intercession of Saints, but it was the departed for the living, 163.
,, 250—Attempt of the Bishop of Rome to domineer ecclesiastically, but rebuked, 163.
,, 257—Hallowing Priests' vestures, altar-cloths, and church ornaments, 164.
,, 260—Monasticism, 164. Sign of the Cross, 165. Discipline and Public Penance led to Indulgences, 166.
,, 290—Orders of the Priesthood, 166.
,, 300—Altars, 167. Sacrifice (the meaning of the word), note ^{2}, 167. Relics of Martyrs, of Pagan origin, 167. Consecration of Churches, and Ceremonies, 168
,, 325—First General Council, 168. Ecclesiastical Jurisdiction of Metropolitan Bishops declared, 168. The position of Rome and Constantinople defined, 168, 169. Celibacy of Priests mooted, 169. Friday a fast-day, 171.
,, 347—The supposed decree of the Council of Sardis as to authority of Bishop of Rome, 171. Contradicts the previous council of Antioch, 172.
,, 350—The derivation of the term "The Mass," 172. Its history, of Pagan origin, 173.
,, 366—The Appellate Jurisdiction of the Church of Rome under an order of the Emperor Valentinian, 173. Extended only to the West, 173. Did not extend to criminal cases, 174. Reasons for this precedence to Rome, 174.
,, 370—Apostrophes to Saints, which led to their Invocation, 174. Angel Worship condemned by the Council of Laodicea, 175.
,, 380—Praying for the Dead in general use, but no reference to Purgatory, 176. Paintings in churches opposed, 176.
,, 386—First Decree (if not spurious) against the Marriage of Priests, 177. Examples of married Priests, Bishops, and Popes, 177. Cyprian and Augustine as to corruptions and innovations, 178.

CONTENTS.   xiii

A.D. 390—First Private Confessions, 179. The Penitentiary Presbyter, 179.
,,   397—Mass ordered to be said fasting, 180.
,,   400—Speculation on an intermediate future state the origin of Purgatory, 180.
        When the Bishop of Rome was first styled simply as "Pope," 181 (see
        A.D. 1073).
,,   417—Pascal candles, 181.
,,   419—First interference in the election of a Bishop of Rome, 181.
,,   431—First civil Law passed granting asylum to fugitives in churches, 182
        (see A.D. 620). The origin of the "Keys" as a papal emblem of, 182.
,,   434—The right of calling Councils, supposed to be assumed by Sixtus III.;
        the document spurious, and also the documents quoted to establish
        appeals to Rome, 183.
,,   450—Interference by the Bishop of Rome in election of other Bishops, 185.
        But practised by other Bishops, 185. Leo assumes a supremacy in the
        West—resisted by Hilary, 186.
,,   460—Fasts of Lent and Whitsuntide, 188.
,,   470—Invocation of a Saint (first act of), 188. "Mother of God" used in
        Prayers, 188. Commemoration changed to Invocation, 188.
,,   492—Soaking or dipping bread at the Eucharist, 189. The introduction of
        half communion, but restrained by Bishops Leo and Gelasius, 189.
        Gelasius denied the conversion of elements in the Eucharist, 190.
,,   500—Images first used as historical monuments, 191.
,,   528—Extreme Unction introduced, but not as a sacrament, 191.
,,   529—Order of Benedictine Monks founded, 192.
,,   535—Processions before festival of Easter, 192.
,,   536—Clergy exempted from civil jurisdiction, 192.
,,   538—Turning the face to the east, and its history, 193. Feast of Purification—
        Candlemas, 194. Burning tapers in honour of the Virgin, 194. Pro-
        cession of Wax-lights, 194.
,,   595—Title of Universal Bishop assumed by the Bishop of Constantinople and
        opposed by the Bishop of Rome, 194. The pagan origin of the title
        "Pontifex Maximus," and "Summus Sacerdos," 195.
,,   600—Invocation of Saints recognised, 196. The ora pro nobis introduced, 196.
        Invocation of Saints of Pagan origin, 196. Progress of Purgatory and
        Masses for the Dead, 197. The Office of the Mass, 198. Pontifical
        habits — Processions and Pictures of the Virgin Mary—Perfumes—
        Candles—Fasting, 198.
,,   604—Ritualistic use of Lamps and Wax-tapers, of Pagan origin, 198.
,,   607—Spiritual Primacy, 199.
,,   610—Dedication of Temples to Saints—All Saints, 200. Tonsure, its Pagan
        origin, 200.
,,   617—Invocation of Saints introduced into the Latin Liturgy, 201.
,,   620—Law making churches a place of protection confirmed, 201 (see A.D. 431).
,,   631—Invention and Exaltation of the Cross, 202.
,,   666—Service in Latin, 202.
,,   682—First act of absolving a subject from his allegiance to the King, 202.
,,   685—To this date election of the Bishop of Rome vested in the Emperor, 203.
,,   700—Private or Solitary Masses, 204. The Wafer, 205.
,,   750—Absolution after Confession, 205.
,,   752—Elevating the Bishop of Rome on the shoulders, on his election, 206.

CONTENTS.

A.D. 754—Image Worship condemned, 206. Invocation of the Virgin Mary and the Saints first enjoined under Anathema by a Council, 206.
" 763—First act of compulsory oral confession, 206. Ecclesiastical Order of Canons; hence Secular and Regular Canons, 206.
" 768—Tithes made compulsory, 207.
" 770—Decree on Image Worship by a Provincial Council, 207.
" 787—Image Worship decreed by a General Council, 207. Lighting tapers, 208. Remarks on the progress of Transubstantiation, 208.
" 795—Incense introduced, 211.
" 800—The Temporal Supremacy of the Bishop of Rome established, 211. The Forged Decretals, 215.
" 818—Transubstantiation progresses, but receives a check, 215.
" 845—Confirmation instituted as a sacrament, 217.
" 850—Unction sanctioned and made a sacrament, 218.
" 852—Sprinkling of Holy Water on people, cattle, etc., 218 (see *ante*, A.D. 113).
" 855—Feast of the Assumption, 218.
" 869—Tradition written (not oral) established as of authority, 218.
" 884—Canonization of Saints, 219. Invocation of Saints authorized, 220.
" 956—The first time a Pope changed his name on his election, 220.
" 965—Baptism of Bells, 221.
" 1000—Before this date the modern Romish doctrine of Absolution unknown, 221. Consecrations, 222. The Little Office of the Virgin, 222. Sacrificing Priests, 222. The Sacrament of the Eucharist changed into a Sacrifice, 223.
" 1003—Feast of All Souls, founded on Paganism, 223.
" 1022—Penance commuted for money, 223.
" 1055—Redemption of Penances, 224. Whipping, 224.
" 1059—Berengarius' forced recantation, 225. Transubstantiation recognised 225.
" 1060—Election of Bishops of Rome restricted to the unanimous consent of the Cardinals, Clergy, and Laity, 225.
" 1070—Purgatory progresses, 226.
" 1073—The title of Pope exclusively applied to the Bishop of Rome, 226 (see A.D. 400).
" 1074—Compulsory Celibacy, 226. The opinions of Roman Doctors on the Subject, 227. Deposition of Sovereigns, 229.
" 1090—Chaplets—Paternosters, 229.
" 1095—Communion in one kind prohibited by Council, 230 (see A.D. 1414)
" 1098—Order of Cistercians founded, 230. Carthusians (A.D. 1084)—Carmelites (A.D. 1185), 230.
" 1123—Decree against Marriage of Presbyters, Deacons, etc., 231.
" 1130—Sacraments defined to be Seven, 231.
" 1140—The Festival of the Conception introduced, but opposed, 231 (see A.D. 1476). The three parts of Penance, Contrition, Confession, and Satisfaction, first defined, 232.
" 1151—Gratian's Decretals—Canon Law, 232.
" 1160—No Saint to be acknowledged, as such, unless canonized by a Pope, 233. Indulgences, 234.
" 1182—The Election of Popes restricted to the Cardinals by General Council, 234.

CONTENTS.

A.D. 1215—Auricular Confession established, 235. A heathen custom, 235. Prayers in a tongue not understood by the people, not the practice of this age, 236. Transubstantiation confirmed, 238. Pixes, 238.
,, 1217—Elevation and adoration of the Host, 239.
,, 1229—The Bible forbidden to the Laity, 242.
,, 1230—Little Bell added to the Mass, 242.
,, 1237—Salve Regina, 243.
,, 1238—The Pope of Rome excommunicated by the Patriarch of Antioch, 243.
,, 1245—Cardinals' red hats and cloaks, 243.
,, 1264—Feast of "Fête Dieu," or *Corpus Christi* Day; its history, 243. Ecclesiastical Treasure and Works of Supererogation, 245.
,, 1300—First Jubilee, 245. Indulgences extended to souls in Purgatory, 246.
,, 1317—Clementine Constitutions, Ave Maria, 246.
,, 1360—Procession of the Host, derived from the heathens, 246.
,, 1362—The first use of the triple crown, 247. The coronation of Popes, 247.
,, 1366—The Rose of Gold, 248.
,, 1390—The Sale of Indulgences, 248.
,, 1414—Half Communion, 249 (see A.D. 1095, p. 230).
,, 1438—The Pragmatic Sanction, the rampart of the Gallican Church against Rome's usurped power, 250.
,, 1439—Seven Sacraments, 250. The Primacy asserted by Council of Florence, 251. Repudiated by the Greeks, 252. Pope called Vicar of Christ, 253.
,, 1470—Rosary of the Virgin Mary, and origin of the term, 253.
,, 1476—Feast of the Conception, 254. A history of the doctrine of the "Immaculate Conception," 254.
,, 1478—The Inquisition, 258.
,, 1495—Dispensations to marry within prohibited degree. 259.
,, 1515—The Great Sale of Indulgences, and Reformation, 259.
,, 1540—The Order of the Jesuits, 259.
,, 1545—Council of Trent, 260.
,, 1546—Tradition, 260. Apocryphal Books, 260. Original Sin and Justification, 261.
,, 1547—Priestly Intention, 262. Seven Sacraments confirmed, 263.
,, 1551—Doctrine of Attrition, 264.
,, 1552—The Lord's Prayer allowed to be said to the Saints, 265.
,, 1563—Purgatory confirmed, 265.
,, 1564—When a new Creed was published, and the following were added as *Articles of Faith*, for the first time, 265:
    1. All Observances and Constitutions of the Church of Rome, 266.
    2. The Interpretation of Scriptures according to the sense of the Church of Rome, 266.
    3. The Interpretation of Scriptures only according to the unanimous agreement of the Fathers, 266.
    4. All the received and approved Ceremonies of the Church of Rome, and all other things defined by Œcumenical Councils, 267.
    5. The Church of Rome to be the Mother and Mistress of all Churches; obedience to the Pope of Rome, as successor of St. Peter and Vicar of Christ, 267.

PART III.

THE OLD AND NEW CREEDS CONTRASTED.

The Acts and Objects of the Reformers, 271. Creeds: Irenæus, Tertullian, Origen, Cyril of Jerusalem, Nicene-Constantinopolitan, 272—276. *Filioque*, 276. Councils of Ephesus and Chalcedon oppose innovations, 276. The truths handed down by the Church of Rome in contrast with her errors, 278. Cyprian and Tertullian on the claims of Custom and Antiquity, 280.

APPENDICES.

APPENDIX A.—Extract from the Work of Bertram of Corby, 287.
APPENDIX B.—Bull of Pope Pius IV., 293.

INTRODUCTION.

The incident which led to the preparation of the present volume has already been adverted to in the preface. It is a reply to the allegation of a Roman Catholic bishop "that he was the representative, in this country, of no new system of religion, and the teacher of no new doctrines." A copy of a previous edition of the work, on its first appearance, was duly forwarded to the rev. doctor, calling in question his broad assertions.

When a professed minister of the gospel presents himself before a mixed audience, and voluntarily makes a bold and startling statement, he is supposed to be prepared with evidence to support that statement; and, when questioned, to be ready to vindicate what he believes, or asserts to be, the truth. Acting, however, on the principle of his sect, the bishop in question maintained a strict silence.

The writer is aware that a priest of the church of Rome makes it a rule not to enter into a discussion with a layman, because he is a layman. The same objection, however, may be raised to any ordained Protestant minister; for, in the priest's estimation, his ordination is invalid, and, therefore, he also is a layman: his challenge may, therefore, with equal show of reason, be rejected. The Romanist may thus escape all explanation when called upon to act on the precept of St. Paul, "to prove all things" (1 Thess. v. 21), and, on the injunction of St. Peter, to be "ready always to give an answer to every man that asketh you a reason of the hope that is in you."

But the claim to the title of "priest" by the Roman priesthood is very questionable; and, when examined on the theory of their own Church, they would have some difficulty in proving that they themselves are anything but laymen.

They derive their title from their ordination, come down to them through an alleged regular and unbroken succession from the apostles. The act of ordination, being a sacrament of their Church, must necessarily be performed by a duly ordained priest, who is also a bishop; and the chain must be perfect in every link from the beginning. By the eleventh canon passed at the seventh session of the Council of Trent it was declared, that intention in the officiating priest to perform a sacrament is necessary to its validity:—

"If any one shall say that intention (at least of doing what the Church does) is not required in ministers when they perform and confer sacraments, let him be accursed."

And further, the same Council declares that even if the officiating priest be in deadly sin, provided he performs the essentials which belong to the administration and conferring of the sacrament, nevertheless a true sacrament is conferred, and if any one deny this also, he is anathematized.[1]

Hence, therefore, the very logical conclusion of Cardinal Bellarmine, that—

"None can be certain, by the certainty of faith, that he

[1] "Si quis dixerit, in ministris, dum sacramenta conficiunt et conferunt, non requiri intentionem saltem faciendi quod facit ecclesia, anathema sit." "Si quis dixerit, ministrum in peccato mortali existentem, modo omnia essentialia quæ ad sacramentum conficiendum aut conferendum pertinent, servaverit, non conficere, aut conferre sacramentum; anathema sit."—Can. et Decr. Concl. Trid. sess. VII. "De Sacramentis in Genere," can. xi., xii. p. 79. Paris, 1842.

receives a true sacrament, since a sacrament cannot be celebrated without the minister's intention; and no one can see the intention of another."[1]

Since the sacrament of Orders depends for its validity on the intention of him who ordains, what certainty has the Roman priest of the intention of the bishop who ordained him? What proof has he of the validity of his ordination? But Bellarmine goes a step further:—

"If we consider in bishops their power of ordination and jurisdiction, we have no more than a moral certainty that they are true bishops."[2]

The higher we go, we multiply the chances, and in proportion decrease the moral certainty.

Thus, then, according to Bellarmine, no single priest of the Romish church can have more than a moral certainty that he is a priest. But we may go further and say that he cannot have even this moral certainty. This is no imaginary position or "theological deduction;" the subject was formally discussed at the seventh session of the Council of Trent on passing the eleventh and twelfth canons just referred to.

One of the essentials is intention in the priest. Will it be argued that a priest in deadly sin can have the true intention? Hear what Ambrogio Caterino, bishop of Minori, said at the Council of Trent, when those decrees were under discussion:—

---

[1] "Neque potest certus esse, certitudine fidei, se percipere verum sacramentum, cum sacramentum sine intentione ministri non conficiatur, et intentionem alterius nemo videre possit."—"Bell. Disput. de Justificatione," lib. iii. c. 8, sec. 5, tom. iv. p. 488. Prag. 1721, and Paris, 1608, tom. iv. col. 946, A.

[2] Bellar. de Milit. Eccles. lib. iii. c. x. ad Secundum, s. 37, tom. ii. p. 82. Prag. 1721.

"But supposing the necessity of mental intention—if a priest, charged with the care of four or five thousand souls, was an unbeliever, but a hypocrite, who, whether in the baptism of children, or in the absolution of penitents, or in the consecration of the eucharist, had no intention of doing what the church does, we must say that all the children were damned, the penitents not absolved, and all those who have received the communion have received no advantage from it."

And he added:—

"If any said that these cases were rare—would to God that in this corrupt age there were no cause to think that they are very frequent. But, even admitting them to be very rare, or even unique; yet suppose, for example, a bad priest, who is a hypocrite, and who has no intention of administering true baptism to a child, and that afterwards this child should become bishop of a great city, and during a long succession of years he has ordained a great number of priests, we must admit that, this child not being baptized, will not have received ordination, and consequently, all those whom he may have ordained will have received nothing, and that thus there will be in this great city neither sacrament, nor penance, nor eucharist, since these cannot exist without ordination, nor ordination without a true bishop, nor any bishop if he has not been previously baptized; and thus, by the malice of a single minister, a million sacraments will be rendered nugatory."[1]

[1] "Que cependant en supposant la nécessité d'une intention intérieure si un prêtre chargé du soin de quatre ou cinq mille âmes était un incrédule mais grand hypocrite, qui, soit dans le baptême des enfants, soit dans l'absolution des pénitens, soit dans la consécration de l'Eucharistie eut intention de ne point faire ce que fait l'Eglise, il faudrait dire que tous les enfants sont damnés, les pénitens nonabsous, et que tous ceux qui ont communié, n'en ont retiré aucun fruit." * * * * "Et si quelqu'un disait que ces cas sont rares, plût à Dieu," ajoutait-il, "que dans ce siècle corrumpu il n'y eût pas lieu de croire qu'ils sont assez fréquens! Mais même en admettent qu'ils sont fort rares, et même uniques, qu'on suppose par exemple un mauvais prêtre, hypocrite et qui n'ait point l'intention d'administrer le véritable baptême à un enfant, et qu'ensuit cet enfant devienne Evêque d'une grande ville, et que pendant une longue suite d'années, il ait ordonné un grand nombre de prêtres; il faudra dire que cet enfant n'étant point baptisé, n'aura point reçu d'ordination, et que par conséquent tous ceux qu'il aura

This is the testimony and opinion of a Roman Catholic bishop!

But to place the matter on still higher grounds—the essence of the title is based on the supposition that "orders" are a sacrament. We deny that "orders" were considered, even by the Roman church, a sacrament, properly so called, for the first six centuries of the Christian era; or that "intention" was considered requisite to give validity to a sacrament, for fifteen centuries after Christ. Bellarmine admits that Dominicus Soto said that " episcopal ordination is not truly and properly a sacrament;"[1] and if not truly and properly a sacrament, then those who ordained during the first six centuries of the Church could not have had the true intention of performing a sacrament.

Here, then, are two essentials, wanting in former ordinations; which, according to modern notions, must, if wanting, render them invalid! It is the fashion with Romish priests to question "Anglican orders;" it would be as well for them to look at home and examine their own title to "orders."

Irrespective, however, of all such abstract questions, when the truth of an assertion made by a minister of the gospel is publicly challenged in a respectful and dignified

---

ordonnés lui même n'auront rien reçu, et qu'ainsi il n'y aura dans cette grande ville ni sacrement ni pénitence, puisqu'il n'y en peut avoir sans ordination, ni ordination sans un véritable Evêque, ni aucun Evêque s'il n'a auparavant été baptisé, et qu'ainsi par la malice d'un seul ministre on rendra nuls un million de sacrements."—" Histoire de Concil de Trente, écrite en Italien [par Paul Sarpi] traduite de nouveau en François, avec des notes, etc., par Pierre François le Courayer," tom. i. lib. ii. pp. 432, 433. Amst. MDCCLI. Father Paul was the principal of the Order of Servites (A.D. 1600). Courayer was a Romish divine, Canon Regular and Librarian of the Abbey of St. Généviève. The third volume of this edition contains a Defence of the Translation by the author.

[1] Bellarm. tom. iii. p. 718. Prag. 1721.

manner, it behoves that man as publicly to vindicate what he believes to be the truth. A conscientious belief in that truth will lead him to "condescend to men of low estate," with the hope of convincing them of their error.

With these few preliminary observations, the writer submits the result of a long and careful examination of facts and documents, which has left in his mind the sincere conviction that the Roman religion is a monstrous delusion, invented to bring man under the subjection of a priesthood which has for many years traded on the credulity of mankind at the imminent risk of the salvation of immortal souls.

PART I.

THE DEVELOPMENT OF DOCTRINES.

THE DEVELOPMENT OF DOCTRINES.

CHAPTER I.

SUPREMACY.

"Neither be ye called masters; for one is your Master, even Christ. But he that is greatest among you shall be your servant. And whosoever shall exalt himself shall be abased; and he that shall humble himself shall be exalted."—MATT. xxiii. 10—12.

A ROMAN Catholic prelate in this country lately delivered an address on the occasion of the consecration, by him, of a piece of ground allotted for the burial of members of his church, in which he is reported to have solemnly maintained that he stood before his hearers as the representative of no new system of religion, the exponent of no novel doctrine; and that the doctrines now taught by his church are the same as those which were preached in this country "by men sent by the pope to convert our poor Saxon forefathers," and as handed down by the apostles. This broad assertion of an alleged historical fact must rest or fall on the evidence adduced to support it.

It is on this assertion that issue is joined, and to its disproof the following pages are devoted.

I. We begin with the subject of prime importance, "Supremacy."

Cardinal Bellarmine says that the doctrine of the Pope's Supremacy is the "sum and substance of Christianity."[1] He says again:—"The Supremacy of the bishop of Rome may be proved by fifteen several names or titles, as, namely, the 'Prince of Priests,' the 'High Priest,' the 'Vicar of Christ,' the 'Universal Bishop,' and the like."[2]

Proof is challenged that any of these titles were given to the bishop of Rome exclusively, from the days of the first bishop of Rome to and including Gregory I., which embraces a period of 500 years.[3] The early Fathers would have shrunk from giving the bishop of Rome the titles of "Prince of Priests," "The High Priest," due alone to Christ. Such an exclusive title, as applied to any one bishop, was never contemplated by the Scriptures. All the people of God are called in Scripture "a royal priesthood." When, however, the term "High Priest" was ever used, it was equally applicable to all bishops. We have a remarkable instance of this recorded in the "Acts of the Councils" by the Jesuit Labbeus, wherein Anacletus, a bishop of Rome, of the second century, in his second

---

[1] "De quâ re agitur, cum de primatu Pontificis agitur? Brevissime dicam, de summâ re Christianâ." In Lib. de Sum. Pont. in Præfat. sec. ii. Edit. Prag. 1721.

[2] Ibid. Lib. ii. c. 31, sec. i.

[3] Some curious details are given by the learned Benedictine, Dom de Vaines (in his *Dictionnaire Raisonné de Diplomatique*, Paris, 1774, p. 161), on the gradual development of the pope's titles). In the first four centuries the title of Pope (Papa) was usually given to bishops indiscriminately. In the ninth century, bishops of France were reprimanded by Gregory IV. for calling him Papa and Frater. Gregory VII., in the eleventh century, was the first who restricted the term Papa to the Bishop of Rome. The title, Vicar of Peter, is not earlier than the ninth century: in the thirteenth, the bishops of Rome limited that of the Vicar of Christ to themselves: it had been previously borne by other Bishops. See Wordsworth's "Letters to Mr. Gondon." Letter II., p. 43. London, 1848.

epistle, writes—"The High Priests, *that is, Bishops*, are to be judged of God."[1]

As to the title of "Universal Bishop," it was specially repudiated by the bishops of Rome, Pelagius II., and Gregory I., when assumed by John, bishop of Constantinople, *for the first time in the church*, and afterwards by his successor, John Cyriacus.

Pelagius II. (A.D. 590) denounced the assumption of the title of "Universal" as an unlawful usurpation, and testified that none of his predecessors assumed such a profane appellation:—

"Regard not," he said, "the name of *universality* which John has unlawfully usurped to himself, for let none of the Patriarchs ever use this so *profane appellation*. You may well estimate what mischief may be expected rapidly to follow, when even among priests such perverted beginnings break forth; for he is near respecting whom it is written, He himself is King over all the sons of pride."[2]

And his immediate successor, Gregory I., expressed himself no less strongly:—

"My fellow priest John attempts to be called the Universal Bishop. I am compelled to exclaim: O times! O manners! Priests seek to themselves names of vanity, and glory in new and profane appellations. Do I, in this matter, defend only my own proper cause? Do I vindicate an injury specially offered to myself? Do not I rather take up the cause of *God*

---

[1] "Summi Sacerdotes, id est, Episcopi, a Deo judicandi." Conc. Labb., tom. i.; Anacleti Papæ, Epist. ii. col. 521. C. Paris, 1671.

[2] "Universalitatis nomen, quod sibi illicite usurpavit, nolite attendere:— nullus enim patriarcharum hoc tam profano vocabulo unquam utatur.—Perpenditis, fratres carissimi, qui de vicino subsequatur, cum et in sacerdotibus erumpunt tam perversa primordia. Quia enim juxta est ille, de quo scriptum est: 'Ipse est rex super universos filios superbiæ.'" Pap. Pelag. II. Ep. viii.; Labb. et Coss., tom. v. col. 949, 950. Paris, 1671.

Omnipotent, and the cause of the church universal? Far from the very hearts of Christians be that name of blasphemy in which the honour of all priests is taken away, while it is arrogated madly to himself by a single individual."[1]

And, again, the same bishop said:

"No one of my predecessors ever consented to use this so profane appellation; for if a single patriarch be styled *Universal*, the name of Patriarch is taken from the others. But far, very far, be it from a Christian mind, that any person should wish to snatch himself a title, whence he may seem, in any even the smallest degree, to diminish the honour of his brethren."[2]

"What," exclaims the same Gregory to his presumptuous brother of Constantinople; "what wilt thou say to Christ, the true Head of the universal church, in the examination of the last judgment—thou who attemptest to subjugate all his members to thyself by the title of Universal? In the use of so perverted a title, who, I ask, is proposed for thy imitation, save he, who, despising the legions of angels constituted in a common authority with himself, endeavoured to break forth to the summit of an isolated dignity. To consent to the adoption of that wicked appellation is nothing less than to apostatize from the faith."[3]

---

[1] "Consacerdos meus Johannes vocari *Universalis Episcopus* conatur. Exclamare compellor ac dicere: O tempora! O mores! sacerdotes vanitatis sibi nomina expetunt, et novis ac profanis vocabulis gloriantur. Nunquid ego, hac in re, proprium causam defendo? Nunquid specialem injuriam vindico, et non magis causam Omnipotentis Dei et causam universalis ecclesiæ? Sed absit a cordibus Christianorum nomen illud Blasphemiæ, in quo omnium sacerdotum honor adimitur, dum ab uno sibi dementer arrogatur." Pap. Greg. I. Epist. lib. iv.; Epist. xx.; Opera, tom. ii. p. 748. Bened. Edit. 1705.

[2] "Nullus unquam decessorum meorum hoc tam profano vocabulo uti consensit; quia, videlicet, si unus patriarcha *Universalis* dicitur, Patriarcharum nomen cæteris derogatur. Sed absit, hoc absit a Christianâ mente, id sibi velle, quenquam arripere, unde fratrum suorum honorem imminuere, ex quantulacunque parte videatur!" Pap. Gregor. I., Epist. lib. v. Ep. xxv. Opera. tom. ii. p. 771. Edit. Bened. 1705.

[3] Tu quid Christo, universaliu scilicet ecclesiæ capiti, in extremi judicii es dicturus examine, qui cuncta ejus membra tibimet conaris *Universalis* appellatione supponere? Quis, rogo, in hoc tam perverso vocabulo, nisi ille ad imitandum proponitur, qui despectis angelorum legionibus secum socialiter

And, once again, he says:—

"I, indeed, confidently assert that whosoever either calls himself, or desires to be called, *Universal Priest*, that person, in his vain elation, is the precursor of Antichrist, because, through his pride, he exalts himself above the others."[1]

This title, then, so late as A.D. 601, was not given to, or assumed by the bishop of Rome, though it was, notwithstanding the above denunciations, assumed by Gregory's successor, Boniface III., in A.D. 605.

Simon Vigorius, an eminent Roman-Catholic French writer of the sixteenth century, properly defines the value of the expression. He says:—

"When the western Fathers call the Roman bishops, Bishops of the Universal Church, it is not that they look upon them as universal bishops of the whole church, but in the same sense that the patriarchs of Constantinople, Antioch, Alexandria, Jerusalem, are called so, either as they are universal over the churches under their Patriarchate, or that in the Œcumenical Councils, they preside over the whole church."[2]

In this sense we must understand the words of Gregory Nazianzen, when he said of St. Athanasius "That, in being made bishop of Alexandria, he was made bishop of the

---

constitutis, ad culmen conatus est singularitatis, erumpere?—In isto tam scelesto vocabulo consentire, nihil est aliud quam fidem perdere." Pap. Gregor. I. Epist. lib. v.; Epist. 8. Opera, tom. ii. p. 742. Edit. Bened. 1705.

[1] Ego vero fidenter dico, quia quisquis se *universalem sacerdotem* vocat, vel vocari desiderat, in elatione suâ Antichristum præcurrit quia superbiendo cæteris præponit. Pap. Greg. I. Epist. lib. vii.; Epist. xxiii. tom. ii. p. 881. Bened. Edit. Paris 1705, and Lab. et Coss. tom. v. col. 1027, *et seq.* Paris, 1671.

[2] Cum occidentales Patres pontifices Romanos vocant Universalis Ecclesiæ Episcopos id more earum ecclesiarum facere, et ea ratione, non quod putent totius orbis universalis, universales esse episcopos, sed eadem qua Constantinopolitanus, Alexandrinus, Antiochanus, Hierosolymitanus, dicuntur universales; aut ut universales ecclesiarum quæ sunt sub eorum Patriarchatu, aut quod in Conciliis Œcumenicis totius ecclesiæ præsint. Opera omnia Simonis Vigorii, Paris, 1683; ad responsionem Syn. Concil. Basil. Commarl. pp. 37, 38.

whole world:"[1] and of Basil when he spoke of him as "having the care of the churches, as much as of that which was peculiarly committed to him."[2]

The title "Vicar of Christ" was never applied to a bishop of Rome exclusively before the Council of Florence, 1439; and, even then, it was expressly stated to be so applied "reserving the rights of the bishop of Constantinople." The spiritual power was to be exercised only "according as it is contained in the acts of general councils and in the holy canons,"[3] which acts and canons we shall presently briefly notice. We find this title in Cyprian's 12th Epistle; but it is applied to all bishops. So also it was used in the Synod of Compiegne, under Gregory IV., A.D. 833:—

"It is convenient that all Christians should know what kind of office that of bishop is—who, it is plain, are the Vicars of Christ, and keep the keys of the kingdom of heaven."[4]

And so at the Synod of Melun, under Sergius II., A.D. 845:—

"And although all of us unworthy, yet we are 'the Vicars of Christ, and successors of the Apostles.'"[5]

As a matter of *doctrine* or *faith*, it is not necessary, at the present day, to hold that the pope is the vicar of

---

[1] Orat. xxi. tom. i. p. 377. Edit. Morell. Paris, 1630.
[2] Ep. 69, tom. iii. Ben. Edit., p. 161.
[3] "Quemadmodum etiam in actis œcumenicorum conciliorum et in sacris canonibus continetur." Conc. Lab. et Coss. tom. xii.; Conc. Florent. Sess. x. col. 154, *et seq.* Paris, 1671.
[4] "Omnibus in Christianâ religione constitutis scire convenit quale sit ministerium episcoporum—quos constat esse Vicarios Christi et clavigeros regni cœlorum," etc. Coucil. General. apud Binium, tom. iii. p. i. p. 573. Col. Agripp., 1606, and Lab. et Coss., tom. vii. col. 1686. Paris, 1671.
[5] "Nos omnes licet indigni, Christi tamen Vicarii, et Apostolorum successores." Bin., p. i. p. 607, tom. iii. Edit. as above, and Lab. et Coss., tom. vii. col. 1818. Edit. as above.

Christ. Dens, in his Theologia,[1] says that "it is *probably* a matter of faith that a modern pontiff is the vicar of Christ, but not a matter of *obligatory* faith."[2] And, in page 22, he further states:—"It is, however, to be noted, that a modern pontiff being the successor of Peter and vicar of Christ is *not a matter of obligatory faith,* for *that* is not sufficiently propounded to the whole church with the necessity of believing it." If this be so, then a Romanist may disbelieve that the pope is successor of Peter and vicar of Christ. Not only, therefore, is the supremacy not proved by the assumption of this title, or by the alleged fact of the pope being successor of Peter, but the whole fabric and superstructure of Popery, resting as it does on these assumed facts, stands on a rotten basis.

We will go further. We assert that for 1000 years after Christ the title of Pope was not the exclusive privilege of the bishop of Rome. Pope Hildebrand (Gregory VII.) was the first who declared that this title should be exclusively applied to the bishop of Rome.[3] Cyprian, bishop of Carthage, was addressed, even by presbyters of Rome, as "Pope Cyprian." Cyril of Alexandria addressed Athanasius as "Pope Athanasius," and so Jerome addressed Augustine, bishop of Hippo, in Africa, as "Pope Augustine;" and many other similar examples might be adduced. Nay,

---

[1] A book of admitted authority, and used as a text-book at Maynooth College, to instruct the students in their theological studies, dedicated to Archbishop Murray, and published with his expressed approbation, "Ejus cum approbatione susceptam." As we shall have again to quote Dens, we may here mention that Peter Dens is stated, on the title-page of this work, to have been an ecclesiastic of high consideration in Belgium in the middle of the last century, Licentiate of Theology in Louvain, Canon of the Metropolitan Church at Mechlin, and President of the Archiepiscopal Seminary there; whence, in June, 1758, his fourth volume of this book was published, and dedicated to the Archbishop of Mechlin.

[2] Dens' *Theologia*, vol. ii. p. 19. No. xiv., Dublin Edit., 1832.

[3] "Biographie Universelle," Paris, 1817. Art. Gregoire VII., p. 396.

so far from the bishop of Rome being the head of the Christian church, the authority of Gregory I. did not extend even over Italy.[1] The archbishop of Milan was wholly independent of Rome up to the days of Hildebrand, about A.D. 1073. The bishop of Aquilia resisted the attempts of Gregory I. to establish by armed force his jurisdiction (A.D. 590). Ravenna, even so late as 649, was independent of Rome, and its archbishop, Maurus, received the pall from the Emperor.[2] Vitalian, bishop of Rome, endeavoured to exercise a supremacy over him, by summoning him to appear at Rome, but Maurus refused to obey.

Our first proposition is, therefore, that the present claim and titles of the bishop of Rome, so far as the modern doctrine of Supremacy is concerned, are new.

II. The Council of Trent, Seventh Session, in the third canon on "Baptism," declared the church of Rome to be "The Mother and Mistress of all Churches;" and by the 13th Article of the present Romish Creed, every Roman Catholic is called upon to declare the Roman church to be "the Mother and Mistress of all Churches." Our second proposition is, that this allegation, now made part of the creed of a Christian church, never was required to be believed before the publication of the pope's Bull in 1564, and that it is not true as an historical fact. It is, therefore, a new doctrine, imposed as an Article of Faith by the Roman church since 1564. The Creed of Pope Pius IV. did not exist before that date. The only symbol of faith required to be subscribed even by Roman Catholics,

---

[1] Bingham, in his "Ecclesiastical Antiquities," shows that in the early times the jurisdiction of the pope of Rome extended only to the lower part of Italy, the Islands of Sicily, Corsica, and Sardinia. Book ix. cap. i. secs. 9—12.

[2] "Hist. Revennant, Hieronymo." Rubeo, lib. iv. p. 205. Venet. 1590.

was the Nicene Creed. The church of Rome was not mistress of the early Christian churches, and as a matter of fact, she is not so now—she is neither mistress of the Greek and other eastern churches, nor of the church of England and other Protestant churches.

As an *historical fact*, the Greek church, represented by the successive bishops of Constantinople, and the African church, represented by its bishops, were never subject to the ecclesiastical jurisdiction of the bishop or see of Rome. Cyprian, bishop of Carthage, A.D. 250, has sufficiently defined the Roman episcopate. From him we learn that a precedence was given to the see of Rome, "because Rome for its magnitude ought to precede Carthage,"[1] and this was written by Cyprian to the bishop of Rome. Regaltius, the famous commentator on Cyprian's works, said that "Rome was called by Cyprian the principal church, because it was constituted in the principal city;"[2] holding, for this reason, a precedence of *rank*, but not any superior *Ecclesiastical jurisdiction*.

The first General Council of Nice, A.D. 325, by the sixth canon reserved to every church its independent honour and dignity, and this old custom was to prevail in Lybia, Egypt, Alexandria, as in Rome.[3] By the second canon of the next General Council, that of Constantinople, A.D. 381, the sixth canon of Nice was confirmed.[4] And by

---

[1] "Quoniam pro magnitudine suâ debeat Carthaginem Roma præcedere." Ep. 49, alios; Ep. 48, ad Cornel, p. 54. Paris, 1836.
[2] "Ecclesia principalis, id est, in urbe principali constituta." Regalt. in Cypr., Ep. 55, p. 84. Paris, 1666.
[3] Honos suus cuique servetur ecclesiæ—Ita ut Alexandrinus Episcopus horum omnium habeat potestatem, quia et urbis Romæ Episcopo parilis mos est." Surius Concil., tom. i. p. 342. Colon. Agripp., 1567, and Labb. et Coss., tom. ii. col. 32. Paris, 1671.
[4] Lab. Concil., tom. ii. p. 947. Paris, 1671, and Surius, tom, i. p. 487. Col. Agrip., 1567.

the third General Council, that of Ephesus, A.D. 431, the see of Cyprus was declared to be independent *of all other bishops*.[1] The fourth General Council, that of Chalcedon, A.D. 451, determined that the archbishop of Constantinople should have the same primacy of honour as the bishop of Rome; but certain privileges were given to the bishop of Rome, not on account of any supposed Divine right, but because it was the seat of empire.[2] The ninth canon in question on the subject of appeals declared:—" But if a bishop or clergyman have a dispute with the metropolitan of the province, let him have access either to the exarch of the diocese, or to the throne of the *imperial Constantinople*, and let it be judged there."[3] Here we have an appeal to a secular tribunal! a proceeding considered by Romanists as heretical. The fifth General Council, the second of Constantinople, A.D. 553, speaking of Leo, bishop of Rome and Cyril of Alexandria, said, "The Synod giveth like honour to the bishops of Rome and Alexandria."[4] The sixth General Council, the third of Constantinople, A.D. 680, by the thirty-sixth canon, decreed "That the see of Constantinople should enjoy equal privileges with the ancient see of Rome;"[5] and it is worthy of remark that this council declared that if any city, in respect of the *civil state*, be reconstituted and exalted by the princely power, that the order also of *ecclesiastical matters* should follow, that is, it should be chief also in

---

[1] Lab. Concil., tom. iii. p. 802; and Surius, tom. i. p. 608.
[2] "Sedi senioris Romæ, propter imperium civitatis illius, etc. Can. 28, Con. Lab., tom. iv. p. 769. Paris, 1671, and Surius, tom. ii. p. 209.
[3] " Εἰ δὲ πρὸς τὸν τῆς αὐτῆς ἐπαρχίας Μητροπολίτην Ἐπίσκοπος ἢ κληρικὸς ἀμφισβητοίη καταλαμβανέτω ἢ τὸν ἔξαρχον τῆς διοικήσεως, ἢ τὸν τῆς βασιλευούσης Κωνσταντινοπόλεως θρόνον, καὶ ἐπ' αὐτῷ δικαζέσθω." Ibid., can. 19 et 17.
[4] "Qui æqualiter, ab hac synodo, pro statu orthodoxæ fidei honorati sunt." Ibid., action. i.
[5] "Decernimus ut thronus C. P. æqualia privilegia cum antiquæ Romæ throno obtineat." Surius, tom. ii. p. 1046.

ecclesiastical as in civil matters : proving incontestably that whatever privileges Rome enjoyed it was on account of her civil position. We may refer to the seventh General Council, that of Nice, A.D. 787, and draw attention to the fact that Adrianus, bishop of Rome, writing to Tharasius, bishop of Constantinople, as recorded in the proceedings, seventh General Council, A.D. 787, thus addressed him: "To my beloved Brother Tharasius, Universal Patriarch, etc. ;"[1] Constantinople being at this time the seat of Empire, and thus it was declared in the Imperial Constitutions that "the city of Constantinople hath the prerogative of old Rome."[2] And Nilus, the Greek patriarch, thus challenged the bishop of Rome, "If, because Peter died at Rome, thou count the Roman see great, Jerusalem shall be far greater, seeing our Saviour Jesus Christ there undertook his living death."[3] It will be observed here that Nilus did not refer to the figment of Peter's supposed episcopate,—an invention of a later date,—but only to his *death* at Rome.

It is worthy of note, with reference to the Greek church, that the Greek bishops maintained their independence. At the Council of Florence, 1439, a desperate attempt was made to induce certain Greek bishops, who were present, to recognise the Papal supremacy. They were by dint of force, fraud, and bribery, prevailed on to join in articles of agreement or union. It will be remembered that this Council claimed a primacy "over the whole world."[4] But when the Greek deputies returned to Constantinople, the church there indignantly repudiated all that had been done,

[1] "Dilecto Fratri Tarasio, universali Patriarchæ." Surius, Concl. tom. iii. p. 72. Colon. Agripp., 1567.
[2] "Urbs Constantinopolitan. veteris Romæ prærogativa lætetur." Cod. lib. i. Tit. v. l. vi. Honor. Theodos.
[3] Edit. Cl. Salmas., Honov., 1608, p. 94.
[4] Lab. et Coss., Concil., tom. xiii. col. 515. Paris, 1671.

which repudiation was confirmed by a council held at Constantinople, A.D. 1440. The proceedings of the Florentine Council were declared null;[1] Gregory the Patriarch, who was inclined to the Latins, was deposed, and Athanasius chosen in his stead. At this council the bishops of all the principal Greek sees were present, thus making the protest of the Greek church universal and complete.

There is no pretence whatever for alleging that, in the apostolic times, the church of Rome was either Mother or Mistress of the Seven Churches of Asia. Antioch claimed greater antiquity than that of Rome, where Peter is said to have presided six years before he and Paul together (according to Irenæus), while founding the church of Rome, appointed Linus to be the *first* bishop of that See. It was at Antioch that Christians were first so called (Acts xi. 26). But the church at Jerusalem was the recognised Mother of all Churches, and thence the Apostles first preached. For many years afterwards, she was so recognised, as is recorded in the proceedings of the Great and General Council of Constantinople,[2] and subsequently by Jerome, a presbyter of Rome.[3]

"It was not so at the beginning," nor is it true now, that the church of Rome either was or is, *The Mother and Mistress of all Churches.*

[1] Con. Constant., Sess. 2, Ibid., tom. xiii. col. 1367. Paris, 1671, and see Percival's "Roman Schism." London, 1836, p. 93.

[2] "Τῆς δε γε μητρὸς ἁπασῶν τῶν ἐκκλησιῶν τῆς ἐν Ἱεροσολύμοις." Epist. Synod. Concil. Const. apud Theodoret. Hist. Eccles., lib. v. c. 9, p. 207. Cantab., 1720.

[3] "Sed in *Hierosoluma*, primum fundata ecclesia, totius orbis ecclesias seminavit." *Hieron.* Comment. in Esai. ii. 3. Opera., tom. iv. p. 7. Basil Edit., 1537.

CHAPTER II.

CANON OF SCRIPTURE.

"It depends upon the mere will and pleasure of the bishop of Rome to have what he lists sacred, or of authority, in the whole church."—*Cardinal Baronius,* "Annales ad Ann.," 553, u. 224.

LET us now test the assertion, that the Roman priests in this country are the "representatives of no new system"—"the preachers and representatives of no novel doctrines"—with reference to the teaching of their church on the CANON OF SCRIPTURE.

Romanists admit the Scriptures to be the word of God, and, combined with tradition, to be the rule of faith of their church, subject to certain restrictions. It is of the utmost importance, therefore, to ascertain what is included in the "word of God." There is a remarkable unanimity on the canon of Scripture among all classes of Protestants of the present day; but their teaching differs materially from that taught by the Roman church.

To state what the Papal church does teach, let us go to head quarters, the "Council of Trent." In April, 1546, at the Fourth Session, believers were called upon for the *first* time, on pain of "anathema" (that is, of being absolutely, irrevocably, and entirely separated from the communion of the faithful), to admit into the sacred canon of Scripture "the Apocrypha." The decree is as follows:—

"The sacred and holy Œcumenical and General Synod of Trent—perceiving that this truth and discipline are contained in the written Books, and the unwritten Tradition, which [books and traditions], received by the Apostles from the mouth of Christ himself, or from the Apostles themselves, the Holy Ghost dictating, have come down even unto us, transmitted, as it were, from hand to hand; [the Synod] following the *example of the orthodox Fathers*, receives and venerates with *equal piety and reverence* all the books of the Old and New Testament—seeing that one God is the author of both—*and preserved by a continuous succession in the church*. And it (the Synod) has thought it meet that a catalogue of the Sacred Books be inserted in this decree, *lest doubt* arise in any one's mind as to which are received by this Synod."

Then a list is appended, in which are included not only the books of the Old and New Testament, admitted by Protestants of the present day, but, beyond these, are what we call the Apocryphal Books, such as Tobit, Judith, Wisdom, Ecclesiasticus, Baruch, and "the rest of the Book of Esther and Daniel"—that is, from after the 3rd verse of the 10th chapter of Esther to the end of the 16th chapter; and from and including the 13th and 14th of Daniel (so-called), including the Story of Susanna, Bel and the Dragon, and the Song of the Three Children, as they at present stand in the Douay version.

Here, then, we have it boldly asserted that the "orthodox Fathers" and the Catholic church "by continuous succession" held the Apocryphal Books, and the other books enumerated in the decree, "with equal piety and veneration." This is notoriously untrue; and if there is any subject on which the "orthodox Fathers" and a succession of divines in the Roman church ever agreed, it was the rejection of the Apocrypha from the sacred canon of Scripture. In this packed Council, at the Fourth Session, when there were not more than forty-nine bishops present, there was much diversity of opinion. The bishops behaved so clamorously, that it was necessary to direct them to give their votes one by one, and to number them as they were received: so great was the diversity of opinion on this subject, even so late as April, 1546. It is a popular error to suppose that the Trent Council merely *declared* what was previously of faith: so far from this, some of the venerable Fathers came even to blows, and tugged at each other's beards to enforce their own private opinions. It is true they passed their decrees, and *asserted* the authority of Fathers and Apostolic Tradition in their favour; but the assertion was not true. It was and is unsupported by evidence.

St. Paul tells us that "unto the Jews were committed the oracles of God," and this he actually wrote to the Romans (iii. 2), as if in prophetic warning: the Jews rejected the Apocrypha; and the early Christians professed to receive the code or canon of the Old Testament from the Jews.

Neither Christ, nor any of the inspired writers of the New Testament, ever quoted the Apocrypha or referred to it.

We have several successive Christian writers, who have left us lists of the sacred canon of Scripture, as accepted in their respective periods. We now name some of the leading Fathers of the early Christian church, and other divines (all claimed by the church of Rome), in each successive century, who rejected the Apocrypha, and who, therefore, bear evidence to the belief of the church in their respective ages. The references given in a note at the end of this chapter are easily accessible.

The modern church of Rome, through the Council of Trent, A.D. 1546, hurled a curse against those who rejected the books of Maccabees, Ecclesiasticus, Tobit, Judith,

Baruch, Wisdom, as included in the inspired canon of Scriptures.[1] Apocryphal books were rejected from the Sacred Canon, expressly by word, or indirectly by giving a list excluding them, by [2]—

In the Second Century—Melito, bishop of Sardis.

In the third—Origen.

In the Fourth—*Saints* Athanasius, Hilary, Cyril of Jerusalem, Cyprian, Gregory of Nazianzen, and Eusebius, bishop of Cesaræa, Amphilochius, and the bishops assembled at the Council of Laodicea,[3] confirmed by a decree of the General Council of Chalcedon, and by the sixth General Council in Trullo. can. 2, and therefore binding on the church of Rome.[4]

In the Fifth—*Saints* Jerome, Epiphanius, and Augustine.

In the Sixth—Junilius (an African bishop), and some add Isidore, bishop of Seville.

In the Seventh, we have no less authority than Pope Gregory the Great himself. Even the Vatican edition [5] of

---

[1] "Si quis libros ipsos [Hester, Danielis, Baruch, Ecclesiastici, Sapientiæ, Judith, Tobiæ, duorum Maccabæorum] pro sacris et canonicis non susceperit, anathema sit." Concil. Trid., Sess. iv. decret. de can. Scrip., p. 27. Paris, 1848.

[2] Some few of the writers here referred to admit in their list "Baruch," but these exceptions will be noticed in the note of editions at the end of this chapter.

[3] It may be useful here to remark that, with regard to the Council of Laodicea, the books of Baruch and Lamentations, and Epistles, are inserted in some copies. (Labb. et Coss., tom. i. p. 1507-8. Paris, 1671). They are found in the version of Gentian Hervet; but in the Latin copies of previous date they have no place. (See Merlin and Crab. apud Cosin Scholast. Hist. of the Canon, sec. lxi., note). Neither Aristenus nor Caranza have them in their transcript. (See Beveridge's Synodicon. tom. i. p. 481); and Caranza Summa Conciliorum (Paris, 1677, p. 140), published with permission and approbation. And as to the 6th Gen. Council, see Binius Concil., Laod. p. 305, tom. i. Paris, 1636.

[4] The third Council of Carthage, A.D. 397. Can. 47. This Council admits some of the Books, but omits Baruch and the two books of Maccabees, that is to say, no Greek copies admit them, though Dionysius Exiguus has added them to his collection. Lab. et Coss. Concil., tom. ii. col. 1177. Paris, 1671. See the learned Bishop Beveridge's note on this canon.

[5] Rome, 1608. Ex Typogr. Vatican. tom. ii. p. 899.

Gregory's Works testifies that he rejected the Apocrypha from the Sacred Canon.

In the Eighth—Saint John Damascene, the founder of School Divinity among the Greeks, and Alcuinus, abbot of St. Martins, Tours, France.

In the Ninth—Nicephorus, Patriarch of Constantinople, and the "Ordinary Gloss" begun by Alcuin or by Strabus, and enlarged by divers writers.

In the Tenth—The Monk Flaviacensis and Ælfrick, abbot of Malmesbury.

In the Eleventh—Peter, abbot of Clugni.

In the Twelfth—Hugo de Sancto Victore, Ricardus de Sancto Victore, Robert, abbot of Duits, the author of the "Gloss upon Gratian," and the English translation of the Bible of this date in the College Library, Oxford.

In the Thirteenth—Hugo Cardinalis and Saint Bonaventure.

In the Fourteenth—Richard Fitz Ralph, archbishop of Armagh and Primate of Ireland; Nicholas Lyra, and Wycliffe.

In the Fifteenth—Alphonsus Tostatus, Thomas Waldensis, and Dionysius Carthusianus.

In the Sixteenth, we have the famous Cardinal Cajetan. This illustrious prelate of the Roman church wrote a Commentary on the Historical Books of the Old Testament, which he dedicated to Pope Clement VIII. This book appeared only twelve years before the meeting of the Trent Council. In the dedicatory epistle, the cardinal adopts Jerome's rule relative to the broad distinction made by him between the Canonical Books, properly so called, and the Apocryphal. His words are:—

"Most blessed Father,—The *universal Latin Church* is most

deeply indebted to St. Jerome, not only on account of his annotations on the Scripture, but also because he distinguished the Canonical Books from the non-canonical, inasmuch as he thereby freed us from the reproach of the Hebrews, who otherwise might say that we were forging for ourselves books or parts of books belonging to the ancient canon which they never received."[1]

Jerome (A.D. 418) distinctly adhered to the books constituting the Jewish canon, and expressly rejected the several Apocryphal books by name,[2] and this is admitted by Cardinal Bellarmine himself.[3]

But what does Cardinal Bellarmine, one of the greatest controversial writers the church of Rome has produced, say to these authorities? The facts are too notorious to be denied; so he admits them, as already stated, but blunderingly "confesses and avoids" (as lawyers say) the difficulty. "It was no sin (he said), no heresy in them [Augustine, Jerome, Gregory, etc.] to reject these books, because no General Council in their days had decreed anything touching them."[4] This may be the best reason that can be advanced; but it does not support the Trent theory.

Thus, then, we have taken some leading names of men from each successive century, all (except Wycliffe) claimed by the church of Rome as members of her communion, who rejected the Apocrypha. We come, then, to the following conclusions—that, down to April, 1546, the Apocryphal books formed no part of the canon of Scripture enjoined by the church: that they became a part of the canon only

---

[1] Cajetan Epis. dedic. ad P. Clem. VII. ante Comm. in lib. Hist. V. T. Parisiis, 1546.
[2] Hier. Ep. ad Paulinum. Oper. Ben. Edit. 1693. Tom. iv. col. 571-4; and Præfat. in Libros Solom. tom. i. pp. 938, 939.
[3] De Verbo Dei. lib. i. c. x. sec. xx. tom. i. p. 20. Edit. Prag. 1721.
[4] Ibid. Id., sec. vii. p. 18.

CANON OF SCRIPTURE. 19

since that date: that the Council of Trent then invented this new code, and that Romanists, in maintaining that the Apocrypha forms a part of the sacred canon of Scripture, represent a new system and teach a novel doctrine.

Our readers will reasonably ask, Had not the Trent Fathers some authority for what they did? We now propose to examine the alleged authorities, for the subject is an important one.

References to editions of the "Fathers" mentioned in pages 16, 17.

Melito, A.D. 177 [he rejects all]. In Epist. ad Onesium, apud Euseb. Eccles. Hist. iv. c. 26, p. 191. Cantab., 1700; Bell. de verbo Dei. lib. i. c. xx. p. 38, sect. 15. Prag. 1721.

Origen, A.D. 200 [he rejects all]. In Expositione primi Psalmi, apud Eusebium. Hist. Eccles., lib. vi. c. 25, pp. 289, 290. Edit. Reading, Cantab. 1720. [But see Dupin, vol. i. p. 28. London, 1692, as to Esther and Ruth.]

Cyprian, A.D. 250 [or Ruffinus], excludes them all. See Bell. de verb. Dei. lib. i. c. 20, p. 38, tom. i. Prag. 1721; Ibid. can. lib. ii. c. 11, p. 67. Colon. 1605.

Athanasius, A.D. 340 [rejects all but Baruch]. Epist. in Alex. Aristeni Epp. quæ dicuntur Canonicæ, Synopsi., Beveridge's Pandect. ii. Oxford, 1672; Athan. Oper. in Synops. tom. ii. p. 39. Paris, 1627.

Hilary, A.D. 350 [rejects all] Prolog. in Lib. Psalm. sect. 15, p. 145. Edit. Wirceburg, 1785; Bell. de verbo Dei., lib. ii. c. 1, sect. 15, tom. i. p. 38. Prag. 1721.

Cyril of Jerusalem, A.D. 370. Numbers 22 books and rejects the Apocrypha, but in these he is supposed to number "Baruch and the Epistles of Jeremiah." Catech. iv. sect. 20. Oxon, 1703.

Gregory of Nazianzen, A.D. 370 [he rejects them all]. Ex Metricis ejus Poematibus, p. 194, tom. ii. Paris, 1630, and see Beveridge's Pandect. tom. ii. p. 178. Oxford, 1672.

Eusebius, A.D. 315, see above. Eccl. Hist. lib. iv. c. 26., lib. vi. c. 25, p. 289, 90. Cantab. 1700. Chron. lib. ii. ex Hier. versione, c. 10, p. 59. Colon, 1605.

Laodicea, Council of, A.D. 367. Can. lx.; Labbe. et Coss. tom. i. col. 1507. Paris, 1671 [rejects all], but see note above, and Bin. Concil. Laod. p. 305, tom. i. Paris, 1636.

Amphilochius, A.D. 370 [who rejects them all]. Ex Iambis ad Seleucum. Beveridge's Pandect. ii. p. 179. Oxford, 1672.

Epiphanius, A.D. 390 [excludes them all]. De Mens. et Ponder, tom. ii. p. 161. Colon. 1682.

Jerome, A.D. 392 [rejects them all]. (Symbolum Ruffini), tom. iv. p. 143; Præfatio in Proverbia Solomonis, tom. iii. 8, i. k; Præfatio in Hieremian; ibid. 9, c; Præfatio in Danielem; ibid. 9, g; Præf. in librum Regum.; ibid. p. 5, m, 6, a, b, c, Edit. Basil, 1525. Bell. de verb. Dei., lib. i. c. 10, sect. xx, p. 20, tom. i. Prag. 1721.

Chalcedon, Council of, A.D. 451, which confirmed the canons of the Council of Laodicea, art. 15, can. i.; Lab. Conc. iv. col. 755. Paris, 1671.
Augustine, A.D. 420 [excludes them all from the sacred canon]. De Mirab. Sacræ. Scrip. lib. ii. c. 34, p. 26, tom. iii, pt. i. Paris, 1686. De Civ. Dei, l. 18, c. 36 p. 519, tom. vii. Paris, 1685. Aug. contra. Secundum Ep. Gaud. lib. i. c. 31, p. 821. Edit. Bass. 1797.
Junilius, A.D. 545 [he excludes Judith, Wisdom, and Maccabees]. De part. divinæ leges. lib. i. cap. 3, p. 80, tom. xii. Bibl. Patrum. Venet, 1765.
Gregory I. A.D. 601, followed the list of Jerome. Greg. Mor. lib. 19, on 39th chap. of Job; Bened. Edit. 1705, and Romæ, 1608, tom. ii. p. 899; see Occam. Dial, pt. 3; Tract. i. lib. 3, c. 16. Lugd. 1495.
Damascene, A.D. 787 [rejected them all]. Orth. fid. lib. iv. c. 18, p. 153. Basil, 1539. See Canus. Loc. Theol. lib. 2, c. x. p. 59. Colon. 1605.
Alcuinus, A.D. 790 [rejected them all]. Advers. Elepant. lib. i. col. 941. Paris, 1617.
Nicephorus, A.D 800 [rejected them all]. Nicep. Patr. C. P. Canon. Script. in Operibus Pithei, cited by H. Lynd, Via Devia, sec. 5, p. 159. Edit. 1850, London.
N.B.—For the remaining references, which, being of so late date, are only valuable as showing a succession of testimony, the reader is referred to H. Lynd's Via Devia, sect. 5. London, reprint 1850, and Birkbeck's Port. Evidence. Lond. 1849, vol. 2. (See Table of Contents, p. iii.)

CHAPTER III.

CANON OF SCRIPTURE—(*continued*).

"As the church is evidently more ancient than the Scriptures, so the Scriptures were not authentic, save by the authority of the church."— *Eckii, Enchiridion de Ecclesiâ et ejus Autoritate,* etc., p. 21. Coloniæ. 1567.

THE authorities usually relied on in support of the assertion that "the orthodox Fathers" received the Apocryphal and the other books "with equal piety and reverence," and thus preserved them by a continuous succession of witnesses in the church, are:—

    1. The Council of Sardis, A.D. 347.
    2. The Council of Carthage, A.D. 397.
    3. Saint Augustine, A.D. 397.
    4. Pope Innocent I., A.D. 405.

5. Pope Gelasius, A.D. 494.
6. The Council of Toledo, A.D. 675.
7. The Council of Florence, A.D. 1439.
8. The Trent Council, A.D. 1546.

I. *The Council of Sardis.* Father Calmet (A.D. 1730) was the first, we believe, who advanced this council as an authority. Independently of the fact that the genuineness of the decrees of this alleged council is challenged, we assert that these decrees, such as they are, give no list of canonical books whatever. Dupin, the famous French ecclesiastical historian, who has ransacked all the Councils, and advanced all the authorities *he* could find, does not refer to this council as an authority.

II. *The Council of Carthage.* This council is supposed, by the 47th Canon, to have included the Apocrypha in the canon or list of Scripture. Our objections to this authority are the following.

Taking for granted, for the moment, that the decree is genuine—this council was not a General, but only a Provincial Council, and cannot, therefore, be cited to establish a doctrine, or bind the church universal. It can only be cited to establish a local custom. Cardinal Bellarmine objected to the citation of this council on another subject. He said, "This Provincial Council cannot bind the bishop of Rome, nor the bishops of other provinces,"[1] because the 26th Canon of this same council declared that the bishop of Rome was not to be called Chief Priest, and the council otherwise opposed the Roman Supremacy. Surely this was an heretical council.

But we may be reminded of Calmet's argument, that the

[1] Bell. de Pont. Rom., lib. ii. c. xxxi. sec. viii. p. 387, tom. i. Prag. 1721.

canons of this council were confirmed by the council of Constantinople, in Trullo, A.D. 695. Be it so! But, alas! for the over zeal of Calmet, who relies on this proof. Was he not aware that this latter council was wholly condemned by popes, as we are informed by the Jesuit Fathers, Labbe and Cossart?[1] A rather awkward mistake this! But, alas! again, for consistency—this same council in Trullo *also* confirmed the canons of the council of Laodicea![2] which expressly rejected the Apocrypha. Did the two hundred and eleven bishops in Trullo confirm two conflicting lists? It is more reasonable to suppose that they confirmed those of the earlier council, whose decrees had never been questioned, but, on the contrary, had already been confirmed by the General Council of Chalcedon.

But it may be also objected, that the Council of Laodicea was equally a Provincial Council. We admit it; but the 60th Canon of this council, which recites the Canonical Books,[3] was confirmed by the General Council of Chalcedon, A.D. 451,[4] and is therefore binding on every member of the Romish church. And while some Romanists prefer the authority of Carthage over Laodicea, because Leo IV. (A.D. 847) is stated to have confirmed the decrees of the former, they overlook the fact that Leo IV., in the same place, confirmed the decrees of the Council of Laodicea also, and thus make a pope confirm two different lists. An additional reason is thus afforded for supposing that the canon of the later council, that of Carthage, was forged, and not known to Leo IV., and the recognition falsely attributed to him.

[1] Lab. et Coss. Concl. Genl., tom. vi. col. 1316. Paris, 1671.
[2] Lab et Cos. Concl. Genl., tom vi., col. 1140, can. ii. Paris, 1671.
[3] Binius Concl., Conc. Laod. can. lx., tom. i. p. 304. Paris, 1636.
[4] See Cosin's "Scholast. Hist. of the Canons," sec. lxxxv. London, 1672.

The second difficulty Romanists have to contend with is, that the list now professed by their church does not agree with the list supposed to be given in the 47th Canon of the Council of Carthage, the canon relied on.[1] For instance, the books of Maccabees are not found in any of the Greek copies or manuscripts of this council, but only in Latin translations, which argues a forgery somewhere. Then, again, by a strange blunder, the council has enumerated *five* books of Solomon—that is,—besides Proverbs, Ecclesiastes, and the Song of Songs, which are in the Hebrew Canon, and, what is called in the Septuagint, the Wisdom of Solomon, attributed to him,—but also "the Book of Jesus the Son of Sirach," written eight hundred years after the death of Solomon.

Sericius was at this date (A.D. 397) bishop of Rome, Cæsarius and Atticus being Consuls, as the council itself relates; and yet the canon which is alleged to contain the list of Canonical Books refers to Pope Boniface, who was not bishop until 418, twenty years after,[2] a very cogent reason for supposing that the man who forged the canon lived so long after the council was held, that he forgot who was bishop of Rome at the time.

Romanists are not at all agreed among themselves as to the genuineness of *this particular canon.* Cardinal Baronius, the famous annalist, was obliged to admit that— "Not all the canons of this council are established; but they are allowed in *divers other* Councils of Carthage, as, namely, that canon wherein the number of Sacred Books is defined;"[3] and Binius, the publisher of the "Councils," said "fifty canons which were attributed to that council, were

---

[1] Labb. et Coss., tom. ii. col. 117   Paris, 1671.
[2] See the List of the Popes. Ibid., tom. xvi. col. 130.
[3] Baron. Annal. Ann. 397, n. 56, p. 249. Edit. Lucæ. 1740.

not all confirmed by it, but by other Councils of Carthage, as, namely, the 47th Canon."[1] So that it is a mistake after all to refer us to the Council of A.D. 397! Take for granted it was another council—say that of A.D. 419, to which the decree is sometimes shifted over—then we have another difficulty. Dupin informs us that this council merely *proposed* the list, and that other churches were to be consulted for its confirmation.[2] But it is quite a mistake to suppose that even this council published a list; and the question is scarcely worth while arguing until Romanists are themselves agreed upon the precise council which did pass the alleged canon or list, and at what date.

So much, then, for this authority.

III. Augustine, bishop of Hippo, is supposed to have subscribed the 47th Canon of the Council of Carthage, above referred to. But we have shown that there was no such canon. Are we to suppose that he professed a different Rule of Faith from that of Jerome? If so, where is the unity of teaching? Augustine was bishop in *Africa;* Jerome a presbyter at *Rome*. But it is certain that Augustine expressly excluded these various Apocryphal books by name from the canon of Sacred Scripture;[3] and he distinguished what he means by the *Divine Canon* from the ordinary canon.[4] Here Bellarmine comes again to the rescue. He says "that St. Augustine was most certain that all Canonical Books were of infallible truth; but was not alike certain that all the Books of Scripture were canonical: for, if he did think so, yet *he knew the point was*

---

[1] Bin. Concl. Carth. III., p. 722. Tom. i. Lutet. Paris, 1636.
[2] Dupin. Vol. i. pp. 8, 9, fol. edit. London, 1699.
[3] Aug. de Civit. Dei. lib. xvii. c. 20, p. 508, and p. 483. Lib. xviii. c. 26, tom. vii. Paris, 1685.
[4] De Mirab. Sacræ. Scrip. Lib. ii. cap. 34, p. 26, tom. iii. Paris, 1680.

not as yet defined by a General Council; and therefore, without any stain of heresy, some books might be received by some persons for Apocryphal."[1] In other words, this is an apology for Augustine for not holding, in A.D. 397, the same belief as the Council of Trent in A.D. 1546! We are quite aware that, in his *"Christian Doctrine,"* Augustine is supposed to give a list of the canon of Scripture, in which the Apocryphal books are included. But this is easily answered; and we prefer to do so in the words of the eminent Romish divine, Cardinal Cajetan, who wrote on this subject as follows :—

" Here we end our commentaries on the Historical Books of the Old Testament; for the remainder—viz., Judith, Tobit, and the books of Maccabees, *are not included by St. Jerome among the Canonical Books,* but are placed along with Wisdom and Ecclesiasticus, among the Apocryphal. Do not be uneasy, tyro, if you should anywhere find those (Apocryphal) books enumerated amongst the canonical, either by holy councils, or by holy doctors; for the words both of councils and of doctors must be reduced to the judgment of Jerome; and, according to his decision, *these books* (the Apocryphal books enumerated), and if there are any others like them in the canon of the Bible, *are not canonical*—that is to say, do not contain rules for *confirming Articles of Faith;* they may, however, be called canonical, as containing *rules for the edification* of the faithful, inasmuch as they have been admitted into this canon of the Bible, and authorized for this very purpose. With *this distinction,* you will be able to discern the meaning of *the words of Augustine* (de Doctr. Christ., lib. ii.), as also the decrees of the Council of Florence, under Eugenius IV., and the Provincial Councils of Carthage and Laodicea, and of Popes Innocent and Gelasius."[2]

[1] Bell. de Verbo. Dei, lib. i. cap. x., sec. vii. p. 18, tom. i. Prag. 1721.
[2] Cajetan in omnes authenticos Vet. Test. Hist. Lib. Comment. p. 482. Parisiis, 1546.

It may be mentioned, by the way, that Cajetan was most highly esteemed by his contemporaries: he was called the "incomparable theologian"—"to whom, as to a common oracle, men were wont to resort in all difficult questions of theology."

Now, what do we learn from this illustrious doctor and cardinal of the *ante*-Trent Roman church! *First*, that the church of Rome, in his day (A.D. 1533), did not admit the Apocrypha into the *sacred* canon of Scripture as of any authority on *questions of faith*, but allowed them to be read for the *edification of the faithful*, assigning to them exactly the same value as that accorded by the church of England, in her Sixth Article, at the present day. On the other hand, the Council of Trent (which now rules the teaching of the church of Rome), twelve years after Cajetan wrote the above, placed the two classes of books exactly on the same level, as being of equal authority in establishing questions of faith, and for which purpose they are now quoted. The same council, too, cursed to all eternity, all who presumed to oppose this, her modern innovation! And *secondly*, we learn from Cajetan in what light we are to regard the word "canonical" when used by Augustine and the other authorities relied on who make a marked distinction between the *sacred* canon, as authority in questions of faith, and the ordinary phrase "Canon of the Bible" (*in canone Bibliæ*, are his words). Since Cajetan wrote, the alleged lists of Carthage, Innocent, and Gelasius have been proved to be spurious.

Augustine (on the sixth Psalm, sec. 9) said, "The *Jews carry the volume* on which the Christian faith is built; they have been constituted our librarians." And his contemporary, Jerome, said—"The church knows nothing of the Apocrypha; recourse *must be had to the Hebrew books*, from which the Lord speaks, and out of which the disciples take their example." [1]

We may here mention that Cardinal Bellarmine, in his extreme anxiety to press Augustine into the service of Rome,[2] quotes a passage from a work entitled "Ad Orosium," to prove "Ecclesiasticus" canonical Scripture; but, when the same tract is quoted against the church of Rome on another of her dogmas, with the short memory peculiar to this Jesuit writer, he says—"It is not St. Augustine's work, as learned men confess." [3] We should not have thought this worth mentioning were not Bellarmine Rome's great controversial authority.

IV. The next authority relied on is a list said to be in a decretal of Pope INNOCENT I., A.D. 405.[4] No one ever heard of this alleged list of Innocent's for 460 years after the date of that letter; and we hear of it for the *first time* in the ninth century, when the mass of forged decretals appeared. We challenge Romanists to prove the contrary. None but a dishonest controversialist would, at the present day, quote this epistle as genuine.

The list stands just at the end, where it was convenient for a forger to add to it, and to render the difficulty still more oppressing, in the earliest copies of this letter we do not find the book of "Tobit." [5]

We should not omit to notice here the testimony of Isidore of Pelusium,[6] quoted by Messrs. Kirk and Berington, in their "*Faith of Catholics*," as a witness in favour of the

[1] Hieron, Præf. in Paralipon.
[2] Lib. i., De Verbo Dei, cap. 14.
[3] Bell. de Miss. lib. ii. c. 12, p. 913, tom. iv. Edit. Colon. 1617.
[4] Ep. ad Exuperium, n. 7, tom. ii. col. 1256, Lab. Concil. Paris, 1671.
[5] Merlin's Councils. fol. clxxxv. Colon. 1535.
[6] L. i. Ep. 369, Cyro., p. 96. Paris, 1633.

Romish canon. We give the quotation as we find it, and we are quite prepared to subscribe to what he says:—

"The sacred volumes, which contain the testimonies of the Divine writings, are steps whereby we ascend unto God. All those books, therefore, that are set before thee in the church of God, receive as tried gold, they having being tried in the fire by the Divine Spirit of truth. But leave aside those which are scattered about *without* that church—even though they may contain something persuasive to holiness."

V. At a council supposed to have been held by Gelasius, at Rome, 494, a list of Canonical Books, it is alleged, was published, which included the Apocrypha. We assert, in the first place, that one of the oldest copies in existence, that in the pope's library, actually gives this council *without any list of the books of Scripture in it!* [1] thus showing the list relied on to be a later addition. But the whole council is such a manifest forgery—resting only on the authority of Isidore Mercator, of the ninth century, an impostor repudiated by all learned men—that no controversialist of the present day would risk his credit as an honest man by seriously advancing such an authority. Dr. Milner, who was bold enough to assert anything to serve his purpose, relied on this as an authority; and so also do Messrs. Kirk and Berington, in their "*Faith of Catholics.*"

VI. Father Calmet also refers us to the Council of Toledo, in Spain, A.D. 675. Surely he must be hard pressed for evidence! At this Provincial Council only seventeen bishops were assembled. They published no list: they merely quoted a passage from the "Book of Wisdom," and this is brought forward to prove the canonical authority of the whole of the Apocrypha! Messrs.

[1] See Berhard in Canones Gratiani. vol. ii. p. 316.

Kirk and Berington quote this council as follows:—" If any one shall say, or shall believe, that other Scriptures, besides those which the Catholic church has received, are to be esteemed of authority, or to be venerated, let him be anathema:"[1] to which we should be quite willing to subscribe, but for the curse.

VII. Father Calmet, and some others, recklessly rely on the Council of Florence, held under Pope Eugenius IV., A.D. 1439. Here is another blunder. This council said nothing at all about the books of Scripture! After the council had closed its sittings, Eugenius drew up some decrees, as "instructions to the Armenians," and which contained a list including the Apocrypha. We have already seen what Cajetan thought of this list. Besides, a pope's decree does not bind the Roman church unless confirmed by a General Council.

This brings us to the middle of the fifteenth century—a period not sufficiently ancient to produce authorities of any value; thus we are brought—

VIII. To the decree of Trent, (1546), as the sole authority on which the Romanist has to rely to support his bold assertion. Cardinal Bellarmine, referring to another equally untenable assertion, says as to this council—" This testimony ought to suffice, if they had no other;"[2] but we, perverse, stiffnecked heretics, think differently.

Sufficient has surely been said to warrant our having called in question the pretensions to antiquity, and authority for the teaching of the Roman church in the question of the "Canon of Scripture."

---

[1] Waterworth's edition. London, 1846, vol. i. p. 335. The reference to the council is—Can. xii. col. 1228, tom. ii. Lab. Council. Paris, 1671.
[2] Bell. de effectu Sacr. lib. ii. c. 25. sect. 4. p. 109, tom. iii. Prag. 1721.

CHAPTER IV.

INTERPRETATION OF SCRIPTURE.

"If any one has the interpretation of the church of Rome concerning any text of Scripture, although he does not understand how the interpretation suits the text, yet he possesses the identical Word of God."—*Card. Hosius de Expresso Verbo Dei*, p. 623. Ed. 1584.

THE interpretation of Scripture is next in importance to the integrity of the Canon. We shall now consider what modern Rome teaches on this head.

In November, 1564, *for the first time*, professors of the Roman religion were practically precluded from all benefit of the Scriptures.[1] By the third article of Pope Pius' Creed, they " promise, vow, and swear most constantly to hold and profess" as follows :—

"I also admit the Scriptures, according to the sense which the Holy Mother Church has held and does hold, to whom it belongs to judge the true sense and interpretation of the Scriptures; nor will I ever take and interpret them otherwise than according to the unanimous consent of the Fathers."

Lest any objection be taken, we have adopted the translation of the eminent Roman Catholic layman, Charles Butler, Esq. In his *"Book of the Roman Catholic Church,"*[2] he says that the Creed, from which the above is extracted, "was received throughout the universal church, and has ever [since its publication] been considered, in every part of the world, as an accurate and explicit summary of the Roman Catholic faith. Non-Catholics, in their admission

---

[1] We have not forgotten the Councils of Toulouse, A.D. 1229, and that of Oxford, 1408, which prohibited the use of vernacular translations; but these were provincial councils.

[2] Page 5. London, 1825.

into the Catholic church, publicly repeat and testify their assent to it, without restriction or reservation." And Dr. Milner, in his "*End of Controversy*" (Letter XIX.), says that this Creed is "everywhere recited and professed to the strict letter."

There are two new propositions here :—

1. This church requires us to admit the Scriptures only according to the sense she puts upon them, to whom (as she pretends) it belongs to judge of their true sense.

2. That we are never to advance an interpretation of them, except the Fathers are all agreed on that interpretation.

Every Romish bishop and priest swears "to God on his Holy Gospels" to "procure as far as lies in his power" that this doctrine " shall be held, and taught, and preached by all who are under them, or are entrusted under their care."

I. With regard to these propositions, we assert that never was such a yoke imposed upon Christians before November, 1564, and therefore on these two points Romish priests in England represent a new system of religion, " anything they may assert to the contrary thereof in anywise notwithstanding."

The church of Rome requires of its members two impossibilities. The Roman church has never published any authoritative interpretation of the Scriptures, nor is there any possibility of ascertaining what interpretation of Scripture she has or does hold. Even the notes invariably appended to the Romish editions, (and indeed without which no editions whatever are allowed), are of no recognised authority. Before a Romanist can advance an interpretation, he must prove that that particular interpretation has always been and still is held by the church. It is not what this priest, what this bishop, or that pope, has said, but what

THE CHURCH says; and we repeat that the church of Rome has never published an authoritative interpretation of even one single chapter of the Bible! The church cannot speak except by the mouth of a General Council, and no General Council has thus spoken out. If any has spoken, let the interpretation be produced.

It is true that Cardinal Hosius said, "If any one has the interpretation of the church of Rome concerning any text of Scripture, although he does not understand how the interpretation suits the text, yet he possesses the identical Word of God." [1] It is right that the cardinal should say, *if any one has!* Were this a secular matter, we should be tempted to say, "first catch your hare." But when we are told where we are to find the church's interpretation, we shall be the better able to judge whether we possess the identical word of God; as yet, we are satisfied that we have the word of God, without the church's interpretation of it.

But when we have found an interpretation, we may discover it to be contradictory to that given by the same church at another period under different circumstances; and this is admitted by no less an individual than Cardinal Cusanus, who was the pope's legate, sent to Bohemia about the middle of the 15th century: "Nor is it surprising," said this prelate, while endeavouring to induce the Bohemians to accept the interpretation of the church as to half communion, "if the practice of the church interprets the Scriptures at one time in one manner and at another in another —for the Scriptures follow the church, which is the earlier of the two, and on account of which Scripture (is given), and not conversely." [2]

[1] Card. Hosius de Expresso Verbo Dei, p. 623. Ed. 1584.
[2] Card. Cusan. Epis. vii. ad Bohem. Opp. tom. ii. pp. 857, 858. Basil, 1565.

We presume that we are correct in defining the church, for the purpose of enunciating an authoritative declaration, to be a General Council. Bellarmine tells us, "A lawful council, by the most general consent, is most properly termed the Church."[1] This is what he calls the "Representative Church."[2] The Trent Council, "a lawful council," according to Romish belief, tried its hand at an authoritative interpretation of the 6th chapter of St. John's Gospel, but could not agree on the matter, and abandoned even the hope of coming to an agreement. Then there is the "Essential Church," which Bellarmine defines in the same place to be "a company of men professing the same Christian faith and sacraments, and acknowledging the bishop of Rome to be the Chief Pastor and Vicar of Christ on earth." Independently of the impossibility of appeal to such a tribunal to obtain the sense of the church, we have here laymen, joined with clerics, made a court of appeal. As yet, such a tribunal has not published the sense of the church on any single text of Scripture. Then there is the "Consistorial Church," which Bellarmine tells us consists of "the pope and cardinals," and is called "The Court of Rome." Here we approach something more tangible. *Directly*, this tribunal has published no interpretation of the Scriptures; but it has *indirectly* sanctioned and published interpretations of isolated texts. "The Sacred Congregation of Rites," at Rome, holds a delegated authority from this tribunal. We shall give a few examples of interpretations (the "sense of the church") sanctioned by them. We have before us the London edition, 1852, of Liguori's "*Glories of Mary*," bearing Dr. Wiseman's own sanction

---

[1] Bell. de Conc. et Eccles. lib. i. c. 18, sec. 5. Prag. 1721.
[2] Ibid. id. lib. iii. c. 2, de Eccles.

and "cordial recommendation to the faithful." In the preface (p. xviii.) we are told—"Remember, dear reader, that it [this book] has been strictly examined by the authority which is charged BY GOD HIMSELF to instruct you, and that that authority has declared that it contains NOTHING[1] worthy of censure." The authority here pointed out is the "Sacred Congregation of Rites," delegated by the "Consistorial Church." In page 215, we have a very original interpretation of the church's sense of that beautiful and encouraging exhortation of St. Paul (Heb. iv. 16), "Let us, therefore, come boldly unto the throne of grace, that we may obtain mercy, and find grace to help in time of need." To this text, set out verbatim, is added, "Mary [*i.e.*, the Blessed Virgin] is that throne of grace to which the apostle Saint Paul, in his Epistle to the Hebrews (iv. 16), exhorts us to fly with confidence, that we may obtain Divine mercy, and all the help we need for our salvation!" Again (page 88), "In the first chapter of the book of Genesis, we read that 'God made two great lights; a greater light to rule the day, and a lesser light to rule the night' (Gen. i. 16)." We are told in this book "that Christ is the greater light to rule the just, and Mary the lesser light to rule sinners!" Again (p. 11), the inspired psalmist exclaimed, "God hath anointed thee with the oil of gladness" (Psalm xlv. 7). We, simple Protestants, believe that David spoke this of our KING, HIGH PRIEST, and REDEEMER, CHRIST: the "Consistorial Church," however, thinks otherwise, for it tells us—"This was foretold by the prophet David himself, for he says that God (so to speak) consecrated Mary, Queen of Mercy, anointing her with the oil of gladness!" Once more. In the "Song of Solomon"

[1] The capitals are in the original.

(i. 6) we read—"They made me keeper of the vineyards." The "Consistorial Church" tells us (p. 23)—"This refers to the Most Blessed Virgin!" And so we might illustrate numerous interpretations of texts of Scripture in this book, by which it is evident that *this* tribunal (the Consistorial Church) has wholly forfeited its reputation as an interpreter of Scripture, and as an exponent of the "sense of the church;" for it is evident that the church has not always held these interpretations.

We now come to what Bellarmine calls "The Virtual Church," that is, "the bishop of Rome, who is said to be the chief pastor of the whole church, and hath in himself eminently and virtually both truth and infallibility of judgment, and upon whom dependeth all that certainty of truth which is found in the whole church." Here, then, we come to something *apparently* practical! But let us see whether we are practically benefited by this ready source of appeal. In the first place, no pope has ever published or sanctioned an interpretation of the Scriptures. Popes, however, have sanctioned *editions* of Scripture; but these were miserably faulty. Clement VIII. published an edition of the Vulgate, and condemned the previous edition of Pope Sixtus V., who had subjected to excommunication any one who should dare to alter his edition, even in the smallest particle, and had declared that the offender was not to be absolved even by a pope!

We have, however, had the advantage of obtaining from some popes infallible interpretations of isolated texts. Take, for instance, the text from Gen. i. 16, the sense of which, as we have seen, the "Consistorial Church" has fixed. Pope Gregory IX. has sanctioned in his Decretals another interpretation. He says:—

"God made two great lights in the firmament of heaven, the greater light to rule the day and the lesser light to rule the night. For the firmament of the heaven, that is, of the universal church, God made two great lights, that is, He appointed two dignities, which are the pontifical authority and the kingly power."[1]

This exposition was addressed by Pope Innocent III. to the emperor of Constantinople, and thus it had the sanction of two popes. It is given in a Decretal Epistle, one of the most solemn papal documents; and Gratian, in the Roman Canon Law, asserts that the Popes' Decretal Epistles are to be counted among the Canonical Scriptures.[2] But hear how contemptuously a Roman Catholic priest, Dr. Doyle, treated the interpretation of Scripture by popes. We transcribe Dr. Doyle's own words:—

"As to the arguments from Scripture or tradition adduced by him [Pope Gregory VII.] or by any of his successors, they are such as will amuse or rather excite the pity of a serious mind. One [Pope Boniface VIII.] wisely observed, that because an apostle said to our Lord, 'Behold, there are two swords here,' the popes have a right to depose kings. Such an inference might appear plausible to him, who was already resolved on an usurpation of right; *but a Christian is forced to blush at such a profanation of the word of God.* Gregory * * * quotes from St. Paul to the Corinthians (1 Cor. vi. 3), 'Know you not that we shall judge angels themselves? how much more worldly things?' and from this passage he claims to be invested with power of invading the rights of kings and emperors, nay, of remodelling the state of society throughout the world; * * * but to offer arguments against such theories *is too humiliating to the common sense of men.*"[3]

[1] Decret. D. Greg. P. IX. de Majoritate et obedientiâ. Tit. 33, p. 424, Turin, 1621; and Gesta Innocentii III. vol. i. 29, ed. 1632.
[2] Cor. Jur. Can. tom. i. Dis. xix. part. i. cap. vi. p. 90. Paris, 1612, and col. 55. Edit. Leipsic, 1839.
[3] Dr. James Doyle, "Essay on the Catholic Claims," etc. Dublin, John Coyne, 1825, pp. 52—57.

The "Virtual Church" is here taken to task by a priest, in no measured terms, for advancing profane interpretations of the Scriptures; and we doubt much if the "Virtual Church" will be considered infallible, when generally known, even by "good Catholics."

There is yet another tribunal, and that is the parish priest. It is a great delusion under which some lay Romanists are labouring, when they are led to believe that the parish priest, as the representative of the church in his district, is enabled to give the church's infallible interpretation of any given text. Whether every parish priest assumes this position we do not know: we have had the advantage of hearing the expositions of some of them, and we can give but a poor report of their infallibility in proposing the church's interpretation: their great authority, Bellarmine, may, we presume, be taken as a type. Take one example of his interpretation, namely, on the text Job i. 14—"The oxen were ploughing, and the asses feeding beside them." "By the oxen (says the cardinal) are meant the learned doctors of the church: by the asses are meant the ignorant people, which, out of simple belief, rest satisfied in the understanding of their superiors."[1] We do not quote this in ridicule; yet, while protesting against this interpretation, we must admit our conviction that there is a great deal of truth in Bellarmine's estimation of the relative position of the parish priest and his flock.

But even the parish priest dares not offer an interpretation of any proposed text, unless it can be shown that his church has held and does hold that particular interpretation: so that, in fact, we come back to the original difficulty in ascertaining what the church has taught and

[1] Bell. Lib. i. de Justif. chap. vii. sec. ix. Prag. 1721.

does teach, for we might show that individual priests have interpreted the same texts differently. This fact is notorious; and the difference is more apparent between the *ante* and *post* Tridentine divines. We conclude, therefore, that, if the Romanist be required to hold that interpretation alone which his church has always held and does hold, he will have an insuperable difficulty put in his way in reading or understanding the Scriptures with any profit to himself; for we challenge the production of such an interpretation.

II. Having treated of that part of the Romish creed which restricts the interpretation of the Scriptures "to the sense which the Holy Mother Church has held and does hold," we now proceed to the continuation of this Article of Faith, to believe which is declared to be necessary for our salvation :—" Nor will I ever take or interpret them [the Scriptures] otherwise than according to the unanimous consent (or agreement) of the Fathers."[1] This additional restriction placed on the Scriptures by the church of Rome was for the *first time* imposed on the Christian world in November, 1564. We challenge Romanists to produce this unanimous agreement of the Fathers on any text of Scripture on which modern Romish controversialists rely in order to support any of the modern doctrines against which Protestants protest.

It is a striking fact that, at the Fourth Session of the Trent Council (April, 1546), the assembled divines took this very subject under their consideration, and passed a decree, in which they stated that, "in order to restrain

---

[1] "Nec eam unquam nisi juxta unanimem consensum Patrum accipiam et interpretabor." Pope Pius' Creed. Art. iii. Concil. Trid. Apud Bullas, p. 311. Romæ, 1564.

petulant spirits, no one, relying on his own skill, shall, in matters of faith, and of morals pertaining to the edification of Christian practice, wresting the sacred Scriptures to his own sense, dare to interpret them *contrary to the unanimous agreement of the Fathers.*"[1]

This is reasonable enough; for he would indeed be a rash man who, "relying on his own skill," should put an interpretation on any given text *contrary* to the universally accepted interpretation of all Christian divines from the time of the apostles, where such interpretation can be ascertained; but this is a very different thing from what the present creed of the Roman church requires, which precludes all interpretations whatever, unless all these Christian Fathers are agreed on that particular interpretation advanced. We may, therefore, safely assume that, down to November, 1564, no Christian was ever required to subscribe such a declaration of faith. It is, therefore, evident that this is a new "Article of Faith," invented by Pope Pius IV., unless, indeed, it be considered as but a modification and an approval of the requirements of the third canon of the fourth Lateran Council, and of the injunctions of Pope Innocent IV. to the authorities of Lombardy.[2]

But how does this rule work, when practically put to the test? Take the leading text, Matt. xvi. 18, relied on by Romanists to establish the supremacy of Peter, and, by assumed deduction, that of the pope of Rome, by declaring that Peter was *the rock* on which Christ was to build his church. Bellarmine asserted that the Fathers were unanimous in this interpretation. This drew forth the rebuke of

---

[1] "Aut etiam contra unanimem consensum Patrum." Sess. iv. Decret. de edit. et usu sacrorum librorum.
[2] Lab. et Coss. tom. xiv. col. 440, *et seq.* Paris, 1671.

a celebrated Roman Catholic writer, Launoy,[1] who, in reply, showed that sixteen Fathers and Doctors interpreted the text in question as referring to Christ, and not to Peter: eight held that the church was not to be built on Peter alone, but on all the apostles equally; whilst only seventeen adopted the modern Roman interpretation. Not *one of them*, however, derived from that text the pope's Supremacy. The Fathers differing, then, in interpretation, this important text must, according to modern Papal theory, remain a dead letter to Romanists.[2] Take another famous text—1 Cor. iii. 15, which is now continually advanced to prove the Romish doctrine of Purgatory. Bellarmine[3] divides the text into five heads, or five great difficulties, and on each head or difficulty he shows various conflicting opinions of the Fathers, and none of them agreeing with the modern Romish interpretation. He, nevertheless, concludes that the text *does* refer to the Romish purgatory; but, so satisfied was Bellarmine that there was no unity of interpretation among the Fathers, that he was constrained to admit that "their writings were not the rule of faith, neither have they any authority to bind."[4] So conscious, indeed, are Romanists of their weakness in this respect, that they have corrupted the genuine text of some of these Fathers, to make them speak modern Popery:

---

[1] Launoii Opera, tom. v. p. ii. pt. 95, Epist. vii. lib. v. Gul. Voello. Col. Alloh. 1731.

[2] The *Reductio ad absurdum* sometimes forcibly proves the fallacy of a proposition. The Romanists contend for *literal* interpretation here and elsewhere. "The *rock*" (say they) "must be *Peter*—it cannot be *the doctrine just before propounded by Peter.*" In this very same chapter, Matt. xvi., in the 23rd verse, Christ addresses Peter—"Get thee behind me, Satan;" therefore Peter was literally *the Devil*; therefore the church of Rome, being founded on Peter, is founded on Satan.

[3] Bell. De Purg. lib. i. tom. i. c. 4. Prag. 1721.

[4] Scripta Patrum non sunt regulæ fidei, nec habent auctoritatem obligandi. Bell. de Concil. author. Lib. ii. c. 12, sec. xii. Prag. 1721.

at other times, they have ordered various passages to be expunged from their works: not unfrequently they palm off spurious productions of later date, as the works of an early Father; and when the evidence against them is too palpable, they do not hesitate to reject the authority altogether. For instance, take one of the most esteemed of all the Fathers, Augustine, who referring to the text 1 Cor. iii. 15, said—"By this fire is meant the fire of tribulation in this world." Bellarmine says—"This opinion of his we have rejected."[1] Again, Augustine says—"Those words of St. Luke, 'I will not henceforth drink of the fruit of the vine,' are to be understood of the sacramental cup"—and deduced that there was no change of the substance of the elements; Bellarmine again therefore opposed him, and said—"He did not well consider of that text, which appears by this that he passed it over lightly."[2]

Another curious illustration we have in the works of the Jesuit Maldonatus. Augustine said—"The Israelites ate of the same spiritual meat, but not the same corporeal which we eat; for they ate manna, we another meat; but both the same spiritual meat." Maldonatus said—"I am verily persuaded that if Augustine had been living in these days, and had seen the Calvinists so interpret St. Paul, he would have been of another mind, especially being an utter enemy to heretics."[3] Once more, Augustine said—"Christ spoke these words: 'This is my body,' when he gave a sign of his body." Harding, the opponent of Jewel, made a curious explanation, peculiarly characteristic of Romanists and Romanism. He explains this most palpable contradiction to

---

[1] Bell. de Purg. lib. i. cap. v. sec. 36. Prag. 1721. I am indebted for some of these facts to Sir H. Lynd's "*Via Devia.*"
[2] Bell. de Euch. lib. i. cap. xi. sec. 61.
[3] Mald. in Joh. vi. n. 50, p. 1476. Lug. 1615, and col. 732, Mussip. 1596.

the Romish theory thus:—"St. Augustine, fighting against the Manichees, oftentimes useth not his own sense and meaning, but those things which by some means, however it were, might seem to give him advantage against them, so as he might put them to the worst."[1] So that a Romanist would even wilfully misinterpret Scripture if thereby he could secure an advantage over his opponent—so that "the end sanctifies the means!"

Thus we might go on. In fact, the "unanimous agreement of the Fathers" is not only not to be found, but when a Father disagrees from modern Romanism, the point in question is at once repudiated, the interpretation rejected, and the book expurgated or prohibited.

Cornelius Mus, indeed, most ingenuously confessed that he would rather give more credit to one pope in matters of faith, than to thousands of Augustines, Jeromes, or Gregories.[2]

There is, however, another peculiarity which we desire to note on this article of the Romish creed. We have not yet met with one Papal controversialist, who has undertaken to vindicate this particular doctrine of his church. While all the other points of faith are combated for and defended as either Scriptural or apostolic, this one stands alone, undefended, unsupported, and unvindicated.

[1] Jewel. Art. xii. p. 346. Lond. 1609.
[2] Ego ut ingenue fateor, plus uni summo Pontifici crederem, in his quæ fidei mysteria tangunt, quam mille Augustinis, Hieronymis, Gregoriis, etc. Cornel. Musaeus Episc. Bitunt. in Ep. ad Roman. i. cap. 14, p. 606. Venet. 1588.

CHAPTER V.

TRANSUBSTANTIATION.

"That we may in all things attain the truth, that we may not err in anything, we ought ever to hold it a fixed principle, that what I see white I believe to be black, if the Hierarchical church so define it to be."[1]—*Ignatius Loyola.*

In this chapter we propose to consider the doctrine of Transubstantiation, which teaches that there is a conversion of the whole *substance* of the bread into the body, and the whole *substance* of the wine into the blood of Christ, after the priest has pronounced the words of consecration.[2] Nothing is supposed to remain of the pre-existing elements but what Romanists call the accidents—namely, the size, shape, and smell, of bread and wine. The bread and wine cease to exist, but in their place comes "entire Christ," the true body, blood, bones, nerves, soul, and divinity,[3]— the very same body which was crucified, was buried, rose again, and ascended into heaven,—under the "appearance" of bread and wine.

---

[1] "The Spiritual Exercises of St. Ignatius Loyola, translated from the authorized Latin," by Charles Seager, M.A., "to which is prefixed a Preface by the Right Rev. Nicholas Wiseman, D.D.," pp. 180. London, 1847.

[2] "Atque in sanctissimo Eucharistiæ sacramento esse vere, *realiter* et *substantialiter* corpus et sanguinem, una cum anima et divinitate Domini nostri Jesu Christi, fierique conversionem totius substantiæ panis in corpus, et totius substantiæ vini in sanguinem."—Pope Pius' Creed. "*Ordo Administrandi Sacramenti,*" p. 67. London, 1840. And Can. i. Decree concerning this sacrament. sess. xiii. Council of Trent.

[3] "Continetur totum corpus Christi, scilicet *ossa, nervi,* et alia."—Thos. Aquin. *Summa,* tom. iii. 2. 76, c. i., Lyons, 1567. "Comprehendens carnem, *ossa, nervos,* etc." Dens' Theo. tom. v. p. 276. Dublin, 1832. "Jam vero hoc loco a pastoribus explicandum est, non solum verum Christi, corpus, et quidquid ad veram corporis rationem pertinet, velut ossa et nervos, sed etiam totum Christum in hoc sacramento contineri." Catech. Concil. Trid. pars. ii. sec. xxxi. de Euchar. Sacr. p. 235. Paris, 1848.

Dr. Butler, in his Catechism, "revised, corrected, enlarged, etc., approved and recommended by Dr. Doyle" (Dublin edition, 1848), thus sums up this last proposition.

"Q. (p. 59) Are both the body and blood of Christ under the appearance of bread and under the appearance of wine?

"A. Yes; Christ is whole and entire true God and true man, under the appearance of each.

"Q. Are we to believe that the God of all glory is under the appearance of our corporeal food?

"A. Yes; as we must also believe that the same God of all glory suffered death under the appearance of a criminal on the cross.

"Q. (p. 60) Is the mass a different sacrifice from that of the cross?

"A. No. The same Christ who once offered himself a bleeding victim to his heavenly Father on the cross, continues to offer himself, in an unbloody manner, by the hands of the priest on their altars."

And again, as the wine has been denied to the laity, it is asserted that in the bread alone, without the wine, the body and blood, soul and divinity, of Christ are received; nay, further, if one consecrated wafer be broken, then, even in each separate piece, "entire Christ" is still alleged to exist without extra benediction.[1] However startling the proposition may be, nothing can be more plain and *literal* than the language of the Romish church; there is nothing typical, or symbolical, or spiritual, in the doctrine. A literal, carnivorous process is to be gone through; the idea is repulsive, but the system suggests it. This process of manducation was (if the doctrine be true) properly defined in the

---

[1] "Si quis negaverit, in venerabili sacramento Eucharistiæ sub unaquaque specie, et sub singulis cujusque specici partibus, separatione facta, totum Christum contineri, anathema sit."—Con. Trid. de Sacra. Euchar. Sacra. sess. xiii. can. iii., p. 118. Paris, 1848.

decree of Pope Nicholas II., at a council held at Rome, 1059, as recorded in the Decretals or Book of Canon Law of the Roman church. When Berengarius[1] was compelled to recant his alleged heresy in denying Transubstantiation, he was compelled to admit that the body and blood of Christ were *sensibly* not only in the sacrament, but verily handled by the priest, and broken and rent with the teeth of the faithful.[2]

The council at Rome, under Pope Nicholas, was, as was just said, held A.D. 1059; but as some Romanists of the present day may declare that the declaration then made was *ante*-Tridentine, and therefore obsolete, it may be stated that the same proposition was revived by Cardinal Archbishop Bellarmine, who lived some time after the Council of Trent. He endorsed what was required of Berengarius. He said:—

"We truly and properly say that the body of Christ is removed, lifted up, and set down, put on the paten or on the altar, and carried from hand to mouth, and from mouth to the stomach: as Berengarius was forced to acknowledge in the Roman council under Pope Nicholas, that the body of Christ was *sensibly* touched by the hands of the priest and broken."[3]

---

[1] Berengarius was archdeacon of Angers, in France, and Scholasticus and Master of the Chair of Divinity of the same church.

[2] "Corpus et sanguinem Domini sensualiter non solum sacramento, sed veritate manibus sacerdotum tractari frangi, et fidelium dentibus atteri."— Gratian Corp. Jur. Can. tom. i. p. 2104, par. iii. Dist. 2, c. 42. Paris, 1612. See Baronii Annales, ad ann. 1059, sec. 18.

[3] "Itaque vere et proprie dicimus, Christi corpus in Eucharistiâ attolli, deponi, deferri, collocári in altari vel in pixide, transferri a manu ad os, et ab ore ad stomachum. Denique in concilio Romano sub Nicholo II. compulsus est Berengarius confiteri, corpus sensualiter sacerdotum manibus tangi et frangi."—Bellarm. de Eucharistiâ, lib. ii. cap. ii. ratio 5 et seq., tom. ii. Prag. 1721.

We have been unable to consult the *first* edition of Bellarmine's work, which, no doubt, quoted the whole decree, including the "dentibus atteri," *torn with the teeth*. These words are omitted from the second and all subsequent editions. The words are given, as in the last note above, in the latest edition of the canon law. Leipsic, 1839. Pars. iii. Dist. ii. c. 42. It is

On what is this Popish theory based? Not on Scripture. Christ, it is true, when he had pronounced a blessing, took bread and said, "This is my body." But what did he mean by the words?[1] Romish controversialists of the present day, boldly declare that it is under a literal interpretation and sanction of this text that they believe in the doctrine of Transubstantiation, and that such has always been the sense of their church. Assertions, however, in controversy go for nothing. The allegation is modern. No doctrine can be based on a text the literal interpretation of which is disputed; and not one of the old Fathers can be cited who alleged the doctrine of the *conversion of elements* resting on the literal interpretation of these words.

On the conversion of the substance of the elements—*the* question at issue—Cardinal Cajetan, who wrote about twelve years before the Council of Trent met, lays it down that such a doctrine is not to be found in the Gospels, but is received expressly from the church.[2] His words are rather startling. He says:—

"There appears nothing out of the Gospel that may enforce

worthy of observation, that Bellarmine, immediately previous to the quotation from the decree of Nicholas II., drawing our attention, as it were, to the ancient and modern belief in the days of Augustine, of the fourth century, and Nicholas II. of the eleventh, quotes the following passage from Augustine:—"Augustinus serm. 2, de verbis Apostoli:—'Quod in sacramento visibiliter sumitur, in ipsa veritate *spiritualiter* manducatur.' Denique in concilio Romano sub Nicholo II. compulsus est Berengarius confiteri, Christi corpus *sensualiter* sacerdotum manibus tangi et frangi." Thus Augustine speaks of a *spiritual*, Nicholas II. a *sensual* eating!

[1] If *literal* interpretation is to be carried thus far, the Romanist must in the eucharist *swallow the chalice*. For St. Paul says—"As often as ye eat *this bread*, and drink *this cup*," 1 Cor. xi. 26.

[2] ".. Dico autem ab ecclesiâ cum non appareat ex evangelio coactionum aliquod ad intelligendum hæc verba proprie quod Evangelium non explicavit expresse ab ecclesiâ accepimus, viz., conversionem panis in corpus Christi."—Cajetan in iii. q. 75, ar. 1, p. 130, col. 1. Venet, 1612. And Index. Expurg. Quiroga. p. 98. Madrid, 1667.

us to understand Christ's words properly, yea, nothing in the text hinders but that these words ('this is my body') may as well be taken in a metaphysical sense, as those words of the apostle, 'the rock was Christ;' that the words of either proposition may well be true, though the things there spoken of be not understood in a proper sense, but in a metaphysical sense."

And he adds—

"That part which the Gospel hath not expressed—viz., the conversion of the bread into the body and blood of Christ, we have *received expressly from the church.*"

The Jesuit Suarez admitted that Cardinal Cajetan taught that the words, "this is my body," do not of themselves sufficiently prove Transubstantiation without the authority of the church, and therefore, by the command of Pius V., that part of his commentary is left out in the Roman edition of his works.[1]

Fisher, the Romish bishop of Rochester, and a great opponent of the Reformers, specially stated that "there are no words in St. Matthew's Gospel whereby it may be proved that in the mass is made the very presence of the body and blood of Christ." He goes so far as to say that "it cannot be proved by any Scripture."[2] And Cardinal Bellarmine was compelled to admit that—

"It is not altogether improbable that there is no express place of Scripture to prove Transubstantiation without the declaration of the church, as Scotus said; for although the Scrip-

---

[1] "Ex Catholicis solus Cajetanus in commentario hujus articuli, qui jussu Pii V. in Romanâ editione expunctus est, docuit, secius ecclesiæ auctoritate verba illa (Hoc est corpus meum) ad veritatem hanc confirmaudam non sufficere."—Suarez. tom. 3, disp. 46, sec. 3, p. 515, edit. Mogunt, 1616.

[2] "Hactenus Matthæus, qui et solus Testamenti novi meminit, neque ullum hic verbum positum est quo probetur in nostra missa veram fieri carnis et sanguinis Christi præsentiam."—"Non potest igitur per ullam Scripturam probari."—J. Fisher, Contra capt. Babyl. c. 10, n. 8, et O. fol. lxxx. Colon. 1525.

tures seem to us so plain that they may compel any but a refractory man to believe them, yet it may justly be doubted whether the text be clear enough to enforce it, seeing the most acute and learned men, such as Scotus was, have thought the contrary."[1]

But another illustrious Romish bishop, Peter Ailly (or, as he is generally called, Cardinal De Alliaco, who was Doctor of Divinity in 1380, and Chancellor of the University of Paris in 1389, and made bishop of Cambray in 1396, and cardinal in 1411), said :—

"That manner or meaning, which supposeth that the substance of bread to remain still, is possible, neither is it contrary to reason, nor to the authority of Scripture; nay, it is more easy and more reasonable to conceive, *if it would accord with the determination of the church.*"[2]

It may be observed in passing, that Cardinal Cajetan draws a parallel between the text (1 Cor. x. 4) "that rock was Christ," and the text in question, as Augustine did in his work, "The City of God." Augustine says—"All symbols (significantia) seem *in a manner* to sustain the persons of those things which they signify; as the apostle says, 'the rock was Christ,' because that rock of which this is spoken signified Christ."[3] And he carries out the same

[1] "Secundo dicit Scotus, non extare locum ullum Scripturæ tam expressum, ut sine ecclesiæ determinatione evidenter cogat transubstantionem admittere, atque id non est omnino improbabile. Non etiam si Scripturæ, nobis tam apertæ videantur, ut cogant hominem non protervum, tamen merito dubitari potest cum homines doctissimi et acutissimi qualis imprimis Scotus fuit, aliter sentiant."—Bell. de Euchar. lib. iii. cap. 23, tom. iii. sec. 2, p. 337. Prag. 1721.

[2] "Putet quod ille modus sit possibilis nec repugnat rationi, nec auctoritati Bibliæ, imo facilior ad intelligendum et rationabilior, quam, etc." In 4 Sentent, q. 6, art. i. fol. ccxvi. Edit. Paris (without date). [We are indebted for some of these references to Sir H. Lynd's " *Via Tuta.*"]

[3] "Quodammodo omnia significantia videntur earum rerum quas significant sustinere personas, sicut dictum est ab apostolo, Petra erat Christus, quoniam Petra illa de qua hoc dictum est significabat utique Christum." De Civit. Dei, lib. xviii., cap. 48, Edit. Paris, 1685, and tom. v., col. 1120, Edit. Basil, 1569.

idea in his commentary on St. John's Gospel (Tract xlv.) "See how the signs are varied, faith remaining the same. There (*i.e.*, in the wilderness) the *Rock* was Christ; to us that which is placed on God's altar is Christ." [1] And, to drive the matter home, he said, "Christ did not hesitate to say, 'This is my body,' when he gave a *sign* of his body." [2] These words are too plain to require any comment.

It will be observed, therefore, that the doctrine of *Transubstantiation* stands solely on the *dictum* or authority of "the [Romish] church." The word [3] itself first authoritatively appeared in the proceedings of the Council of Lateran, held under Pope Innocent III. (Nov. 1215), in the first part of the seventy chapters alleged to have been drawn up by Innocent himself, relating to the extirpation of heretics. These constitutions are denied by some to be the work of the council, and are said to be by Pope Innocent alone. If so, the doctrine will scarcely be admitted even to have received at this time conciliar sanction. Indeed, it is quite common in the present day for Romanists to deny that these canons, and especially the "third" of these chapters (which anathematizes heretics, and orders them to be delivered up to the secular power to be punished), had the sanction even of this council.[4]

[1] "Quid enim illi bibebant? Bibebant enim de spirituali sequente petrâ; petra autem erat Christus. Videte, ergo, fide manente, signa variata. Ibi petra Christus, nobis Christus quod in altari Dei ponitur." Edit. Basil, 1569, tom. ix. col. 333.
[2] "Non enim Dominus dubitavit dicere, Hoc est corpus meum, cum signum daret corporis sui." Cont. Adimantum. c. xii. p. 124, tom. viii. Paris, 1688.
[3] The *doctrine* had been already announced in the several Councils of Versailles and Paris, 1050; of Tours, 1054; Rome, 1058 and 1079; at which several synods, Berengarius was condemned for denying the change of substances.
[4] Those who deny that the statutes of Lateran IV., and especially the third canon, ever were sanctioned by the council, call Collier as a witness

That eminent scholastic divine, the acute and learned John Duns Scotus,[1] as Bellarmine calls him, gave it as his opinion that [2] "before the Council of Lateran, Transubstantiation was not believed as a point of faith," and indeed he clearly and plainly confessed that, "properly speaking, Transubstantiation *is not a change.*"[3] Was Scotus justified in the assertion, that before that period this doctrine was not taught by the church? Take another very famous theologian, called "the Master of the Sentences," Peter Lombard, archbishop of Paris (A.D. 1150). If Transubstantiation be true, the so-called sacrifice on the Popish altar and the sacrifice on the cross are one and the same, and the former is not a *commemoration* of the latter. What was his opinion? He asks, "Can that which the priest transacts be rightly called a sacrifice or immolation, and is Christ daily immolated or was he only once immolated?" He answers the question thus:—

"That which is offered and consecrated by the priest is called a sacrifice and oblation, because it is a memorial and representation of the true sacrifice and holy immolation accomplished upon the altar of the cross. Christ died once upon the cross,

that it is not to be found in the Mazarine copy, coeval with the council. An unfortunate witness: for whilst Collier states, erroneously, that the third canon is not found with the others, he assigns to the others a place in the *Mazarine copy!* The fact is, that the third canon *is* found in the Mazarine copy; a *portion* of it having been removed *mechanically*. Should any one get possession of the MS. of Hume's History of England, and tear out a portion of his history of Charles I., or James II., he might as justly contend, and on the very same grounds, that the history of these monarchs "is not found in the Hume MS." See the Rev. John Evan's "Statutes of the Fourth Lateran Council:" London, 1843.

[1] Duns Scotus was professor of theology at Oxford in 1301, and afterwards removed to Paris in 1304, where he was placed at the head of the theological schools.

[2] "Unum addit Scotus, quod minime probandum, quod ante Lateranense Concilium non fuisset dogma fidei."—Bell. lib. iii. de Euchr. cap. xxiii. sec. 12, p, 337, tom. iii. Prag. 1721. Scotus, fol. 55, p. 2, col. 2. Venet, 1597.

[3] "Dico proprie loquendo, quod transubstantio non est mutatio." In 4 Sent. Art. xi. sec. 1, ad propositum. Edit. as above.

and was there in himself sacrificed; but He is daily sacrificed in the Sacrament, because in the Sacrament a commemoration is made of that which was done only once."[1]

To go up to an earlier date, Gelasius, bishop of Rome (A.D. 492), wrote:—

"Certainly, the sacraments of the body and blood of the Lord, which we receive, are a Divine thing; because by these we are made partakers of the Divine nature. Nevertheless the *substance or nature of the bread and wine ceases not to exist;* and, assuredly, the *image* and *similitude* of the body and blood of Christ are celebrated in the action of the mysteries."[2]

Cardinal Baronius and some other zealous Romanists have endeavoured to deny the authenticity of this passage by attributing the work to Gelasius of Cyzicus (of the fifth century nevertheless); and Rome, ashamed of its teacher, has placed the passage in question in the Roman Expurgatory Index.[3] There are, however, honest men in this Church, such as Dupin and others, who admit its authenticity.

To go still higher, Theodoret, bishop of Cyrus (A.D. 430), wrote[4] that "the mystical signs do not depart from their

[1] "Quæritur si quod gerit sacerdos proprie dicatur sacrificium vel immolatio: et si Christus quotidie immoletur, aut semel tamen immolatus sit? * * * * illud quod offertur et consecratur, a sacerdote, vocari sacrificium et oblationem: quia memoria est, et repræsentatio veri sacrificii, et sanctæ immolationis factæ in arâ crucis. Et semel Christus mortuus in cruce est, ibique immolatus est in semetipso: quotidie autem immolatur in sacramento, quia in sacramento recordatio fit illius quod factum est semel."
—Pet. Lombard. Sentent, lib. iv., distinct. 12, p. 745, ed. Mogunt. 1632.

[2] "Certe sacramenta qua sumimus corporis et sanguinis Domini Christi Divina res est, propter quod et per eadem Divinæ efficimur consortes naturæ. Et tamen esse non desinit substantia vel natura panis et vini: et certe imago et similitudo corporis et sanguinis Christi in actione mysteriorum celebrantur."—Gelas. de Duabus in Christo naturis, contra. Eutychen. et Nest. in Bib. Patr. tom. iv., par. i. col. 422, Paris, 1589; and p. iii. tom. v. p. 671. Colon. 1618.

[3] See Mendbam's *Literary Policy of the Church of Rome*, p. 121. Second edition, London, 1830.

[4] "Neque enim signa mystica recedunt à naturâ suâ, manent enim in priore substantiâ, figurâ, et formâ, et videri et tangi possunt."—Theodor. Oper. Dialog. lib. ii. cap. 24, p. 924. Paris, 1608.

nature, but remain in their former substance, figure, and form." This passage has also been tampered with.¹

Again, we have Chrysostom (A.D. 406), who, in his Epistle to Cesarius, said :—

"Before the bread is consecrated, we call it bread; but when the grace of God, by the priest, has consecrated it, it is no longer called bread, but is esteemed worthy to be called the Lord's body, *although the nature of bread still remains in it.*" ²

Cardinals Perron and Bellarmine, feeling the force of this formidable passage, accused Peter Martyr (A.D. 1548) of having forged the treatise in question, and actually asserted that the epistle never existed; though they do not undertake to explain how it is that this same epistle was quoted as the genuine production of Chrysostom, by John Damascene (A.D. 740), Anastasius (A.D. 600), and the Greek Father Nicephorus (A.D. 800), as shown by Wake. To this we may add the words of the French ecclesiastical historian, Dupin, " It appears to me that one ought not to reject it as a piece unworthy of St. Chrysostom." ³

Again, we have Ephrem, of Antioch (A.D. 336), who testified as to the belief in his day :—

"The body of Christ, which is taken by the faithful, *neither departs from its sensible substance*, nor remains separated from intellectual grace on the other hand." ⁴

---

¹ See Faber's *Difficulties of Romanism*. B. ii. c. iv. p. 274. London, 1853.

² "Sicut enim antequam sanctificetur panis, *panem* nominamus: Divina autem illum sanctificante gratia, mediante sacerdote, liberatus est quidem appellatione *panis*; dignus autem habitus est *Dominici Corporis appellatione, etiamsi natura panis in ipso* permansit." Chrysost: ad Cæsarum Monachum. Oper. Chrysost. tom. iii. p. 744, fol. Bened. Edit. Paris, 1721.

³ "Il me semble meme que l'on ne doit pas rejetter comme une piéce indigne de S. Chrysostom."—Dupin, Nov. Bib. des auteurs Eccles. tom. iii. p. 37. Paris, 1698.

⁴ "Τὸ παρὰ τῶν πιστῶν λαμβανόμενον σῶμα Χριστοῦ, καὶ τῆς αἰσθητῆς οὐσίας οὐκ ἐξίσταται, καὶ τῆς νοητῆς ἀδιαίρετον μένει χάριτος." Ephraem. Theopolitan. apud Phot. Bibl. cod. ccxxix. p. 794. Edit. Rathomag. 1653.

This passage has also been perverted in the Latin version of the Jesuit editor with native adroitness.[1]

The signal failure of all the attempts to prove these passages to be either spurious, or to tamper with them, or to put them in the Roman Index as prohibited, establishes our case triumphantly.

Without further evidence, we are now in a position boldly to challenge Romanists to disprove the allegation—that the doctrine of Transubstantiation is a modern invention of their church.

We proceed now to what is called the " Real Presence."

Romish controversialists artfully attempt to separate the consideration of this doctrine from that of transubstantiation; but with them they are one and the same. *Their* " real presence" means the presence of the body, blood, (and as the Roman catechism adds) bones and nerves, soul and divinity, of our Lord, in the consecrated host. They assert, however, that the early English divines and all the early Fathers of the church, held *a* real presence of Christ. That is true; but that presence was a real *spiritual* presence without any idea of a transubstantiation or change of the substance of the elements, which is the very essence of the alleged real presence in the host. It is equally true, that the early Christian writers often referred to the elements as the *body* and *blood* of Christ; and asserted that the body and

---

[1] "Qui locus in se perspicuus, misere corruptus fuit ab Andrea Scotto Jesuita, cum videret ejus sanam interpretationem evertere transubstantionem. Ideo verba illa τῆς αἰσθητῆς οὐσίας οὐκ ἐξίσταται, vertit *sensibilis essentiæ non cognoscitur*, cum notum sit, verbum ἐξίσταμαι, idem esse ac *degenero, de statu dejicior*, etc.; verba autem sequentia de baptismo, τὸ ἴδιον τῆς αἰσθητῆς οὐσίας τοῦ ὕδατος λέγω, διασώζει; quorum perspicuus est sensus, *servat proprium sensibilis substantiæ aquæ dico*. Sic infeliciter et veteratorie interpolat: *hocque substantiæ visibilis proprium est, per aquam, inquam, salvat:* ubi nullus est sensus." Riveti *Critici Sacri*, lib. iv. cap. xxvi. p. 1148. Roterodami, 1652.

blood are received at the sacrament. And so did also Dr. Watts, in his hymns :—

"The Lord of life this table spread
With his own flesh and dying blood." (vi. b. 3.)

Again—

"Thy blood, like wine, adorns thy board,
And thine own flesh feeds every guest." (xix. b. 3.) [1]

And yet no one accuses Watts of holding the Popish doctrine of the real presence. But who can say that a hundred years hence it will not be said of him by Papists—if Popery then exist—that he believed in transubstantiation?

On the other hand, it is equally clear that many of the early Fathers expressly stated that they understood the words of our Lord not literally, but figuratively; and the consecrated elements are spoken of by them as *types*, or *figures*, or *symbols*, or *representations* of the body and blood of Christ—language wholly incompatible with the idea of a real corporeal presence of Christ. Thus, it is said in the Clementine Liturgy, as set forth in the "Apostolic Constitutions :"

"We moreover give thanks, O Father, for the precious blood of Jesus Christ, which, on our behalf, was poured out, and for his precious body, of which also we celebrate these elements as the *antitypes*, He himself having commanded us to set forth his death." [2]

Origen (A.D. 216), in his commentary upon Matt. xv. 11, after showing that it is the prayer of faith which

---

[1] Quoted by Dr. Cumming in the Hammersmith Discussion. London, 1848, p. 214.

[2] "Ἔτι εὐχαριστοῦμεν, Πάτερ ἡμῶν, ὑπὲρ τοῦ τιμίου αἵματος Ἰησοῦ Χριστοῦ τοῦ ἐκχυθέντος ὑπὲρ ἡμῶν, καὶ τοῦ τιμίου σώματος, οὗ καὶ ἀντίτυπα ταῦτα ἐπιτελοῦμεν, αὐτοῦ διαταξαμένου ἡμῖν καταγγέλλειν τὸν αὐτοῦ θάνατον." Clem. Liturg. in Const. Apost. lib. vii. o. 25, Cotel. Patr. Apostol. Amstel. 1724.

is said over the elements, which becomes profitable to the soul, concludes:

"... For it is not the *matter of the bread*, but the word that is said over it, which profiteth him who eateth it worthily of the Lord. Thus much concerning the *typical* and symbolical body."[1]

The following quotations may be added to those already given, selected from the many at our disposal.

Irenæus, bishop of Lyons (A.D. 178):—

"Wherefore also the oblation of the Eucharist is not *carnal* but *spiritual*, and in that respect pure. For we offer unto God the bread and the cup of blessing, giving thanks unto him, because he has commanded the earth to produce these fruits for our food: and then, having finished the oblation, we invoke the Holy Spirit, that he would make this sacrifice, both the bread the body of Christ, and the cup the blood of Christ, in order that they who partake of these *antitypes* may obtain remission of sins and life eternal. Wherefore they who bring these oblations in remembrance of the Lord, approach not to the dogmas of the Jews; but worshipping spiritually they shall be called the sons of wisdom."[2]

Clement of Alexandria, A.D. 190:—

"The Scripture has named wine a mystic symbol of the holy blood."[3]

Tertullian, A.D. 195:—

"The bread which He had taken and distributed to his dis-

---

[1] "...Καὶ οὐκ ἡ ὕλη τοῦ ἄρτου ἀλλ' ὁ ἐπ' αὐτῷ εἰρήμενος λόγος, ἐστιν ἃ ὠφελῶν τὸν μὴ 'ἀναξίως τοῦ κυρίου ἐσθίοντα αὐτὸν. Καὶ ταῦτα μὲν περὶ τον τυπικου καὶ συμβαλικου σώματος." Orig. comment. in Matt. vol. iii. p. 500. Ben. Edit. Paris, 1733.

[2] "Προσφέρομεν γὰρ τῷ θεῷ τὸν ἄρτον καὶ τὰ ποτηριον τῆς εὐλογίας, εὐχαριστοῦντες αὐτῷ, ὅτι τῇ γῇ ἐκέλευσε ἐκφῦσαι τοὺς καρποὺς τούτους εἰς τραφὴν ἡμετέραν, καὶ ἐνταῦθα, τὴν πρασφορὰν τελέσαντες, ἐκκαλοῦμεν τὰ Πνεῦμα τὸ Ἅγιον, ὅπως ἀποφήνῃ τὴν θυσίαν ταύτην, καὶ τὸν ἄρτον σώμα τοῦ Χριστοῦ, καὶ τὸ ποτήριον τὰ αἷμα τοῦ Χριστοῦ, ἵνα οἱ μεταλαβόντες τούτων τῶν ἀντιτύπων, τῆς ἀφέσεως τῶν ἁμαρτιῶν, καὶ τῆς ζωῆς αἰωνίου, τυχωσιν. Οἱ οὖν ταύτας τὰς προσφορὰς ἐν τῇ ἀναμνήσει τοῦ Κυρίου ἄγοντες, οὐ τοῖς τῶν Ἰουδαίων δόγμασι προσέρχονται, ἀλλὰ, πνευματικῶς λειτουργοῦντες, τῆς σοφίας υἱοὶ κληθήσονται. Iren. Fragment. in Append. ad Hippol. Oper. tom. ii. pp. 64, 65. Hamburgi, 1716.

[3] Μυστικὰν ἄρα συμβολον ἡ γραφὴ αἵματος ἁγίου οἶνον ὠνόμασεν. Clem. Alex. Pædag. lib. ii. c. 2. Oper. p. 156. Colon. 1688.

ciples He made his body, by saying, 'This is my body,' that is, *the figure* of my body."¹

And again :—

"Nor the bread, by which he represents his body."²

Eusebius, bishop of Cesaræa, A.D. 325 :—

"Christ himself gave the *symbols* of the Divine economy to his own disciples, commanding that the image of his own body should be made. He appointed them to use bread as a symbol of his own body."³

Cyril of Jerusalem, A.D. 363 :—

"With all assurance let us partake, *as it were*, of the body and blood of Christ: for, in the *type of bread*, the body is given to thee; and, in the *type of wine*, the blood is given to thee; in order that thou mayest partake of the body and blood of Christ, becoming with him joint body and joint blood."⁴

Gregory of Nazianzen, A.D. 370 :—

"... How could I dare to offer to Him that which is from without, the antitype of the great mysteries."⁵

Macarius of Egypt, A.D. 371 :—

"In the church are offered bread and wine, *antitype* of Christ's flesh and blood; and they who partake of the visible bread eat the flesh of the Lord *spiritually*."⁶

---

1 Acceptum panem et distributum discipulis, corpus suum illum fecit, Hoc est corpus meum dicendo, id est, *figura* corporis mei. Tert. Adv. Marci. lib. 5, p. 458. Parisiis, 1675.

2 .. nec panem, quo ipsum corpus repræsentat. Idem. ibid. lib. i. sec. ix.

3 Πάλιν γὰρ αὐτὸς τὰ σύμβολα τῆς ἐν θέου οἰκονομίας τοῖς αὐτοῦ παρεδίδου μαθηταῖς, τὴν εἰκόνα τοῦ ἰδίου σώματος ποιεῖσθαι παρακελευόμενος.—Ἄρτῳ δὲ χρῆσθαι συμβόλῳ, τοῦ ἰδίου σώματος παρεδίδου. Euseb. Demons. Evan. lib. viii. c. 2, p. 236. Paris, Stephan. 1544.

4 Ὥστε, μετὰ πάσης πληροφορίας, ὡς σώματος καὶ αἵματος μεταλαμβάνωμεν Χριστοῦ, ἐν τύπῳ, γὰρ ἄρτου δίδοταί σοι τὸ σῶμα, καὶ, ἐν τύπῳ οἴνου, δίδοταί σοι τὸ αἷμα, ἵνα γένῃ μεταλαβὼν σώματος καὶ αἵματος Χριστοῦ, σύσσωμος καὶ σύναιμος αὐτοῦ. Cyril. Hieros. Cat. Myst. sec. iii. p. 300. Ed. Paris, 1720.

5 Πῶς ἔμελλον θαρρῆσαι προσφέρειν αὐτῷ τὴν, ἔξωθεν, τὴν τῶν μεγάλων μυστηρίων 'ἀντίτυπον; Gregor. Nazianzen. Orat. i. oper. i. tom. i. p. 38. Paris, 1630.

6 Ἐν τῇ ἐκκλησίᾳ, προσφέρεται ἄρτος καὶ οἶνος, 'ἀντίτυπον τῆς σαρκὸς αὐτοῦ καὶ τοῦ αἵματος, καὶ οἱ μεταλαμβάνοντες ἐκ τοῦ φαινομένου ἄρτου, πνευματικῶς τὴν σάρκα τοῦ Κυρίου ἐσθίουσι. Macar. Ægypt. Homil. xxvii. p. 168. Lipsiæ, 1698.

Ambrose, bishop of Milan, A.D. 385 :—

"In the law was the shadow; in the gospel is the *image*; in heaven is the reality. Formerly a lamb was offered, a calf was offered; now Christ is offered.—Here he is in an *image*; there he is in reality."[1]

Jerome, a presbyter of Rome, A.D. 390 :—

"He did not offer water, but wine, as a *type* of his blood."[2]

Augustine, bishop of Hippo in Africa, A.D. 400 :—

"The Lord did not doubt to say, 'This is my body,' when he gave the *sign* of his body."[3]

"These are sacraments in which, not what they are, but what they show forth, is the point to be always attended to: for they are the *signs of things*, being one thing and signifying another thing."[4]

Theodoret, bishop of Cyrus in Syria, A.D. 424 :—

"The mystic *symbols*, after consecration, pass not out of their own proper nature.—Place, then, the *image*, by the order of the archetype, and thou wilt see the *similitude* : for it is meet that the *type* should be similar to the reality."[5]

We cannot complete these extracts more appropriately than by adding the decision of Pope Gelasius, A.D. 496 :—

---

[1] Umbra in lege: imago in evangelis: veritas in cœlestibus. Aute, agnus offerebatur, offerebatur vitulus: nunc Christus offertur.—Hic, in imagine: ibi, in veritate." Ambros. Officior. lib. i. c. 48, Oper. col. 33. Paris, 1649.
[2] "In typo sanguinis sui non obtulit aquam sed vinum." Hier. lib. ii. adversus Jovinianum, tom. ii. p. 90. Paris, 1602.
[3] See note 2, p. 49.
[4] "Hæc enim sacramenta sunt, in quibus, non quid sint, sed quid ostendant, semper attenditur: quoniam signa sunt rerum, aliud existentia, et aliud significantia. Aug. cont. Maxim. lib. ii. sec. 3. tom. viii. col. 725. Bened. Edit.
[5] Οὐδὲ γάρ, μετὰ τὸν ἁγιασμὸν, τὰ μυστικὰ συμβολα τῆς οἰκείας ἐξίσταται φύσεως.—Παράθες τοίνυν τῷ ἀρχετύπῳ τὴν εἰκονα, καὶ ὄψει τὴν ὁμοιοτητα, χρὴ γὰρ ἐοικέναι τῇ ἀκηθείᾳ τὸν τυπον. Theod. Dial. ii. Oper. cap. 24, fol. 113, veros ed. Tiguri, 1593.

"Assuredly the *image* and *similitude* of the body and blood of Christ are celebrated in the action of the mysteries." [1]

Having brought our extracts from divines up to the end of the fifth century, no reasonable person can doubt that the modern Roman theory of the real carnal presence was unknown to the early Christian church.

For every single passage that may be adduced by Romanists, referring to the elements as the body and blood of Christ, we can place beside it one or more extracts from the same Father who spoke of the consecrated elements as the *images, types,* or *symbols,* of the same body and blood which modern Romanists assert to be *really* and *substantially* present. If this be true, and most certainly it is, we can safely assert that "the real presence" of modern Romanism is evidently different from the real [*spiritual*] presence maintained by the early Christian writers. It may indeed be admitted that some of these Fathers held the doctrine of consubstantiation, subsequently revived by Luther, but condemned by the Romish church. It is nevertheless true that transubstantiation and the Romish doctrine of the real presence are equally inventions of the modern Papal church, and were not held by *the church* as an accepted doctrine for, at the very least, eight hundred years after Christ. And we challenge proof to the contrary.

A striking fact in corroboration of this proposition is, that the Greek church, which was formerly in communion with the Western churches, never did, nor does it now, hold the doctrine of transubstantiation. This was made plain at the Council of Florence (A.D. 1439), where the Greeks alleged

---

[1] Certe imago et similitudo corporis et sanguinis Christi in actione mysteriorum celebrantur. Gelas. de duab. Christ. natur. cont. Nestor. et Eutych. in Biblioth. Patr. tom. iv. p. 422. Paris, 1589.

that " the body and blood of Christ are truly mysteries; not that these are changed into human flesh, but we into them." [1]

In denying that conciliar sanction for the doctrine of transubstantiation can be found, we really take the view most favourable to Romanists; for, in the other case, we have the boasted unity of the church at once destroyed, and a council, and a General Council, ignoring the opinion of Rome's dearest sons. We must, in such a case, come to the conclusion either that these men affirmed " they knew not what," or that the *church* does not at all times hold the same doctrine. " Utrum mavis "—alas for Rome and infallibility in either case!

CHAPTER VI.

INVOCATION OF SAINTS.

"The sacred Scriptures do not teach, even in effect or by implication, that prayers are to be made to the saints, etc. Therefore it is sufficiently clear that many things belong to the [Roman] Catholic Faith which have no place in the sacred page."—*Dominic Banhes. In Secundum Secundæ Thom.* Q. i. Art. x., Concil. ii. col. 521. Venet. 1587.

IN considering the Romish doctrine of the Invocation and Worship of Saints, the question should be carefully freed from the evasions and subtleties attempted to be introduced into it. The question is, not whether saints or angels

---

[1] See the whole of this proposition stated in Sir H. Lynd's " *Via Devia.*" New edition. London, 1850, p. 191, sec. viii., and wherein Binius' perversion of the text is exposed. The word used at the Council of Florence is τελεῖοῦσθαι, which Binius falsely translated "Transubstantiari." Binius in Concil. Flor. sess. xxv. p. 839, tom. viii. Paris, 1636.

in heaven offer up their prayers for us who are on earth; but whether (as declared by the Trent Council at its Twenty-fifth Session) it is "a good and useful thing suppliantly to invoke them (mentally or verbally), and to flee to their prayers, help, and assistance," or in any way to rely on their "merits" for assistance. This decree points to a direct invocation of saints for their intercession, aid, and help, and assumes that they can hear or perceive our verbal or mental prayers.

Dr. Delahogue, the Maynooth Professor, admits that the worship rendered to saints is a *religious* worship, "though the Tridentine Fathers did not use that word." [1]

This theory must presuppose two important propositions:—

First, that the particular saint invoked is actually in a beatific state, and—

Second, that the departed spirit has a knowledge, directly or indirectly, of our prayers, either verbal or mental; in fact, that the spirit is neither in hell, nor in purgatory, but actually in heaven, and also in effect is omniscient and omnipresent.

I. And, firstly, Cardinal Bellarmine, on this very subject, in the 20th chapter of the first book *"De Beatitudine et Cultû Sanctorum,"* informs us (as his opinion of course), by way of excuse for the patriarchs of the Old Testament not

---

[1] Trait. de Mysterio S.S. Trinitatis. Autore L. A. Delahogue. R. Coyne. Dublin, 1822. Appendix de Cultu Sanctorum, p. 218. It is proper here to state, that Veron, in his "*Rule of Catholic Faith,*" pp. 96, 97, Birmingham, 1833, says, that it is not an article of Romish faith that this veneration is to be called a *religious* veneration; but he admits that their "writers differ on the question. Marsilius thinks that the honour which is shown to God and the saints is the exercise of one and the same virtue," but of different degrees. "Derlincourt (he says) goes farther, and maintains, in a pamphlet written expressly on this subject, that a *religious* honour ought to be given to the Blessed Virgin."

being invoked, that until Christ's death they were not in a state of beatitude; "for," says he, "it belongs to perfect beatitude to know these things."

We ask any Roman Catholic what proof he has that the particular saint he invokes is actually in that beatific state, so as to be able to have cognizance of our mental or verbal prayers, and that the alleged saint does not, in fact, himself require that assistance which the devotee is asking of him.

Some Romanists declare themselves satisfied if the individual invocated be but canonized by a pope. Cardinal Bellarmine, and others of his school, declare that in the act of canonization the pope is infallible.[1] But there are difficulties in the way before we can accept this theory.

It was decreed by Alexander III. that no one should be acknowledged as a saint and invoked, unless he had been declared to be a saint (in other words, canonized) by the bishops of Rome; and the reason given was, lest idolatry be committed by invoking one not in a state of happiness.[2] The church of Rome *must* claim for herself infallibility, if she takes upon herself so daring and presumptuous a task as to anticipate God's decree, by authoritatively declaring that such an one is a happy spirit in heaven, bearing in mind also the inevitable result, should an error be committed. But *if*, as Veron asserts, canonization be not a *doctrine* of the church of Rome, it may be disbelieved.

Again, the alleged proofs on which the claim to canonization depends are questions of fact, supposed to have been investigated. But if the pope, even in General Council, may err in deciding matters of fact, then the whole system of saint

[1] Bellarmine's "Church Triumphant," vol. ii. p. 871. Cologne, 1617.
[2] Polydore Virgil. In Rer. Invent. Book vi. c. vii. fol. cxxii. London, 1551.

worship being based on false principles, will be rotten from the foundation, and must fall.

It is true that Dens, enlightened by the dictum of Alexander III., tells us why the church of Rome *ought* to be believed to be infallibly right in her judgment concerning the character of any person when she decrees a canonization. He says that, were she not infallibly correct in her judgment, "the whole church would be involved in a superstitious worship, should he be invoked as a saint who is associated with the damned in hell."

If such a process of reasoning be admitted, any other act of idolatry might be sanctioned, merely because the church of Rome sanctioned it. But the question is, Are Romanists themselves bound to believe that a saint, officially canonized, is really in heaven? and that the pope is right in his decision? and that Romanists are bound to accept the decision? These questions are put by Dens, in the same place whence we have extracted the last passage:—"Is it to be believed with divine faith that a canonized person is a saint or holy person?" He answers this important question by saying, "That is not clear; * * * it appears that this thing is not a matter of certain faith." [1]

Again, a no less authority, Veron, in his "*Rule of*

---

[1] Dens' Theologia, tom. ii. pp. 138, 139. Dublin, R. Coyne, 1832. The authority of this work we have given before, p. 7, *note*. Mr. Coyne, in his catalogue, stitched into the Priest's "Ordo," or Directory, for the year 1832, informs us that "at a meeting of the Roman prelates, held at Dublin, Sept. 14th, 1808, it was unanimously agreed that Dens Theologia was the best book that could be published, as containing the most secure guidance for those ecclesiastics who could not have access to libraries, or an opportunity of consulting those placed in authority over them;" and the Rev. David O'Croly, a Romish priest, in his postscript to his "Address to the lower orders of the Roman Catholics of Ireland," p. 25, declares that the Theology of Peter Dens is "a standard work of Irish Catholic orthodoxy, and of Roman Catholic orthodoxy universally." It was published in Ireland and on the Continent, permissu superiorum, and *no exception was ever taken to it, either in whole or in part.*"

Catholic Faith,"[1] on the same subject, gives the following important information :—

"The canonization of the saints is not an article of faith; in other words, it is no article of our faith that the saints whom we invoke—for instance, St. Lawrence, St. Vincent, St. Gervase, St. Blase, St. Chrysostom, St. Ambrose, St. Dominic, etc., are really saints, and in the number of the blessed. [He makes one exception only, St. Stephen, who is said in the sacred text to have slept in the Lord.] This is proved—1. From the silence of our creed, and the Council of Trent.—2. It is clear that there is no evidence to prove, either from the written or unwritten word of God, that these persons were saints.—3. Besides, it is not even an article of our faith that such men were even in existence, and therefore much less are we bound to believe that they really lived saintly lives, or were afterwards canonized. All these are, undoubtedly, questions of *fact,* and not of *doctrine.* [And after stating that miracles, the foundation of canonization, were not matters of faith, 'how should a canonization grounded upon them—a judgment of the church as to their sanctity, be an article of Catholic faith?' he proceeds.] No bulls, therefore, of their canonization, though they generally emanate from the popes, as they merely contain a question of fact, declaring that such an one is a saint, are anywise matters of Catholic belief. I may again observe, that neither the pope, nor even a General Council, is guided infallibly in the canonization of a saint. The proof of this is drawn in our general rule of faith, namely, that *all Catholics* [in italics] are agreed that the pope, even in General Council, may err on mere matters of fact, which, as such, depend principally, if not wholly, on the means of information and the testimony of individuals."

[1] Birmingham, 1833, pp. 84, 85. This work was written expressly to remove erroneous notions of the Romish system. The translator, Dr. Waterworth, in his preface, begins by declaring that its "authority is universally acknowledged;" and Dr. Murray, a Romish bishop, in his examination before a Committee of the House of Commons, declared that this book, among others, contained a most authentic exposition of the Romish faith. See Phelan and O'Sullivan's Digest of the Report of the State of Ireland, 1824, 1825. H. Commons' Report, p. 224, 22nd March, 1825.

Now, what is the result? By the creed of Trent, Romanists declare that they "firmly hold that the saints reigning together with Christ are to be venerated and invoked;" and the Trent Council, at its twenty-fifth session, "admonished all those to whom the office of teaching has been entrusted, diligently to instruct the faithful—that the saints, who reign together with Christ, offer up their prayers to God for man; that it is good and profitable suppliantly to invoke them—and that it is an impious opinion which denies that the saints, who enjoy eternal happiness in heaven, are to be invoked."

All this presupposes that the saints are reigning with Christ, a matter of fact first to be ascertained. But no saint must be invocated unless canonized by a pope's bull; and it is not a matter of faith that the individual saint is in a state of beatitude. The alleged fact may therefore be disbelieved, as it is admitted to be a matter of uncertainty. Nevertheless nine-tenths of the religious worship of Romanists is made up of the invocation of one saint or another. What certainty, therefore, have Romanists in acting up to the precepts and customs of their church, when, according to the showing of their own teachers, they may be involved in "superstitious worship," invoking men who may, according to Veron, "never have had any existence;" or who, according to Dens, "may be associated with the damned in hell!" And this is the system, called a religion, which we are declared to be heretics for not embracing!

We therefore ask again, what proofs do Romanists adduce that the person invocated is in heaven? We challenge them to give a satisfactory reply; and, until they do so, cannot admit this proposition. The great final judgment, and the knowledge who are saved and who are condemned, are respectively reserved for the coming of Christ (1 Cor. iv. 5), and must be left to the foreknowledge of God alone.

II. The state of the soul immediately after death and until the day of judgment (whenever that may happen), and its attributes and employments in the invisible world, are mysteries not given to man to know. These were matters of speculation among the early Christian writers, who delivered various opinions on the subject: a proof that the invocation of the departed was not a doctrine of the church in their day! But it is an acknowledged fact, that, before the corrupt practice of invocating departed spirits began, prayers *for* them were offered up. We find, therefore, the writings of Epiphanius (A.D. 370), Cyril of Jerusalem (A.D. 386), etc., quoted by Romanists in favour of *prayers for the dead;* but in all these instances we also find included in the same prayers, in the very same form of words, the patriarchs, prophets, apostles, Virgin Mary, martyrs, etc., a notion wholly incompatible with the doctrine of modern saint worship, which presupposes that the saints are in a beatific state, and are above the want of *our* assistance and prayers.

The early Christians of the second and third centuries commemorated the death of martyrs, etc. (usually at their tombs), on the anniversary of their death, which led to the custom of the departed being included in their prayers, not *to* but *for* them. So certain is this fact, that Dr. Wiseman, in his lectures on "The Principal Doctrines and Practices of the [Roman] Catholic Church," is constrained to admit that—"there is no doubt that in the ancient liturgies the saints are mentioned in the same prayer as the other departed faithful, for the simple circumstances that they were so united *before the public suf-*

frages of the church proclaimed them to belong to a happier order "[1]—that is, declared them to be canonized. But, according to Veron,[2] it was not decided by the Roman church until the beginning of the 15th century, at the Council of Florence (A.D. 1439), "whether the souls of the blessed are received into heaven and enjoy the clear vision of God, before the resurrection and the last day of final judgment." It was, therefore, not until the 15th century that the papal church took upon herself to proclaim any departed individual to belong to a happier order; therefore even a firm believer of this latter Papal assumption is precluded, according to the theory of his church, from believing that any saint could have been lawfully invoked before that comparatively late date.

The custom, however, of praying *for* the departed was introduced about the latter end of the third or beginning of the fourth century, and hence arose the subsequent corruption of Christianity of addressing prayers *to* the departed.

Before that period, we challenge the production of any genuine Father of the church who taught or advocated the invocation of saints.[3] Indeed, the first trace we find of the departed being invoked by particular individuals (for it formed no doctrine of the church) was in orations, not in prayers; and then even such ejaculations were accompanied by doubts and suggestions *if* the person apostrophized heard the speaker. Of this we have notable examples in the orations of Gregory of Nazianzen (A.D. 318), when he invoked the spirits of the dead. In his first Invective against Julian the emperor, he says, "Hear, O thou soul of

---

[1] Lecture XI., vol. ii., p. 66. London, 1851.
[2] Veron's "*Rule of Catholic Faith*," p. 82. Birmingham, 1833.
[3] This subject has been very ably treated by the Rev. J. E. Tyler in his "*Primitive Christian Worship*."

great Constantine, *if thou hast any understanding of these things,* and all ye souls of kings before him who lived in Christ." [1] And again, in the funeral oration delivered on the death of his sister Gorgonia, he introduces the following apostrophe:—" *If* thou hast any care of the things done by us ; *if holy souls receive this honour from God,* that they have any feeling of such things as these, receive this oration of ours," etc. [2] This is the first trace we can find of invocation of the departed. It was introduced, as we have said, raising the very question at issue, whether the departed have any cognizance of our words and acts on earth ; and this is pertinent to our second question, How is a Romanist assured that a departed spirit has any knowledge of the *prayers,* much less of any mental action, of individuals on earth ?

Here, then, are two insuperable difficulties in the way of a Christian before he can adopt the Romish theory. The Romanist must make clear, as a matter of certainty, that the departed whom he invokes are actually in a beatific state, and that they are endowed with two, at least, of the attributes of the Divinity, viz., *Omnipresence* and *Omniscience.*

The text in St. Luke's Gospel (xv. 10), "There shall be joy before the angels of God upon one sinner doing penance" (Romish version), is often cited on this subject. But let the context immediately preceding be examined. The man who had lost a sheep, when he found it came home rejoicing; and then calling his neighbours together, told them of his lost sheep being found, and bade them rejoice with him ; so the angels *being informed* of the lost sheep on earth returning, by repentance, to the fold, are also bidden to rejoice ;

---

[1] Tom. i. p. 78. Paris, 1778.
[2] Greg. Naz., Orat. ii., in Gorgon., p. 190. Paris, 1630.

not that they of themselves knew of the fact from any prayers being offered to them, but from it being told to them by the great Shepherd who has brought back the lost sheep into the true fold. And this interpretation is borne out by a note in the Douay Bible, appended to Ecclesiastes ix. 5— "The dead know nothing more"—which is as follows: "*Know nothing more,* viz., as to the transactions of this world, in which they have now no part, *unless it be revealed to them.*" Besides, the text from Luke has reference to angels (ἀγγελοι)—the messengers of God—not departed spirits. What reason have we for believing that Pope Pius V., who anathematized our Elizabeth, or the exterminator, Dominic, the haughty and traitorous a'Becket, or Thomas Aquinas, who taught the doctrine of killing heretics if they persisted in their refusal to believe Rome's doctrines (all invocated by Romanists as saints), are angels in heaven?

It is yet a matter of doubt in this so-called infallible church how or in what manner saints have any knowledge of our prayers. Bellarmine, in the treatise already quoted, book i. cap. 20, on "The Beatitude of Saints," declares that there are four theories held by doctors:—

"1. Some say that they know from the relation of the angels, who at one time ascend to heaven, and at another time descend thence to us.

"2. Others say that the souls of the saints, as also the angels, by a certain wonderful swiftness that is natural to them, are in some measure everywhere, and themselves hear the prayers of the supplicants.

"3. Others say the saints see in God all things, from their beatitude, which in any way appertain to themselves, and hence even our prayers that are directed to them.

"4. Others say, lastly, that the saints do not see in the Word our prayers from the beginning of their blessedness, but that our prayers are *only then revealed to them by God* when we pour them forth."

And so again, Gabriel Biel, a great schoolman and divine (A.D. 1460), gives it as his opinion that the saints, of their own knowledge, do not hear our prayers by reason of their great distance from us, and that it is no part of their beatitude that they should know what is going on here, nor that it was "altogether certain" that they do know of our prayers; and he concludes by saying that it was "probable—but that it by no means followed of necessity"—that God reveals our prayers to them.[1] And so Veron, in his "*Rule of Catholic Faith*,"[2] says, "that it is not of faith that the saints in heaven hear the prayers of the living." But he asserts that they do in fact hear "our prayers which are revealed to them *probably* by the Almighty, or made known to them in various ways explained by St. Augustine," etc.

Let Romanists tell us how they know that our prayers are revealed to departed spirits. That we should pray to saints with the doubt in our minds whether they hear us, or with the belief that God reveals to them the fact that some one on earth is asking their aid, is a complication and corruption of Christianity worthy of the darkest ages, and reserved for Rome to consummate.

III. Romanists of the present day, in accepting this doctrine, with all its uncertainties and difficulties, nevertheless declare that they profess no *new doctrine*.

Have Romanists the sanction of Scripture or apostolic tradition? We maintain that they have neither.

---

[1] Gab. Biel in the Canone Missæ., Lect. 31. Lugdun. 1527.
[2] Birmingham, 1833, pp. 81, 82.

Some remarkable admissions on the part of Romanists themselves may be introduced here.

Cardinal Bellarmine admits that, before the coming of Christ, invocation of saints was not practised:—

"It is to be noted (he says) because the saints which died before the coming of Christ did not enter into heaven, neither did see God, nor could ordinarily take knowledge of the prayers of such as should petition unto them; therefore it was not the use in the Old Testament to say, St. Abraham, pray for me."[1]

And another Romanist, Eckius, writes, to the same effect, but he adds that the doctrine is not even taught in the New Testament.[2] And Veron, in his "*Rule of Catholic Faith,*"[3] says:—

"Moreover, although it be revealed in the word of God, *at least in the unwritten word*, that the saints are to be invocated, and it follows, therefore, that they hear us, still the close connexion does not make this consequence, however just and necessary, a revealed doctrine or an article of faith."

The *consequence*, however, depends on the supposition that the saints are to be invocated, and so assumes the whole matter in dispute.

It is admitted, therefore, notwithstanding the forced interpretation given to some texts by over-zealous controversialists, that the doctrine of invocation of saints is not revealed in, or enjoined by, either the Old or New Testament,—the written word. To us Protestants such an admission is a surrender of the whole question; for of what value can any custom be, however ancient, if not sanctioned

---

[1] Bellar. de Sanct. Beat., lib. i. c. 19, sect. 2, p. 412, tom. ii. Prag. 1751; and tom. ii. p. 833. Ingolstadii, 1601.
[2] Eckius, Euch. cap. de Sanct. Ven., pp. 179, 180. Coloniæ, 1567.
[3] Birmingham, 1833, p. 82. Father Waterworth's Translation.

by the word of God? But Veron tells us that it is at least sanctioned "in the unwritten word," namely, the assumed apostolic tradition of the church, which, with Romanists, is of equal authority with the written word. Worthless as this assertion is, it can nevertheless be shown to be groundless.

According to Bellarmine, all these alleged traditions, "although not written in the Scriptures, are nevertheless written in the monuments of the ancients, and in ecclesiastical books;"[1] and we shall have presently to record Dr. Wiseman's declaration to the like effect.[2] The question reduces itself, therefore, to a matter of fact, capable of proof one way or the other.

Now, as to this alleged tradition, there is the startling fact, that the invocation of saints was only first used in public liturgies under Boniface V., A.D. 618. We challenge the production of any genuine, well-authenticated liturgy, of anterior date, which contains any prayers to saints. This is strong negative testimony against the alleged antiquity of the custom. But further, Justin Martyr (A.D. 150), Clement, bishop of Alexandria (A.D. 180), and Tertullian, his contemporary, have handed down to us the public forms of Christian service and religious exercises of the primitive Christians. In these no trace whatever can be found, or mention made of prayers to saints, but to God alone through the mediation of Christ. In this fact we have strong grounds for believing that invocation of saints was not, in the second century, either a doctrine or practice of the church.

[1] "Etsi enim non sint scriptæ traditiones in divinis litteris, sunt tamen scriptæ in monumentis veterum, et in libris ecclesiasticis." Bell. de Verbo Dei non Scripto, lib. iv. c. 12. Edit. Prag. 1721.
[2] Lectures. No. iii. vol. i. p. 61. London, 1851. See our chapter on "Purgatory."

Irenæus, bishop of Lyons, martyred A.D. 165, testified as follows:—

"The church throughout the whole world does nothing by invocation of angels, nor by incantations, nor other depraved and curious means; but, with cleanliness, purity, and openness, directing prayers to the Lord who made all things, and calling upon the name of Jesus Christ our Lord, it exercises its powers for the benefit, and not for the seducing of mankind."[1]

An endeavour is made to explain away this striking passage, by the assertion, that Irenæus was alluding to evil spirits. This is an assumption not warranted by the context; besides, *angels* are absolutely named by him, and he makes an opposition to this by telling us whom Christians did invoke—that they directed their prayers to the Lord who made all things, and they called on the name of Jesus. We are not left in uncertainty, for we find passages of an unequivocal nature which leave no doubt as to the singleness of worship of the early Christians, and the acknowledgment by them of one only Mediator between God and man, Christ Jesus, without any subtle distinction of a mediator of mercy and a mediator of grace. Indeed, as to the "Monuments of the Ancients," Delahogue, the Maynooth Professor, is constrained to admit that—

"If any monuments of the invocation of saints are not found in the first and second centuries, that ought not to appear strange; for, as persecutions were then raging, the pastors of the churches were more anxious to instruct and to prepare the faithful for martyrdom than to write books. Besides, very few monuments of those ages have reached us."[2]

[1] Ecclesia per universum mundum,—nec invocationibus angelicis faciat aliquid, nec incantationibus, nec aliquâ pravâ curiositate, sed mundè, et purè et manifeste orationes dirigentes ad Dominum, qui omnia facit et nomen Domini nostri Jesu Christi [invocans, virtutes] secundum utilitates hominum, sed non ad seductionem perfecit. Irenæus, Oper. lib. ii. c. 35, sec. 5, p. 166. Paris, Benedictine Edit. 1710 [sic Agit Fevardentius].

[2] Si autem in primo et secundo sæculo multa non reperiantur invocationis

And to the like effect Cardinal Perron said :—"No trace of the invocation of saints can be found in the authors who lived nearest to the times of the apostles;" but he " accounts for this fact," in a like most convenient, but not convincing manner, " by the circumstance that most of the writings of that early period have perished."[1] Under this plea any modern invention or absurdity might be sanctioned. But the cardinal has forgotten that, in those writings which are extant, there is ample evidence to prove what has been before asserted.

It should be noted here, as a fact in the history of angel worship, that about the year 366 a sect called Angelites seem to have gained many followers in Phrygia. They dedicated oratories and chapels to St. Michael, to whom they prayed, and whom they called the Chief Captain of God's Host. This heresy became so important, that a council, assembled at Laodicea in Phrygia, passed a decree against it.

This decree was as follows—"We ought not to leave the church of God and invocate angels (*angelos*)."[2] The Romish canonists, Merlin and Crabbe,[3] feeling the force of this evidence against their modern teaching, artlessly, though deceivingly, altered *angelos* to *angulos*, and make this learned assembly decree that " we must not leave

Sanctorum monumenta, id mirum videri non debet; tunc enim, furentibus persecutionibus pastores ecclesiarum de instruendis et ad martyrium præparandis fidelibus magis soliciti erant, quam de libris scribendis. Præterea paucissima illorum sæculorum monumenta ad nos pervenerunt. Tractatus de Mysterio S.S. Trinitatis, Delahogue. R. Coyne, Dublin, 1822. Appendix de Cultu Sanctorum, etc., p. 233.

[1] See Stillingfleet's *Rational Account of the Grounds of the Protestant Religion*, pt. iii. c. 3, sec. xix. p. 590. Fol. Camb. 1701.

[2] Non oportet Christianos Ecclesiâ Dei derelictâ, abire atque Angelos nominare. Can. 35. Concil. Laodic. Binius. Concil. tom. i. p. 301. Lutet, Paris, 1636. Can. 35. Labb. Concil. tom. i. col. 1504. Paris, 1671.

[3] Non oportet Christianos, derelictâ Ecclesiâ Dei, abire in Angulos. Conciliorum quatuor Gen. etc. Edit. J. Merlinus. Fol. 68, Edit. Coloniæ, 1530. Conciliorum omnia, etc. P. Crabbe. Fol. 226, Edit. 1538.

the church of God and have recourse to angles" (or corners)!

With regard to the testimony of the early Christian writers, called the Fathers of the church, we have yet to record another remarkable and important admission of Romanists, which cuts at the root of the whole system if attempted to be based on the traditions of the church. We have seen that Dr. Wiseman accounts for the fact, that the early Christians, in their prayers for the departed, included patriarchs, prophets, apostles, martyrs, the Virgin Mary, etc., by asserting that the suffrages of the church had not then declared them to belong to a happier order; and also that Veron admitted it was not until A.D. 1439, at the Council of Florence, that the church made the declaration that the holy departed were in heaven. Bearing in mind the theory laid down by Cardinal Bellarmine, that it is essential that the saint invocated should be in the actual enjoyment of heaven, we draw attention to the candid acknowledgment of a Romish writer, Franciscus Pagna. He states that we are assured by three eminent Romanists, the celebrated Franciscan Castrus, also Medina, and Scotus, that "it was a *matter in controversy* of old whether the souls of the saints, before the day of judgment, did see God and enjoy the Divine vision; seeing many worthy men, and famous both for learning and holiness, did appear to hold that they do not see and enjoy it before the day of judgment, until, receiving their bodies together with them, they should enjoy Divine blessedness." He then enumerates the Fathers who held this opinion. Again, Stapleton, the celebrated Romish controversialist, and Regius Professor of Divinity at Douay (A.D. 1598), admitted that "these so many famous ancient Fathers [naming them] did not assent to this sentence which now in the Council of Florence was at length, after *much disputing, defined as a doctrine of faith,* that the souls of the righteous enjoy the sight of God before the day of judgment; but did deliver the contrary sentence thereto."[1]

The following admonition of Augustine on this important subject, may be regarded as conclusive testimony as to the opinion prevailing in the early part of the fifth century:—

"Let not our religion be the worship of dead men, because if they lived piously they are not so disposed to seek such honours; but they wish Him to be worshipped by us, by whom being enlightened they rejoice that we are deemed worthy of being partakers with them. *They are to be honoured, then, on the ground of imitation, not to be adored on the ground of religion;* and if they lived ill, wherever they be, they must not be worshipped. This also we may believe, *that the most perfect angels themselves, and the most excellent servants of God,* wish that we, with themselves, should worship God, in the contemplation of whom they are blessed. * * * Therefore, *we honour them with love, not with service.* Nor do we build temples to them; for they are unwilling to be so honoured by us, because they know that, when we are good, we are as temples to the most high God. Well, therefore, is it written, that a man was forbidden by an angel to adore him."[2]

[1] Fr. Pagna. in part ii. Directorii Inquisitor. Comment. xxi. Stapleton. Defens. Ecclesiastic. Auctor. contra Whitaker, lib. i. cap. 2. Antvp. 1596. Quoted by Usher, *Answer to a Challenge,* etc., cap. ix. p. 375. Camb. 1835.

The following is the list of names referred to by one or other of the two last named, to which we add the dates, etc.:—

(A.D.) 100. Clemens Romanus, bishop; 150. Justin, the martyr and saint; 165. Irenæus, bishop of Lyons; 200. Tertullian; 230. Origen, pupil of Clement, bishop of Alexandria; 300. Lactantius; 348. Prudentia; 370. Ambrose, bishop of Milan; 370. Victorinus; 416. Chrysostom; 420. Augustine; 430. Theodoret; 1050. Œcumenius; 1070. Theophylact; 1118. Euthymius; 1130. Bernard, the last of the Fathers.

It is evident that none of these could have known of the modern Romish theory of saint worship. A clear fact, thus admitted by Romanists themselves, is worth a thousand arguments founded on subtleties, theories, and suppositions.

[2] Non sit nobis religio cultus hominum mortuorum, quia si pie vixerunt, non sic habentur ut tales quærant honores; sed illum a nobis coli volunt, quo illuminante lætantur meriti sui nos esse consortes. Honorandi ergo sunt

We need not weary our readers, nor occupy space, in going over the ground already so thoroughly traversed, by quoting extracts from the writings of Fathers in successive centuries, by exposing the perversions and misquotations advanced by Romanists.

The following points may be regarded as conclusively established:—

In the first place, negatively, that the Christian writers, throughout the first three centuries and more, never refer to the invocation of saints and angels as a practice with which they were familiar; that they have not recorded or alluded to any forms of invocation of the kind used by themselves or by the church in their day; and that no services of the earliest times contain hymns, litanies, or collects, to angels, or to the spirits of the faithful departed.

In the second place, positively, that the principles which they habitually maintained and advocated are irreconcilable with such a practice.

As to the worship or invocation of the Virgin Mary, which forms the principal item in modern Romish devotions, it has been shown by the Rev. J. E. Tyler, after a diligent and impartial investigation of the records of the early councils, and the works of the early Christian writers to the end of the first five hundred years, that they all testify, "as with one voice, that these writers and their contemporaries knew of no belief in the present [*supposed*] power of the Virgin Mary, and of her influence with God; no practice, in public

propter imitationem, non adorandi propter religionem.. Quare honoramus eos caritate non servitute; nec eis templa construimus. Nolunt enim se sic honorari a nobis, quia nos ipsos, cum boni sumus, templa summa Dei esse noverunt. Lecte itaque scribitur, etc. Augustine on "*True Religion,*" tom. i. p. 786. Benedictine Edition. Paris, 1700. There is a similar passage in Augustine's book De Civit. Dei, lib. 8, c. 27.

or private, of praying to God through her mediation; or of invoking her for her good offices of intercession, and advocacy, and patronage; no offering of thanks and praise made to her; no ascription of divine honour or glory to her name. On the contrary, all the writers of those ages testify that, to the early Christians, God was the only object of prayer, and Christ the only Mediator and Intercessor in whom they had put their trust."

CHAPTER VII.

IMAGE WORSHIP.

"As to the images of saints, it is certain that, when the gospel was first preached, there was for some time no use of images among Christians, especially in churches."—*Cassander. Consult. Art.* xxi. *de Imag.*, p. 163. Lugd. 1608.

THERE is no point of doctrine on which the Romanist is more tender than that of "Image Worship," or the use of images in his religious exercises. Idolatry, or idol worship, is a grave charge to be brought against a professed Christian. Without using hard words or calling names, let us for a moment dispassionately examine what is taught by orthodox members of the Papal church on this point of their faith.

At the twenty-fifth session of the Council of Trent (A.D. 1563), "all bishops and others sustaining the office and charge of teaching" were directed "especially to instruct the faithful that images of Christ, the Virgin, and other saints are to be had and retained, particularly in churches;

* * * and that *due* honour and veneration are to be awarded to them." The decree does not define what is the nature of this " due honour :" but it specially permits us to kiss the image, to uncover the head, and to prostrate ourselves before it.[1] The council having left this important matter to the *teaching* of bishops, priests, etc., their opinions on the subject, as might be expected, are divided. The illustrious champion of Romanism, Cardinal Bellarmine, in his second book on "*Sacred Images*,"[2] tells us that there are different opinions on the question proposed—" With what sort of worship are images to be honoured?" The first opinion he rejects, namely: "That the faithful ought to do no more, with regard to images, than to *worship before them* the prototype, the exemplar, the original Being, of which the image is a representation." The second opinion he does not absolutely object to, which is: "*That the same honour* is due to *the image as to the exemplar;* and thence that the image of Christ is to be worshipped with the worship of *Latria* [the species of worship rendered by Romanists to the Most High God], the image of the blessed Virgin with the worship of *Hyperdulia,* and the images of the other saints with the worship of *Dulia.*" He names several "Catholic theologians" who taught this doctrine, and among them Alexander, the "blessed saint" St. Thomas Aquinas, Cardinal Cajetan,

---

[1] "Imagines porro Christi, Deiparæ Virginis et aliorum sanctorum, in templis præsertim habendas, et retinendas, eisque debitum honorem et venerationem impertiendam; non quod credatur inesse aliqua in iis divinitas, vel virtus, propter quam sint colendæ; vel quod ab eis sit aliquid petendum; vel quod fiducia in imaginibus sit figenda, veluti olim fiebat a gentibus quæ in idolis spem suam collocabant; sed quoniam honos qui eis exhibetur, refertur ad prototypa, quæ illæ repræsentant; ita ut per imagines, quas osculamur, et coram quibus caput aperimus et procumbimus, Christum adoremus, et sanctos, quorum illæ similitudinem gerunt, veneremur." Sess. xxv. *Decretum de Invocatione, Veneratione, et reliquiis Sanctorum, et sacris Imaginibus.* Lab. et Coss. concl. tom. xiv. col. 895. Paris, 1671.

[2] Cap. 20. Edit. Prag. 1721.

the "blessed saint" Bonaventure, Marsilius, Almagne, "and others."

With regard to Aquinas, it may be as well to remark, that he justifies himself for giving the self-same worship to the wooden cross which he gives to God himself, by quoting the ritual of his church. His words are:—

"Because Christ himself is adored with Divine honour, it follows that his image is to be adored with Divine honour.— We offer the supreme adoration of the *Latria* to that Being in whom we place our hope of salvation; but we place our hope of salvation in the Cross of Christ, for the church sings: 'Hail, O Cross, our only hope in this time of passion; increase righteousness to the pious, and grant pardon to the guilty.' *Therefore the Cross of Christ is to be adored with the supreme adoration of the Latria.*"[1]

This is no figurative language; for the "Pontificale Romanum" directs that the cross of the pope's legate shall be carried in the right hand, "because *Latria* is due to it."[2]

In justice, however, to Bellarmine, we should add, that he said of the theory taught by Aquinas[3] and his school—"Those who maintain that images are to be adored with divine honour are driven to use such subtle distinctions as they themselves can scarcely understand, much less the ignorant." And so say we. Whether this teaching, sanctioned as it is by such high authorities, is or is not idolatry in its worst sense, is happily not our inquiry. We have merely stated the Romanist's case in his own words, and if he is charged with teaching an idolatrous practice, we are not to blame. But our present object is to prove that what the present Roman

---

[1] Thos. Aquinas, Theo. Sum. part iii. quæs. 25, art. 1—4; Romæ, 1686; and see Lib. iii. Dixt. ix. Salect. iv. p. 126, tom. xxiv. Venice, 1787.

[2] "Quia debetur ei Latria." Pontificale Romanum, p. 468. Edit. Romæ, 1818.

[3] De Relig. Sac. Lit. c. xxii. sec. 4. Prag. Edit. 1721.

church does authoritatively teach as her doctrine is a modern invention.

We have seen that the *church* by her mouthpiece, the Trent Council, has not defined the meaning of the expression "*due* honour." It may be, as Aquinas has it, that supreme worship is to be given to the image of Christ, a less worship to that of the Virgin, and a lower degree to that of saints. But the decree says that these images are to be retained in churches, and "that due honour and veneration are to be awarded to them;" because "the honour which is shown unto them [the sacred images] is referred to the prototypes which they represent, in such wise that by the images which we kiss, and before which we uncover the head and prostrate ourselves, we adore Christ, and venerate the saints, whose similitude they bear." It is argued, therefore, that after all, the worship, whatever it may be, is only a *relative* worship. They do not worship what they see, but the Being represented by the image before them. This is refined Popery, and not much understood by the people; and has led, as we shall see, to absolute idolatry. Let us, however, take the declaration in the most liberal sense; and we shall find that even this species of refined Romanism was expressly condemned by the early Christian writers, as a proposition advanced by the heathens and image-worshippers of their day.

I. And first, on the theory of *relative worship*.

Arnobius, who flourished at the beginning of the third century, was himself a zealous pagan before his conversion to Christianity, and therefore practically knew what he was writing about. He thus remonstrated with the heathen idolaters of his day:—

"You say, 'We worship the gods *through the images*.' What

then? If these images did not exist, would the gods not know they were worshipped, nor be aware of any honour being paid to them by you? What can be more unjust, more disrespectful, more cruel, than to recognise one as a God, and offer up supplication to another thing; to hope for help from a Divine Being, and pray to an image which has no sense?"

Again, he says:—

"But ye say,—You are mistaken; we do not consider materials of brass, or silver, or gold, or other things of which the statues are made, to be of themselves gods or sacred divinities; but in these materials we worship and venerate those gods whom the holy dedication brings in, and causes to dwell in the images wrought by the craftsmen."[1]

Origen, a Father of the third century, in his writings against Celsus, strongly condemned, by anticipation, the same theory. He says:—

"What sensible person would not laugh at a man who * * * * looks to images, and there offers up his prayer to them, or, *beholding them, refers it to the being contemplated in his mind*, to whom he fancies that he ought to ascend from the visible object, which is the symbol of him (whom the image is supposed to represent)?"[2]

Saint Ambrose, bishop of Milan, in the fourth century, also thus speaks of this species of heathen worship:—

"This gold, if carefully handled, has an outward value; but inwardly it is mere ordinary metal. Examine, I pray you, and sift thoroughly the class of Gentiles. The words they utter are rich and grand: the things they defend are utterly devoid of truth: they talk of God—they worship an image."[3]

Saint Augustine, a Father of great authority with

---

[1] Arnob., lib. v. c. ix. and c. xvii. Leipsic Edit. 1816.
[2] Origen cont. Cels., lib. vii. c. xliv. Paris, 1733.
[3] Amb. ad Valen. Epist. cap. i. xviii. Venice, 1781.

Romanists (when he speaks for them), arguing against the nice distinctions made by the heathen idolaters of his day, says :—

"But those persons seem to themselves to belong to a more purified religion who say—'I worship neither an image nor a demon [this does not mean a *devil*, but a departed spirit], but I regard the bodily figure as the *representation of that Being whom I ought to worship.*' * * * And when, again, with regard to these, they [the more enlightened heathens] begin to be pressed hard on the point, that they worship bodies, * * * they are bold enough to answer that they do not worship the images themselves, *but the divinities which preside over and rule them.*"[1]

And, again, he says :—

"But some disputant comes forward, and, very wise in his own conceit, says—'I do not worship that stone nor that insensible image; your prophet could not say they have eyes and see not, and I be ignorant that that image neither hath a soul, nor sees with his eyes, nor hears with his ears. *I do not worship that, but I adore what I see, and serve him whom I do not see.*' And who is he ?—a certain invisible divinity, which presides over that image."[2]

And once again, he says :—

"And lest any one should say, 'I do not worship the image, but that *which the images signify,*' it is immediately added, and they worshipped and served the creature more than the Creator. Now, understand well, they either worship the image or a creature; he who worships the image converts the truth of God into a lie."[3]

Whether Ambrose and Augustine (both saints canonized by the church of Rome) were right or wrong in their con-

---

[1] Aug., in Psalm xciii. part 2, tom. iv. p. 1261. Paris, 1679.
[2] Aug., in Psalm xcvi. tom. iv. p. 1047.
[3] Aug., Serm. cxvii. tom. v. p. 905.

demnation of this theory of relative worship, subsequently revived by the Roman church A.D. 787, at the second Council of Nice, it is evident that the doctrine was not universally admitted by the Christian church until very many years after their day, and therefore must be accounted a novel doctrine.

II. On the second head, as to the introduction of images in churches for religious worship, we may observe generally, that it was the opinion of Lactantius, an eloquent Latin Father, called the Christian Cicero, who wrote at the end of the third century, that, "beyond all doubt, wherever an image is, there is no religion." [1] But, without going to the writings of the early Fathers, whose works are replete with denunciations against the use of images in religious worship, let us take the opinion of modern Romish divines. Two or three instances will suffice.

The great scholar, Erasmus, who was ordained a priest in 1492, said—"Down to Saint Jerome's time (A.D. 400) those of the true religion would suffer no image, neither painted nor graven, in the church; no, not the picture of Christ." And he adds, "No man can be free from show of superstition that is prostrate before an image, and looks on it intentionally, and speaks to it, and kisses it; nay, although he does but (only) pray before an image." [2]

Henry Cornelius Agrippa, a divine of great and varied attainments, who died 1535, said:—

"The corrupt manners and false religion of the Gentiles have infected our religion also, and brought into the church images and pictures, with many ceremonies of external pomp,

[1] Lact. Divin. Instit., lib. ii. c. xix. tom. i. Paris, 1748.
[2] "Usque ad ætatem Hieronymi erant probatæ religionis viri, qui in templis nullum ferebant imaginem, nec picturam, nec sculptam, etc." Erasm. Symbol. Catch. tom. v. p. 1187. Edit. L. Bat. 1703.

none whereof was found amongst the first and true Christians."[1]

To go up to a higher date, Agobard, archbishop of Lyons (A.D. 816), said:—

"The orthodox Fathers, for avoiding of superstition, did carefully provide that no pictures should be set up in churches, lest that which is worshipped should be painted on the walls. There is no example in all the Scriptures or Fathers, of adoration of images: they ought to be taken for an ornament to please the sight, not to instruct the people."[2]

Such testimony we might multiply, but to what purpose? Romanism stands self-convicted.

III. As to councils. Here we have a regular "Papal war." The thirty-sixth canon of the Council of Elvira or Illiberis, Spain, A.D. 305, decreed that "no pictures should be in churches, lest that should be worshipped which was painted on the walls."

In 730, the Council of Constantinople, under the emperor Leo (the Isaurian), passed a decree, not only against the abuse, but against the use of any images or pictures in churches. Perceiving how the Christian church was becoming immersed in gross idolatry, and feeling that the Arabian imposture (Mohammedanism) would be promoted by such an innovation on Christianity, Leo undertook to abolish the sinful practice altogether. He issued an edict, directing that images should be removed from churches and sacred places, and be broken up or committed to the flames, with the threat of punishment for disobedience of orders. Constantine, to whom the image worshippers, in derision, gave

[1] Cornel. Agrippa, de incert. et vanit. Scient., c. lvii. p. 105, tom. ii. Lugd.
[2] Agobard Opera. Lib. de Imag. tom. i. p. 226. Edit. Baluzius, Paris, 1665.

the name of Copronymus, followed in his father's footsteps. In A.D. 754, he summoned another council at the same place, which was attended by 388 bishops, who enjoined the absolute rejection of every image or picture from every church.

In 787, at the seventh session of the second Council of Nice, images, etc., were, for the first time, authoritatively permitted. It was declared that "there should be paid to them the worship of salutation and honour, and not that true worship which is accorded by faith and belongs to God alone;" and that "the honour so paid to them was transmitted to the originals they represent." In this year, the Empress Irene, the Jezebel of that day (who became regent, on the death of her husband, Leo IV., and during the minority of her son, Constantine VI.), convoked the council, and was mainly instrumental in effecting the firm establishment of image worship. She was heathen by instinct, and conceived the idea that this idolatry would soon make the world forget the profligacy of her past life. But, in 794, the Council of Frankfort, by its second canon, condemned the said decree of the second Council of Nice, and all worship of images; as did also, in 815, a Council of Constantinople, which decreed that all ornaments, paintings, etc., in churches should be defaced. In 825, the Council of Paris condemned the decree of the second Council of Nice, declaring that it was no light error to say that even some degree of holiness could be attained through their means. This Council of Paris was continued at Aix-la-Chapelle; the French bishops still resisting the decree of the second Council of Nice, though the pope had approved it. But in 842, at the Council of Constantinople, under the emperor Michael, and Theodora his mother, the decree of the second

Council of Nice was confirmed, the image-breakers anathematized, and images restored to churches.

In 870, at the tenth session of the Council of Constantinople, the third canon again enjoined the worship of the cross and the images of the saints. And at the same place, at another council, A.D. 789, in the fifth session, the decrees of the second Council of Nice were approved and confirmed.

Again, in 1084, at another Council of Constantinople, the decree made in the council of 842, in favour of the use of images, was confirmed.

The worship of images, after this time, appears to have taken such deep root among the people, that, in 1549, the Council of Mayence decreed that people should be taught that images were not set up to be worshipped; and priests were enjoined to remove the image of any saint to which the people flocked, as if attributing some sort of a divinity to the image itself, or as supposing that God or the saints would perform what they prayed for by means of that particular image, and not otherwise.[1]

Such was the fearful idolatry to which the introduction of images into churches led; so that the assembly of French bishops, at the celebrated conference at Poissi, A.D. 1561,

---

[1] The following are references to the above Councils:—
"Placuit picturas in ecclesiâ esse non debere; ne quid colitur et adoratur in parietibus." Council of Eliberi, A.D. 300, can. xxxvi. Labb. et Coss. Conc. tom. i. col. 974. Paris, 1671.
Council of Constant., A.D. 730. Ibid. tom. vi. col. 1461.
Council of Constant., A.D. 754. Ibid. tom. vi. col. 1661.
Council of Nicea II., A.D. 787. Ibid. pp. 449, 899, tom. vii.
Council of Frankfort, A.D. 794. Can. ii. Ibid. tom. vii. col. 1013.
Council of Constant., A.D. 815. Ibid. tom. vii. col. 1299.
Council of Paris, A.D. 825. Ibid. tom. vii. col. 1542.
Council of Constant., A.D. 842. Ibid. tom. vii. col. 1782.
Council of Constant., A.D. 870, session x. Can. iii. Ibid. tom. viii. col. 962.
Council of Constant., A.D. 879, session v. Ibid. tom. ix. col. 324.
Council of Mayence, A.D. 1549. Ibid. tom. xiv. col. 667.

enjoined on the priests to use their endeavours to abolish all superstitious practices; to instruct the people that images were exposed to view in the churches for no other reason than to remind persons of Jesus Christ and the saints; and it was decreed that all images which were in *any way indecent*, or which merely illustrated fabulous tales, should be entirely removed:[1]—a proof of the corruption of the times that such a decree should be needed. And the Council of Rouen (A.D. 1445), in its seventh canon, condemned the practice of addressing prayers to images under peculiar titles, as "Our Lady of Recovery," "Our Lady of Pity," of "Consolation," and the alike, alleging that such practices tended to superstition, as if there was more virtue in one image than in another.[2]

It remained for the Council of Trent (at the twenty-fifth session, A.D. 1563) to confirm, and for Rome to give its authoritative sanction to the worship of images, and their use in churches, as part of the religious worship of Christians.

Such, then, is the rise and progress of image worship in the church, now confirmed by Rome; call it idolatry, or call it what you will, "it was not so from the beginning." "They that make a graven image are all of them vanity." (Isaiah xliv. 9.)

[1] See Landon's "*Manual of Councils*," p. 495. London, 1846.
[2] Labb. et Coss. Concil. tom. xiii. Concl. Rothomagense, Can. vii. col. 1307. Paris, 1671.

CHAPTER VIII.

IMAGE WORSHIP (*continued*).

"Ye shall not add unto the word which I command you, neither shall ye diminish aught from it, that ye may keep the commandments of the Lord your God which I command you."—Deut. iv. 2.

No chapter on image worship would be complete without some observation on the treatment, by priests of Rome, of what we designate the "Second Commandment." And first, a few words on the translations of Exodus xx. 4, 5. The Latin Vulgate translation is as follows:—

"Non facies tibi sculptile, neque omnem similitudinem, quæ est in cœlo desuper et quæ in terrâ deorsum, nec eorum quæ sunt in aquis sub terrâ. Non adorabis ea, neque coles."[1]

The Douay [Romish] translation is:—

"Thou shalt not make to thyself any *graven thing*, nor the likeness, * * * thou shalt not *adore* them nor *serve* them."

And the Protestant authorized version:—

"Thou shalt not make unto thee any *graven image*, or any likeness, * * * thou shalt not *bow down* thyself to them nor serve them."

1. The word *image* is alleged to be a mistranslation.[2]

For a reply let us go first to Rome and the Papal press. Two editions of an Italian translation of the Catechism of the Council of Trent were simultaneously issued at Rome,

---

[1] Biblia Sacra Vulgatæ editionis Sixti. Pont. Max jussu recognita, et Clementis VIII. auctoritate, etc. Venetiis, MDCLXXVII. Apud Nicholaum Pezzana.

[2] See Dr. Doyle's *Abridgment of Christian Doctrine*, R. Coyne, Dublin, 1846, p. 49; and Dr. Dixon's *General Introduction to the Sacred Scriptures*, Duffy, Dublin, 1852, who devotes a chapter to the subject.

with the authoritative approval of Pope Pius V. (A.D. 1567). At page 375, we have the translation given as follows:—

"Non ti farai alcuna *imagine scolpita*, etc. :—non le adorerari, ne le honorerari."

That is :—

"Thou shalt not make thee any *sculptured image*—thou shalt not adore them, nor shalt thou honour them." [1]

Passing over to Austria, we find that in the Austrian "Great Reading Book for German Normal and Upper Schools in the Imperial and Royal Provinces" [2] the commandments are professedly set out as they are given in the Bible, and here the word "bild," *image*, is used. And the correctness of our translation is also confirmed by the "Catechism in use in all the churches in the empire of France." [3] The pupil is requested to recite the commandments "as God gave them to Moses;" here again the translation is "aucune *image* taillée," any cut or graven *image*.

And in England also we have the same translation recognised in "*The Poor Man's Catechism*, by the Rev. John Mannock, A.S.R." In p. 133, section iii., we read—"Thou shalt not make to thyself any *graven image*." And in the foot-note to the Douay translation [4] of Exod. xx. 4, is added :—

All such *images* and likenesses are forbidden by this com-

---

[1] These two editions are in the Library of Trinity College, Dublin. See *Catholic Laymon*, December, 1852, p. 142. Dublin.

[2] Grosses Lehrebuch für die deutschen Normal und Haupt-Schulen in den Kais Königl. Staaten. Religions-Lehre Wien., 1847, p. 69. "Du sollat dir kein geschnitztes Bild machen dasselbe anzubeten."

[3] Catéchisme à l'usage de toutes les Eglises de l'empire Français," Paris, 1806. "D. Récitez ces Commandements *tels que Dieu les a donné à Moïse*"—"tu ne feras aucune *image* taillée," p. 51.

[4] Published by Richardson and Son, with the approval of Dr. Wiseman, dated from Birmingham, 1847.

mandment as are made to be *adored* and *served*," though the text is " *graven thing.*"

We are entitled, therefore, by the admissions of Roman Catholics themselves, to claim for our version accuracy of translation when it uses the word *image*.

2. The second peculiarity to be observed is the use of the word " *adore* " in all the Romish versions, and in all catechisms where this commandment is set out, while our translation renders it " bow down."

The best authority on this subject is, perhaps, Dr. Walton's well-known " Polyglot." [1] Here we have the Hebrew text with an interlinear literal translation of Pagnini compared with the Hebrew by Ben Ariam Notanius, and others. The rendering of the original is *non incurvabis*, which means, that a literal *bending of the body* is prohibited. The Trent Council permits, as we have already shown, a *prostration* before the image; hence the necessity of changing the meaning of the word. The Septuagint translators render it προσκυνήσεις, which literally means a bending of the body.[2]

3. The next peculiarity to be observed is, the division of the commandments in the Romanist Bibles and manuals. When all the commandments are given, the first and second are blended into one and considerably curtailed, and the

---

[1] Folio edition, tom. i. p. 310.
[2] See the word used in the following texts:—Gen. xviii. 2; xxvii. 29; xxxiii. 3, 6, 7; xxxvii. 7; xlix. 8; and Isa. xlv. 14. The original Hebrew signifies to "bow down," and the Greek "to prostrate oneself in homage;" but in a secondary sense *both* words apply to the mental act of adoration and honouring: but if mental *adoration* be forbidden, how much more the *outward* act by which it is signified? It is the outward act by which man is made cognizant of the feeling of adoration in another, and although the outward act may be insincere, yet it *acquiesces* in the propriety of the feeling, and would, of course, be forbidden when it testified to the presence of a forbidden sentiment.

tenth is divided into two. The Bible clearly makes the second commandment a distinct precept from the first. "Thou shalt have no other gods before [or but] me." "Thou shalt not make unto thee any graven image.... Thou shalt not bow down thyself to them [the images], nor serve them." The first forbids the acknowledgment of any other than the one true God. The second forbids the use of images in religious worship. Clearly, these are two distinct commands. Whenever the church of Rome does give the second part, she blends the two precepts into one, and thus endeavours to evade the direct force and prohibition of the command to abstain from the use of all images in religious worship. For instance, in Dr. Doyle's "General Catechism,"[1] are the following questions and answers :—

"Q. Say the Ten Commandments of God.

"A. 1. I am the Lord thy God, thou shalt not have strange gods before me. Thou shalt not make to thyself either an idol or any figure to adore it.

"2. Thou shalt not take the name of the Lord thy God in vain," etc.

And the tenth is divided into two, in order to make up the number thus :—

"9. Thou shalt not covet thy neighbour's wife.

"10. Thou shalt not covet thy neighbour's goods."

It is worthy of observation that this tenth commandment, according to our arrangement, embraces one subject, "Thou shalt not *covet;*" and so obvious is this, that the Trent Catechism is compelled to consider the whole as one, "their subject not being dissimilar," though it designates it as the

[1] Stereotyped edition. Richard Grace, Dublin, 1843, p. 25.

ninth and tenth commandments. There is this further peculiarity: when divided, the commandments are thus given:—

"9. Thou shalt not covet thy neighbour's wife.
"10. Thou shalt not covet thy neighbour's goods."

But the Trent Catechism gives the order thus:—

Of the Ninth and Tenth Commandments.
"Thou shalt not covet thy neighbour's *house;* thou shalt not covet thy neighbour's *wife*, nor his man-servant, nor his maid-servant, nor his ox, nor his ass, nor anything that is his."

So that, following this authority, the division should be—

"9. Thou shalt not covet thy neighbour's house.
"10. Thou shalt not covet thy neighbour's wife."

And, on the principle of making these different precepts, there is sufficient omitted for an eleventh commandment!

The object for adopting this division is obvious: it enables compilers to omit what we place as the second commandment, without any alteration of the numbers, when that omission may suit a purpose.

It is true that Augustine is cited as an authority for this division; but Augustine gives both divisions, as may be found by a reference to his "*Epistola ad Bonifacium*," and the "*Speculum ex Deuteronomia*." Augustine's theory was, that the first *three* precepts contained our duty to God, and by this division he desired to symbolize the Trinity; a mischievous mysticism which brought much evil into the church.[2] On the other hand, we follow the division adopted by the Jews,

---

[1] Cat. Concl. Tridt., Part iii., cap. x. q. 1.
[2] See a very clever pamphlet entitled "*Why does the Church of Rome hide the Second Commandment from the People?*" by Dr. M'Caul.

as testified by Josephus,[1] and also by the Greek church; and among the Fathers, we may reckon on our side Tertullian, Clement of Alexandria, Origen, Gregory Nazianzen, Athanasius, Chrysostom, Jerome, Ambrose, John Cassion, Sulpicius Severus, etc.[2]

4. This leads us to one of the gravest charges we have to bring against Roman Catholics, namely, the entire omission from the Decalogue of what we may now safely call *the* second commandment. This has been done in most of the catechisms, the exception being when the omission is not made, and, in that case, attention is pointedly called to the fact. For instance, in the catechism of Dr. Doyle, above quoted, in p. 26, the following question is asked:—

" Q. Is any *part* of the commandments left out?
" A. No.—But some *words* are omitted."

But in none of those catechisms which do *omit* the second precept or commandment is this question asked! To quote all the examples and references would be need-

[1] Josephus' "*Jewish Antiquities*," book iii. c. v. Works, vol. i. p. 207. London, 1716.
[2] Bishop Taylor, in his "*Christian Law the great Rule of Conscience*," (b. ii. c. ii. Rule vi. vol. xii. p. 360, *et seq.*, Heber's edit. Lond. 1822), quotes Athanasius, Cyril, Jerome, and Hesychius, as making the introduction to be one of the commandments, and those which we call the first and second, to be the second only. Of the same opinion of uniting these two, he quotes Clemens Alexandrinus, Augustine, Bede, and Bernard, the ordinary Gloss, Lyra, Hugo Cardinalis, and Lombard. On the other side, two distinct commandments are made by the Chaldee Paraphrast, and by Josephus, Origen, Gregory Nazianzen, Ambrose, Jerome, Chrysostom, Augustine (or the author of *The Question on the Old and New Testaments*), Sulpicius Severus, Zonaras, and admitted as probable by Bede, followed by Calvin and other Protestants, not Lutherans. Athanasius, in his *Synop. Scrip.*, gives the division as follows:—" The Book hath these Ten Commandments in tables: the *first* is 'I am the Lord thy God;' the *second*, 'Thou shalt not make an idol to thyself, nor the likeness of anything.'" And Cyril (lib. v. cont. Jul.) brings in Julian thus accounting them:—"I am the Lord thy God which brought thee out of the land of Egypt; the *second* after this—'Thou shalt have no other gods besides me; thou shalt not make to thyself (*simulacrum*) a graven image.'"

lessly extending our work; we give only a few. Of catechisms published in England, we have to notice " The Catechism or Christian Doctrine by way of Question and Answer, illustrated by the Sacred Text and Tradition."[1] We read:—

" Q. How many commandments has God given?

" A. Ten.

" Q. Say them.

" A. [N.B. *Placed in inverted commas as a quotation from the Bible*] 'I am the Lord thy God, who brought thee out of the land of Egypt and out of the house of bondage; thou shalt not have strange gods before me. Thou shalt not take the name of the Lord thy God in vain. Remember to keep holy the Sabbath day. Honour thy father and thy mother. Thou shalt not commit adultery. Thou shalt not steal. Thou shalt not bear false witness against thy neighbour. Thou shalt not covet thy neighbour's wife. Thou shalt not covet thy neighbour's goods.' Exod. xx. 3, etc."

Again, in " A Catholic Catechism methodically arranged for the use of the uninstructed, translated from the Italian of the Very Rev. Antonio Rosmini-Serbati, D.D., Founder and General of the Institute of Charity, by the Rev. U. S. Agar,"[2] the commandments are thus given:—

" 1. I am the Lord thy God; thou shalt not have other gods before me.

" 2. Thou shalt not take the name of the Lord thy God in vain.

" 3. Remember thou keep *holy the days appointed*." [!] etc., etc., etc.

Of those published in Ireland, we may cite " Dr. James

[1] Pages 25 and 26. London, C. Dolman, 61, New Bond Street, 1843. This book contains 249 pages, and is alleged to be, on the title-page, " permissu superiorum."

[2] Pages 33 and 34. London and Dublin: Richardson and Son (containing 203 pages). There is no date, but it is now on sale. This translation is dedicated to Dr. Ullathorne, one of the [illegal] Romish bishops in this country.

Butler's Catechism, revised, enlarged, approved and recommended by the four R.C. archbishops in Ireland as a general catechism for the kingdom," [1] p. 36.

"A Catechism: or an abridgment of the Christian Doctrine. By the Most Reverend Dr. Reilly. Dublin: Richard Grace, Catholic bookseller, 1845," p. 20.

Butler's Catechism (title as before), "approved and recommended by the Right Rev. James Doyle, D.D., bishop of Kildare and Leighlin. Dublin: printed by Richard Grace and Son, 1848," p. 36.

The commandments in all these are thus given, at the several pages indicated:—

"1. I am the Lord thy God, thou shalt not have strange gods before me.

"2. Thou shalt not take the name of the Lord thy God in vain.

"3. Remember that thou keep holy the Sabbath day.

*   *   *   *   *   *

"9. Thou shalt not covet thy neighbour's wife.

"10. Thou shalt not covet thy neighbour's goods."

With this evidence of the suppression of God's command against the worship of images, we may be spared the enumeration of examples from foreign catechisms. The curious on this subject may obtain further information by consulting the little pamphlet of the Rev. Dr. M'Caul before cited, where all these foreign catechisms are quoted, and the writer thus sums up his evidence:—

"Here, then, are twenty-nine Catechisms in use in Rome and Italy, France, Belgium, Austria, Bavaria, Silesia, Poland, Ireland,

---

[1] The edition before us is the "27th edition carefully corrected and improved with amendments. Dublin: John Coyne, 1844."

England, Spain, and Portugal, in 27 of which the second commandment is totally omitted; in 2 mutilated, and only a portion expressed. Is not, then, the charge proved, that the church of Rome hides the second commandment from the people?"

Any further comment on this treatment of the word of God by Romanists would be superfluous.

CHAPTER IX.

PURGATORY.

"PURGATORY—The Priests' Kitchen."
Italian Proverb.

IN conversation with an intelligent Italian, a man of eminent ability and professedly a Roman Catholic, we took occasion, among other topics, to speak to him of his religion. We asked him what he thought of the doctrine of purgatory? "Oh! (said he), we call purgatory here (Italy) the priest's kitchen!" The idea is a good one; for purgatory is the foundation for masses, indulgences, and prayers for the dead. Credulous people are taught to believe that the faithful departed are detained in torments, if not in actual flames, till they can be relieved and set free by the help of these religious performances; and priests are paid, and have death-bed bequests made them to do this work, under the representation that they can accelerate the transit of the sufferer from purgatory to heaven. The doctrine is one of very considerable importance to the Romish church, and worth maintaining at all hazards. Those who die in mortal sin go to hell; but those who die in what this church asserts to be venial sins, for which satisfaction has not been made in this life, or for which satisfaction has not been remitted by indulgences, go to purgatory. Again, we are told, " when a man's sins are forgiven him, and *he is justified*, there yet remains an obligation to the payment of temporal punishment, either in this world, or the world to come, in purgatory;"[1] then by indulgences these temporal punishments can be remitted. The mass is also stated to be " propitiatory," and " rightly offered," not only for the living, " but also for those who are *departed in Christ*, and who are not as yet fully purified and purged "[2]—namely, for those in purgatory. And the Trent Catechism tells us that purgatory is a purgatorial, literal *fire*, in which the souls of the pious, being tormented for a defined time, are purged of their guilt, by which means an entrance is gained into heaven.[3] The system is a masterpiece of imposition and priestcraft: and the only surprise is, that men in the nineteenth century can be found to believe in it. There is, first, the arbitrary distinction between venial and mortal sins, the line where one ends and the other begins being judged of by the priest in the confessional: a system wholly unknown to the early Christian church. As God alone knoweth the heart, what an impious assumption in the priest to take upon himself to draw the line! Then comes the absolution from the sin, by the priest, leaving the punishment due to the sin, to be undergone in this life or in purgatory. Conceive for a moment a criminal, found guilty of some offence, being told that he received the Queen's most

---

[1] Concl. Trident. Sess. vi. can. xxx.
[2] Ibid. Sess. xxii. cap. ii.
[3] " Est Purgatorius *ignis*, quo piorum animæ ad definitum tempus *cruciatæ* expiantur." Catech. Concl. Trid. Pars. i. s. v. Purg. Ignis. p. 61. Paris Edit. 1848.

gracious pardon because he had repented and confessed his guilt, but nevertheless that he must still undergo the punishment due to the crime! It would be difficult to make the man appreciate either the value of the pardon or the justice of the proceeding. Yet such is the modern Romish theory, which we challenge Romanists to support by any evidence from the early Christian church.

The proposition of a purgatory was *first* submitted for discussion at the second session of the Council of Ferrara, 15th March, 1438, and before that date it formed no part of any creed, nor was it recognised as the admitted doctrine of the church. It was first admitted as a doctrine of the Romish church at the Council of Florence, 1439.[1]

We may here record a remarkable admission on this subject. The doctrine involves a decision, on the part of those who profess it, as to the state of departed souls; any uncertainty on which head, must also involve an uncertainty in the belief in the doctrine itself. The Benedictine editors of the works of Ambrose (A.D. 370) make the following acknowledgment:—

"It is not, indeed, wonderful that Ambrose should have written in this manner about the state of souls; but it may seem almost incredible how uncertain and how little consistent the holy fathers have been on that question from the very times of the apostles to the pontificate of Gregory XI. and the Council of Florence, that is, in the space of nearly fourteen hundred years. For not only do they differ one from another, as in matters not [yet] defined by the church as likely to happen, but they are not even sufficiently consistent with themselves."[2]

[1] The Council of Florence was a continuation of that of Ferrara.
[2] "Mirum quidem non est hoc modo de animarum statu scripsisse Ambrosium, sed illud propemodum incredibile videri potest, quam in eâ quæstione sancti patres ab ipsis apostolorum temporibus ad Gregorii XI. Pontificatum, Florentinumque Concilium, hoc est toto ferme quatuordecim sæculorum spatio, incerti ac parum constantes exstiterint. Non enim solum alius ab

What better information, what new revelation, had the doctors of the Council of Florence, which the Christians of the time of Ambrose had not? The fact is, the Bible speaks only of heaven and hell, and of no such intermediate place as purgatory. The Bible having ceased to be the guide of the church of Rome, that church, acting on her own authority, invented and then defined what she chose about purgatory, and afterwards assumed the power of assisting souls therein : canonizing this man, and sending another to the " bottomless pit :" impudently claiming antiquity in her favour as sanctioning her teaching, and dogmatically anathematizing every one who would not implicitly believe what she chose to dictate.

On what evidence is this doctrine supported? Dr. Wiseman, in his "Moorfields Lectures,"[1] admits that the doctrine of purgatory cannot be proved *directly* from Scripture ; he admits it to be there laid down " indirectly" only. Dr. Wiseman's theory is important. He says that it is unreasonable to demand that Romanists should prove every one of their doctrines individually from the Scriptures. His church (he alleges) was by Christ constituted the depository of His truths, and that although many were recorded in Holy Writ, still many were committed to traditional keeping. "It is on this authority that the Catholic grounds his belief in the doctrine of purgatory; yet not but that its principle is laid down, *indirectly at least,* in the word of God."

Dr. Wiseman makes purgatory a theological principle deduced from another doctrine of his church, "praying for

alio, ut in hujusmodi quæstionibus necdum ab ecclesiâ definitis contingere amat, dissentiunt : verum etiam non satis cohœrent sibi ipsi." St. Amb. Oper. tom. i. p. 385, Admonitio ad Lectorem. Edit. Bened. Parisiis, 1686.

[1] London, 1851. Lect. xi. vol. ii. p. 53.

the dead;" which he asserts to be both Scriptural and apostolical, and practised by the early Christian church. "This practice" (he says) "is essentially based on the belief in purgatory, and the principles of both are consequently intimately connected together." If he proves the one, he asserts that the other necessarily follows, as a theological consequence and conclusion; "for, if the ancient Christians prayed for the dead, what else could they pray for but to relieve the soul from this distressing position?" This is his argument. It is important here to observe, that Dr. Wiseman gives us a rule whereby to test the genuineness of a doctrine. In the same "Lectures"[1] he says:—

"Suppose a difficulty to arise regarding any doctrine—that men were to differ, and not know what precisely they should believe—and that the church thought it prudent and necessary to examine into this point, and define what was to be held: the method pursued would be to examine most accurately the writings of the oldest fathers of the church, to ascertain what in different countries and different ages was held by them; and then collecting the suffrages of all the world and of all times —not indeed to create new articles of faith—but to define that such and such *has always been the faith of the Catholic church.* It is conducted in every instance *as a matter of historical inquiry*, and all human prudence is used to arrive at a judicious decision."

We will not comment on the hopeless task proposed to us, before we can assert what is, or what ought to be, of faith on a disputed point; but all we require is the admission that the question is resolved into an *historical inquiry—a matter of fact.*

Dr. Wiseman, it will be observed, does not rely on the modern theory of "development."

[1] London, 1851. Lect. xi. vol. i. p. 61.

Now, let us draw attention to the Rev. Father Waterworth's edition of Veron's *Rule of Catholic Faith*,[1] which is "well known and universally acknowledged." The Romish priest, Dr. Murray, in his examination before a committee in the House of Commons,[2] on oath deposed that in this book, among others, was "to be found the most authentic exposition of the faith of the Catholic church."

Veron, in order that the meaning of his church should not be misrepresented, lays down the following rules :—

" I. That, and that only, is an article of Catholic faith, which has been revealed in the word of God, and proposed by the Catholic church to all her children, as necessary to be believed with Divine faith (Cap. i. sec. i. p. 1). It no longer belongs to this heavenly deposit if either of these conditions fail (p. 3).

" II. No doctrine is an article of faith which is grounded on texts of Scripture which have been interpreted in various senses by the holy fathers (Sec. iv. 3, p. 8).

" III. We do not admit as an article of Catholic faith any consequences, however certain, or however logically deduced from premises, one of which is of faith, and the other clear by the mere light of reason (4, p. 8).

" IV. It must be laid down as a certain and undeniable position, that theological conclusions are not articles of faith" (Ibid. p. 10).

Alas! for Dr. Wiseman's theory, which falls foul at once of Rules I. and IV.

With regard to the theory of treating purgatory as a necessary consequence of the custom of praying for the dead, it is admitted that this latter practice, though not

---

[1] Birmingham, 1833. The admitted authority of this we have already proved, *ante*, p. 63, *note*.
[2] Phelan and O'Sullivan's Digest of Evidence and Commons' Report. March 22nd, 1825. Report, p. 224.

Scriptural, is ancient. To what end, asks Dr. Wiseman, did they pray for the dead, if they did not pray for the release of souls from purgatory? *First*, let Romanists produce from the writings of the early Fathers, or the genuine old liturgies, one single prayer or collect, for the delivery of souls out of that imaginary place. No such prayer can be found. Nor is there in the old Roman offices—we mean the vigils said for the dead—one word of purgatory or its pains. Passages are cited indeed from interpolated liturgies, but the fact of their interpolation is admitted. It is likewise true that Dr. Wiseman quotes a passage from the funeral oration delivered by Ambrose on the death of Theodosius, wherein he leads us to suppose that he unceasingly prayed for the deceased emperor; but Dr. Wiseman, with his wonted talent for misquoting the Fathers, actually omits, from the very middle of the passage he pretends to quote, the fact that Ambrose declared he knew Theodosius was then "in the kingdom of the Lord Jesus, and carefully beholding his temple"—"that he had put on the robe of glory"—was "a tenant of Paradise"—"an inhabitant of that city which is above!" Why he omits these passages is obvious—none of his readers would believe *that* to be a popish purgatory, which was spoken of by Ambrose. So also in the passages he cites as from Epiphanius and Cyril of Jerusalem, to prove that these Fathers offered prayers for the dead for the benefit of their souls in purgatory, he omits that in their prayers were included "patriarchs, prophets, apostles, bishops, and martyrs!" By falsifying passages from the Fathers, he may easily make them appear to say that white is black.

This leads us to the *second* head. It is admitted by Romanists that the patriarchs, prophets, apostles, the Virgin

Mary, the martyrs, etc., did not go to purgatory. Now, in almost every prayer for the departed, which is quoted to prove the custom of praying for the dead, the prayer is extended to or includes the above class. If, therefore, Dr. Wiseman's theory is to hold good, then all these went to purgatory, which no Romanist will admit; then it must be also admitted that purgatory is not based on the custom of praying for the dead, as practised by the early church. Dr. Wiseman was quite aware of the difficulty, and he boldly meets it:—

"There is no doubt" (he says) "that in the ancient liturgies the saints are mentioned in the same prayer as the other departed faithful, for the simple circumstance that they were so united before the public suffrages of the church proclaimed them to belong to a happier order."[1]

The *first* act of canonization took place at the Council of Rome, A.D. 993;[2] and, as it is not pretended that the Virgin and the apostles and martyrs did go to purgatory, it is evident that the doctrine of purgatory must be of later date than 993. When were the saints *first* proclaimed to belong to a happier order? We reply not before A.D. 1439, at the Council of Florence.[3] We would ask Dr. Wiseman, Who authorized the church of Rome to proclaim the apostles, prophets, etc., to belong to a happier order, and whether they would not have belonged to "a happier order" without the proclamation of the church of Rome?

On the other hand, if we follow the course suggested by Dr. Wiseman, and examine accurately the writings of the oldest Fathers to ascertain what, in different countries and

---

[1] The Moorfields Lectures. Lect. xi. vol. ii. p. 67. London, 1851.
[2] Labb. et Coss. Concl., tom. ix. p. 741. Paris, 1671.
[3] See *ante*, pp. 66, 75.

in different ages, was by them held, what do we find? We find that the doctrine of purgatory was wholly unknown to the Greek Fathers and the Greek church;[1] and we have the striking fact that the Greek church now practises prayers for the dead, but rejects the doctrine of purgatory! And as to the Latin church, the very first Father, Tertullian, quoted by Dr. Wiseman, destroys his theory. He tells us of a widow who is advised by Tertullian to pray for the soul of her deceased husband. Now, Dr. Wiseman asserts that this practice is sanctioned by Scripture, while Tertullian (his own authority) gives us testimony exactly to the contrary; for he says that, "if we ask for the law of Scripture" as to this custom among others, "none can be found;" but he defends the practice as a traditional custom only.[2] Dr. Wiseman contradicts, at once, Veron's Rule I., and explodes at the same time his own theory! Origen, who, by teaching that all, including the apostles, and even the devil, would pass through fire and be ultimately saved, first paved the way for the introduction of this superstition. His theory was, however, condemned by the fifth General Council, A.D. 553,[3] though Dr. Wiseman has the boldness to quote in his Lectures this very condemned theory as the teaching of the universal church!

This heretical dogma led to the introduction of a speculation, which shortly afterwards sprang up, of a purgatorial fire; but that was not a *present* fiery purgatory, but was

---

[1] "Sed et Græcis ad hunc usque diem [*i.e.*, Concl. Floren. A.D. 1439] non est creditum purgatorium esse." Assert. Lutheran. confutat. per Joan. Roffens, Art. xviii. Colon. 1559. See also the same admission made by Alphonsus à Castro "Adversus Hæres." lib. xii. p. 155. Paris, 1543.

[2] Tertullian de Coronâ Militis, p. 289. Edit. Roth. 1662.

[3] Bals. apud Beveridg. Synod. vol. i. p. 150. Oxon. 1672. And also by Augustine. Aug. lib. de Hæres. c. xliii. tom. viii. p. 10. Edit. Bened. Paris, 1685.

postponed to the judgment day; and Augustine, among others, referred to the belief of a purging fire as a possibility only, not incredible;[1] which, while it proves that he did not believe in the doctrine of purgatory, also proves that it was not then an article of faith. Indeed, he says positively, "Catholic faith, *resting on Divine authority*, believes the first place the kingdom of heaven, and the second hell. A third place we are wholly ignorant of; yea, we shall find in Scripture that it is not."[2]

If the childish and absurd dialogues which pass under the name of Gregory I. be genuine, which is very improbable, then we are mainly indebted to him for a more formal recognition of the doctrine; but even his speculations, and private opinions, and the theory of the seventh century, differ greatly from the modern teaching. His system was, that souls were punished by expiating their *sins;* whereas the doctrine of modern purgatory presupposes a forgiveness of the sin, and that it is a place of punishment after the sin is forgiven.

If Scripture be appealed to, as it is by some advocates less discreet than Dr. Wiseman, to support the doctrine, then we confront them with Veron's Rule II.; for it can be shown from the writings of the Fathers that the texts usually relied on, are variously interpreted by them. And we deny that any of these Fathers advanced a text of Scripture in order to support the papal theory.[3]

[1] "Tale aliquid etiam post hanc vitam fieri *incredibile non est*, et utrum ita sit quæri potest, et aut inveniri aut latere." Aug. in Enchirid. de fide, etc., ad Laurentium, cap. 69, tom. vi. col. 222. Edit. Bened. 1685.
[2] "Tertium penitus ignoramus, immo, nec esse in Scripturis Sanctis inveniemus." Aug. Hypog. 1. 5. tom. vii. Basil, 1529.
[3] For a critical examination of the various texts advanced by Romanists to support the doctrine of purgatory, see Collette's "*Milner Refuted*," Part II. London, 1857.

We, therefore, now challenge Romanists to show that the modern Tridentine doctrine was held by the early Christian church. And, to assist their investigation, we would call their attention to the notable admission on this head made by a zealous opposer of Luther, the learned Fisher, who was Roman Catholic bishop of Rochester, A.D. 1504, and divinity professor at Cambridge. He says:—

"Who will, let him read the commentaries of the ancient Greeks, and, so far as my opinion goes, he shall find very seldom mention of purgatory, or none at all [he having admitted, as already shown, that the doctrine was rejected by the Greeks]; and the Latins [in the Western church] did not receive the truth of this matter altogether, but by little and little; neither, indeed, was the faith either of purgatory or indulgences so needful in the primitive church as now it is."[1]

In advocating this doctrine, therefore, Roman Catholics must give up their claim to antiquity.

CHAPTER X.

PENANCE.

"So that he as God sitteth in the temple of God, showing himself that he is God."—2 Thess. ii. 4.

IN proceeding still further to test the claim to antiquity and the assertion that the Roman priests are the "representatives of no new system of religion, the exponents of no new

---

[1] "Legat qui velit Græcorum veterum commentarios, et nullum, quantum opinor, aut quam rarissime de purgatorio sermonem inveniet. Sed neque Latini simul omnes at sensim hujus rei veritatem conceperunt; neque tam necessaria fuit sive Purgatorii, sive Indulgentiarum, fides in primitivâ ecclesiâ atque nunc est." Assert. Lutheran. Confutat. per Joan. Roffens, Art. xviii. p. 200. Colon. 1559.

doctrine," and "that the doctrines now taught by them are the same as those that were preached in this country when Gregory sent to us" his emissaries, let us take one of the most popular tenets of that church—the doctrine of penance as now taught, and called the "Sacrament of Penance."

I. The Romish church, by her Trent Council, requires us to acknowledge no less and no more than seven sacraments, with all their attendant ceremonies and appurtenances, under pain of no less than eighty-nine distinct anathemas or damnations. Two of the above number we admit to be sacraments—Baptism and the Lord's Supper. The five others are Matrimony, Penance, Extreme Unction, Orders, and Confirmation. The number, *seven*, was first "insinuated" by the Council of Florence, A.D. 1439; and only dogmatically declared to be an article of Christian faith at the seventh session of the Council of Trent, held in March, 1547. It was asserted by an eminent divine of the Romish church, Cassander, after considerable research, that previous to the time of Peter Lombard (the great Master of the sentences), A.D. 1140, the number of the sacraments, as being *seven*, was not determined.[1]

The Roman priesthood represent, therefore, a church holding this new doctrine, not even taught before A.D. 1140; and we challenge them to prove that the early Christian church held, as a doctrine of faith, neither more nor less than *seven sacraments*, or that the Romish doctrine of penance was then considered a sacrament ordained by Christ.

II. The eighth canon of the seventh session of the

[1] "Non temere quenquam reperies ante Petrum Lombardum, qui certum aliquem et definitum Sacramentorum numerum statuerat: et de his septem non omnia quidem Scholastici æquè propriè Sacramenta vocabant." Cassander de numero Sacrament. Art. xiii., p. 951. Paris, 1616. And p. 107, Consultat. Lugd. 1608.

Council of Trent declares that each of these so-called sacraments confers grace *ex opere operato*—by the act performed; which dogma we are now bound to believe under pain of damnation. This also is a novel teaching of the Romish church. For take one of these so-called sacraments—Matrimony. Peter Lombard distinctly denies that grace was conferred by matrimony, and this is attested by another Roman Catholic, Cassander.[1] And so in the Romish canon law, or rather by the author of the Gloss upon Gratian, we are told that the grace of the Holy Spirit is not conferred in matrimony as in the other sacraments.[2] Durandus, a most learned divine of the Roman church, goes still further by saying "that it (matrimony) does not confer the *first* grace, nor does it *increase* grace.[3]

We repudiate, therefore, this novel teaching, added by the Romish church, and which they have added to the creed as a new article of faith.

III. This so-called sacrament of penance is stated to be as necessary to salvation for those who have sinned after baptism, as baptism itself for the unregenerate;[4] and the Trent Catechism says, "There is no sin however grievous, no crime however enormous or however frequently repeated, which penance does not remit." "To it belongs in so special a manner the efficacy of remitting actual guilt,

---

[1] "De Matrimonio Petrus Lombardus negavit in eo gratiam conferri." Cassand. Consult., ut supra., p. 951. Edit. Paris, 1616.

[2] "In hoc sacramento non confertur gratia Spiritûs Sancti, sicut in aliis." Corp. Jur. Can., vol. i. col. 1607. Lugd. 1671. Causa 1, Q. 1, c. 101, and 32, Q. 2, c. 13.

[3] "Ipse vero Durandus hoc argumento utitur; matrimonium non confert primam gratiam, quæ est ipsa justificatio a peccatis; neque secundam gratiam, sive gratiæ incrementum; nullam igitur gratiam confert." See Bellarmine de Matrim. Sacram. Lib. i. c. v. tom iii. p. 506. Colon. 1616. Durand, fol. cccxviii. Paris, 1508.

[4] "Concl. Trid.. Sess. xiv. cap. ii. *ad fin.*

that, without its intervention, we cannot obtain or hope for pardon."[1] The three necessary or component parts are stated to be contrition (or more correctly *attrition*,) confession and absolution, and satisfaction, which are the matter of the sacrament.[2] It is modestly admitted that *contrition* alone (that is, a sorrow and detestation of past sin from a *love to God*, and a determination to sin no more), without confession, absolution, and satisfaction, but with a desire for them, will obtain the grace and pardon of God. But *imperfect* repentance (*attrition*), (that is, a turning from sin, from a selfish motive, such as a fear of punishment,) will not alone obtain pardon; but, nevertheless, when accompanied by confession and absolution, and satisfaction, it will obtain grace and pardon in this so-called sacrament of penance. That is to say, an imperfect repentance of sin in the so-called sacrament of penance is sufficient to obtain pardon of sin![3] Delahogue plainly lays down the rule—"Perfect repentance is not required in order that a man may obtain the remission of his mortal sins in the sacrament of penance."[4]

[1] See Donovan's Translation. pp. 260, 261. Dublin, 1829. Donovan was a Professor at Maynooth College.
[2] Concl. Trid., Sess. xiv. cap. 3.
[3] See Donovan's Translation as above, pp. 269, 270, 271, and Concl. Trid., Sess. xiv. c. 4. "L'attrition est cette douleur qu'on éprouve d'avoir offensé Dieu par un motif moins parfait, par exemple à cause de la noirceur du péché, c'est-à-dire à cause de l'enfer qu'on a mérité et du paradis qu'on a perdu. De sorte que la contrition est une douleur du péché à cause de l'injure faite à Dieu, et l'attrition est une douleur de l'offense faite à Dieu à cause du mal qu'elle nous cause."—Liguori Œuv. Completes, tom. xxviii. Paris, 1842. Instruction pour les Curés et les Missionaires. Chap. v. De la Penitence. Sec. ii. De la Contrition. No. xx. p. 199. Liguori thus states this doctrine—"XXI. Quand on a la contrition, on obtient aussitôt la grace avant de recevoir le sacrement avec l'absolution du confesseur, pourvu que le penitent ait l'intention, au moins implicite, de recevoir le sacrement en se confessant."—Concl. Trent, Sess. 14, c. iv.
[4] "Contritio perfecta non requiritur ut homo, in sacramento pœnitentiæ, peccatorum mortalium remissionem obtineat." Tract. de Sacr. Pœnit. Dublin, 1825.

This is in accordance with the teaching of the Trent Council, which, while it admits that, by means of true repentance, reconciliation to God does take place before the so-called sacrament of penance is received; yet, in order to exalt the church and priesthood, asserts that this reconciliation is not to be ascribed to that repentance unless there is a desire for the sacrament, which is alleged to be included therein. Thus it places the mercy of God and his forgiveness, not upon God's promise to forgive the repentant sinner, but upon the desire to conform to the ordinance of the church of Rome; and again, to give further importance to this ordinance of the Roman church, while it declares that a sinner whose repentance is imperfect will not meet with mercy without penance, it holds out the delusive hope of salvation through it.[1] The reason for all this is, because the power vested in the Deity is sought to be transferred to the priest; for the Trent Catechism proceeds to say that "his (the penitent's) sins are forgiven by the *minister of religion*, through the power of the keys: the priest acting a *judicial*, not a ministerial part, and judging in the causes in which this discretionary power is to be exercised."[2] In fact, the sentence is pronounced by

---

[1] "Docet præterea, etsi contritionem hanc aliquando caritate perfectam esse contingat, hominemque Deo reconciliari, priusquam hoc sacramentum actu suscipiatur; ipsam nihilominus reconciliationem ipsi contritioni, sine sacramenti voto, quod in illa includitur, non esse adscribendam. Illam vero contritionem imperfectam, quæ attritio dicitur, quoniam vel ex turpitudinis peccati consideratione, vel ex gehennæ et poenarum metu communiter concipitur, si voluntatem peccandi excludat, cum spe veniæ, declarat, non solum non facere hominem hypocritam et magis peccatorem, verum etiam donum Dei esse, et Spiritus Sancti impulsum, non adhuc quidem inhabitantis, sed tantum moventis, quo poenitens adjutus viam sibi ad justitiam parat. Et quamvis sine sacramento Poenitentiæ per se ad justificationem perducere peccatorum nequeat, tamen eum ad Dei gratiam in sacramento Poenitentiæ impetrandum disponit." Concl. Trid. Sess. xiv. De Poenit. caput. iv. De Contritione, pp. 136, 137. Paris, 1848.

[2] Cat. Concl. Tridt. Donovan's Translation, pp. 271, 273. Dublin, 1829.

him as a judge.[1] The priest "sits in the tribunal of penance as his (the penitent's) legitimate judge. * * * He represents the character and discharges the office of Jesus Christ."[2] This same Trent Catechism goes on to assert that the Roman priest represents the person of God upon earth, "and therefore they are justly called not only angels, but GODS, because they possess amongst us the strength and power of the immortal God;" giving as a reason, that they not only have the power of "making and offering the body and blood of our Lord," but also "of remitting sins, which is conferred upon them."[3] "So that he as God sitteth in the temple of God, showing himself that he is God," 2 Thess. ii. 4.

The distinction which is drawn between attrition and contrition in the doctrine of penance is one of vital importance, and the Romanists may be confidently challenged to adduce any Scriptural authority for it, or to show that such a distinction was recognised by the early Christian church.

IV. The second "integral part" of this so-called sacra-

---

[1] "Non est solum nudum ministerium, vel annuntiandi Evangelium, vel declarandi remissa esse peccata; sed ad instar actus judicialis quo ab ipso velut a judice, sententia pronunciatur." Concl. Trid. Sess. xiv. de Pœnit. caput. vi. De Ministro hujus Sacramenti, et Absolutione; et Can. ix., whereby all are anathematized who deny this doctrine.

[2] Trent Catech. as above, p. 260.

[3] "Cum episcopi et sacerdotes tanquam Dei interpretes et internuncii quidam sint, qui ejus nomine Divinam legem et vitæ præcepta homines edocent, et ipsius Dei personam in terris gerunt; perspicuum est eam esse illorum functionem, quâ nulla major excogitari possit. Quare merito non solum angeli, sed Dii etiam, quod Dei immortalis vim et numen apud nos teneant, appellantur. Quamvis autem omni tempore summam dignitatem obtinuerint, tamen Novi Testamenti sacerdotes cæteris omnibus honore longe antecellunt; potestas enim tum corpus et sanguinem Domini nostri conficiendi et offerendi, tum peccata remittendi, quæ illis collata est, humanam quoque rationem atque intelligentiam superat; nedum ei aliquid par et simile in terris inveniri queat." Catech. Concil. Tridentini, pars. ii.; *De Ordinis Sacramento*, sec. ii. p. 327. Edit. Paris, 1848.

ment, which is declared necessary for our salvation, is "confession and absolution."

By confession is meant secret oral confession to a priest. This is rendered absolutely necessary by the modern church of Rome. This church, at the fourth Council of Lateran, A.D. 1215, first authoritatively decreed and required every believer of either sex, after arriving at the age of discretion, under pain of mortal sin, to confess at least once a year to a priest.[1] This decree was recognised and confirmed by a decree of the Trent Council.[2] Peter Lombard tells us that, in his day, oral confession to a priest or private confession to God were both advocated, but the doctrine was not defined by the church; and learned men differed on the subject.[3] Mosheim, in his Ecclesiastical History, says that, before the decree of Lateran, "it was left to every Christian's choice to make this confession to the Supreme Being, *or*, to express it in words, to a spiritual confidant and director."[4] And the Roman Catholic historian, Fleury, clearly lays it down, that the invention of compulsory oral confession was the work of Chrodegang, bishop of Metz, A.D. 763, but only as a private discipline for his monastic institution. "This is the first time," writes Fleury, "that I find confession commanded."[5]

No case can be adduced to prove that compulsory oral confession, now alleged to be necessary for all, was a doctrine of the church before A.D. 1215. In this essential point, therefore, she has invented a new doctrine.

V. The absolution which follows the oral confession of

---

[1] Lab. et Coss. Concil. Lat. IV. Can. 21, tom. xi. p. 147. Paris, 1671.
[2] Sess. xiv. Can. viii. De Pœnitentia.
[3] Pet. Lombard, Sent. 1. lib. iv. dist. xvii. pp. 102, 107. Lugdun. 1618.
[4] Mosheim, Eccl. Hist. Cent. xiii. part. ii. cap. iii. sec. 2. See Appendix, No. iv. Maclain's Edition.
[5] Fleury, Eccl. Hist., tom. ix. p. 300. Paris, 1769.

the penitent, consists in the utterance by the priest of the words, *Ego absolvo te*, "I absolve thee." It is clearly laid down by the Catechism of the Council of Trent,[1] that no absolution takes place unless the priest utters those words:—

"Every sacrament [says this Catechism] consists of two things—'matter,' which is called the element, and 'form,' which is commonly called the word. * * * In the sacraments of the new law, the *form* is so *definite* that *any*, even a casual *deviation from it*, renders the sacrament *null*. These, then, are the parts which belong to the nature and substance of the sacraments, and of which every sacrament is *necessarily* composed."

Take away the *form* of this sacrament, the words "I absolve thee," then there will be no sacrament, no pardon, no salvation for those who have sinned after baptism; yet no fact in the history of the church is more certain than this, that these words, "I absolve thee," were never contained in any form of absolution used in the church for more than one thousand years after Christ.[2]

Here, then, is another difficulty. Let the priests of Rome produce such a form if they can. If they cannot, this favourite doctrine—priestly absolution—so earnestly contended for by them, also vanishes like the "baseless fabric of a vision."

VI. By absolution the guilt of sin is supposed to be remitted, but not the punishment due to the sinner. The priest, therefore, imposes as a "satisfaction" some penitential work. These penitential works can, however, be remitted by "indulgences," which are defined to be a "remission of the temporal punishment due to sin *after* the sin

---

[1] Donovan, p. 259. Dublin, 1829.
[2] See "*Catholic Layman*," Dublin, 1854.

is remitted in the sacrament of penance,"[1] by the application to the penitent of a share of the superabundant merits of Christ, of the Virgin Mary, and of the saints, called the "celestial treasure of the church," supposed to be in the custody of the pope, and unlocked and distributed at his pleasure. And these penitential works can even be done by another for the sinner. "One person (says the Trent Catechism) can make satisfaction to God for another, which indeed is, in a pre-eminent sense, a property of this part of penance."[2] Peter Dens says that "it is imposed with good effect as a sacrament, that the penitent shall see to have works of satisfaction performed for him by others." But mark the ingenuity of the evasion: "yet these works performed by others are not part of the sacrament; but the act of the penitent himself attending to it, that these should be performed for him, is part of the sacrament."[3]

To ask a Romanist to prove the antiquity of this piece of priestcraft would be a mockery of religion; it is a modern and vain invention—an attempt to cheat the devil by proxy.

Thus, whichever way we take this so-called sacrament of penance, as a whole or in its parts, it is a modern invention of the Romish church—a piece of priestcraft without its parallel in the Christian church.

[1] Cat. Christian Doctrine, p. 158. London, 1850.
[2] Satisfacere potest unus pro alio, etc. Pars. ii. de Pœnit. Sacr. No. cix. cx., p. 312. Paris, 1848.
[3] Dens' Theol. tom. vi. p. 242. Dublin, 1832.

CHAPTER XI.

INDULGENCES.

* * * * * * * "Omnia Romæ
Cum pretio." JUVENAL, *Sat.* iii. 183, 184.
* * * * * * * "Venalia nobis
Templa, sacerdotes, altaria, sacra, coronæ,
Ignes, thura, preces, cœlum est venale, Deusque."
B. MANTUANI *de Calamit.* lib. iii.

AFTER image worship, "indulgences" is the doctrine on which a Roman Catholic is the most sensitive. So sensitive, indeed, are Romanists when sordid or unworthy motives are attributed, that, in whatever recognised phase we may present their teaching, it will be repudiated when such repudiation is convenient; and the very vagueness in the definition of the doctrine by the church of Rome, in her creed and the decrees of Trent, gives the opportunity for any and every repudiation. The exposures of the nefarious traffic have been so damaging to the papal system, that the anxiety has been to explain away, or soften down, the practical teaching of the church and the express language of popes. Indulgences are a cunningly devised scheme for raising money by "making merchandise of souls." The system is too valuable to be renounced.

I. The priests tell us that it is a popular fallacy and a libel to say that an indulgence is a pardon of sin. They say that it "does not include the pardon of any sin at all, little or great, past, present, or to come;"[1] and yet, in the book of canon law of the church of Rome, we find recorded in

---

[1] Dr. Milner's "*End of Religious Controversy,*" Letter xlii.

the bull of Boniface VIII., on the first issue of a jubilee—
"We grant not only full, and larger, but most full remission of all sins." And so, likewise, Clement VI. declared in his bull that the recipients of the indulgence should obtain "most full pardon of all their sins;" and Sixtus IV. called them "indulgences and remission of sins."[1] One would suppose this to be plain language, and easily understood by those simple-minded people for whose benefit the indulgences were issued. No such thing; for we are told by more modern apologists that such expressions as *venia peccatorum* (pardon of sins) and *remissio peccatorum* (the remission of sins), used in these bulls, "are technical expressions, as familiarly understood by a Catholic theologian as any legal technicality is by a gentleman of the law;"[2] and, in fact, do not mean at all what the words appear to indicate. Really, these gentlemen should not be so sensitive on this point; for, when we come to consider the matter, they are only splitting straws. They will tell us that an indulgence only remits the punishment due to the sin already forgiven. Granted; but by whom is the sin supposed to be forgiven, and when? By none other than the priest in the so-called sacrament of penance: and the penitent, they tell us, must have first fulfilled the proper conditions before he can avail himself of an indulgence—that is, confess and receive absolution. So, whether the sin be forgiven by the indulgence itself, or by means of the prior ordeal, in the so-called sacrament of

---

[1] "Non solum plenam et largiorem, sed plenissimam concedimus veniam omnium peccatorum." Extrav. Commun. lib. v. tit. ix. c. 1. Corp. Jur. Can. tom. ii. p. 316. Paris, 1612. "Suorum omnium obtinerent plenissimam veniam peccatorum." Ibid. p. 317, tom. ii. "Indulgentias et remissiones peccatorum." Ibid. p. 319, tom. ii.

[2] "The Truth, the whole Truth, and nothing but the Truth," by the Rev. T. S. Green [Romish priest at Tixall]. London, T. Jones, 1838, p. 28.

penance, through the absolution of the priest, matters little; for it is the priest who is supposed to forgive the sin judicially, and then the punishment due to the sin is remitted through the indulgence which emanates from the pope. But, to be "technically" correct, we concede that it is not defined by the Roman church that an indulgence does extend to the forgiveness of the sin, though it is equally a fact that Romanists themselves do associate in their minds the forgiveness of sin with the indulgences, and this is candidly admitted by Dr. Hirscher, Professor of Theology in the Roman Catholic University of Freiburg. He says:—

"A further practical and deeply-seated evil, to which the attention of the church must be directed, is the idea entertained by the popular mind concerning indulgences. Say what you will, there it remains: the people understand by indulgences the remission of sins. Explain to them that not the sins, but only the penalties of sin, are affected by indulgences; very well, it is the penalty, and not the guilt of sin, which the people regard as the important thing; and whatever frees them from the punishment of sin, frees them, so far as they care about it, from the sin itself." [1]

Our assertion is, nevertheless, that popes—for instance, Clement VI. and VIII., Boniface VIII. and IX., and Urban VIII.[2]—have, in the most orthodox fashion and in the most solemn manner, extended indulgences to the most full pardon of sins. We have nothing to do with the question of the *fallibility* or *infallibility* of these popes: we merely deal with facts, and challenge contradiction.

II. Other apologists affirm that the indulgence extends

[1] Hirscher, "*State of the Church*," p. 210. Quoted by the Rev. W. E. Scudamore in his "*England and Rome*."—Rivington, London, 1855, p. 399.
[2] See Cherubini. Bullar. tom. i. p. 145, and tom. iii. pp. 23, 75, etc. Luxemb. 1727.

only to the remission of punishment due to the sin forgiven in the sacrament of penance—that is, after attrition, confession, and absolution (by the priest) of the sin; the indulgence, they say, extends only to the remission of the punishment consequent on the sin which has been forgiven, and which otherwise must be undergone to satisfy God's justice. This is a favourite evasion. Dens, in his "Theologia," tells us that an indulgence "is the remission of temporal punishment due to sins, remitted as to their guilt, by the power of the keys, without the sacrament, by the application of the satisfactions which are contained in the treasure of the church."[1] The priest, on pronouncing the absolution, measures out the amount of *satisfaction* to be undergone, called the penal part of the sacrament of penance, and an indulgence in this instance, they tell us, is awarded to remit this penalty of sin. But the assertion that this theory is restricted to the remission of the satisfaction to be performed at the bidding of the priest in the sacrament of penance, is at once put to the rout by the admission of Dens, and also by the fact that it was quite a common thing to grant indulgences for a long period of years. For instance, the following is recorded in the *Hours of the blessed Virgin Mary according to the ritual of the church of Salisbury :*[2]—" This prayer, made by St. Austin, affirming that he who says it daily, kneeling, *shall not die in sin*, and after this life shall go to everlasting joy and bliss. Our holy father, the Pope Bonifacius VI., hath granted to all

---

[1] "Quid est indulgentia ? R. Est pœnæ temporalis peccatis, quoad culpam remissis, debitæ remissio, facta potestate clavium, *extra sacramentum* per applicationem satisfactionum quæ in thesauro Ecclesiæ continentur." Dens' Theologia, tom. vi.; Tract de Indulg., No. 30; De Indulgentiarum Natura. Dublin, 1832.

[2] Edit. Paris, 1526. See Burnet's Hist. of the Reformation. Records, Book i. xxvi. p. 280, vol. iv. Nares' Edition.

them that say devoutly this prayer following, between the elevation of our Lord and the Agnus Dei, 10,000 years' pardon" (fol. 58), or an indulgence for that period. And, in folio 42, we are told that Sixtus IV. granted 11,000 years of pardon to all who should devoutly say a prescribed prayer before "the image of our Lady." And again, in folio 54, we read—"To all them that before this image of pity devoutly say five Pater Nosters, five Ave Marias, and a Credo, piteously beholding those arms of Christ's passion, are granted 32,755 years of pardon; and Sixtus IV., pope of Rome, hath made the fourth and fifth prayer, and hath doubled his foresaid pardon" [*i.e.* 65,510 years]. And, in folio 72, there is this strange form of indulgence :—

"And these prayers written in a table hanged at Rome in St. Peter's Church, nigh to the high altar there, as our holy father the pope evely is wont to say the office of the Mass; and who that devoutly, with a contrite heart, daily say this orison, if he be that day in the state of eternal damnation, then his eternal pain shall be changed him into temporal pain of purgatory; then, if he hath deserved the pain of purgatory, it shall be forgotten and forgiven, through the infinite mercy of God."

It is true that indulgences of thousands of years are not now issued, simply because the absurdity would be too glaring for this advanced age; so they are reduced to days. But what was orthodox and good for Christians in the sixteenth century, must be, according to Romish teaching, good in the nineteenth. The principle is exactly the same. The extreme illustrates the case better. What we maintain is, therefore, that this principle of granting indulgences is wholly incompatible with the doctrine of penance and the remission of the satisfaction imposed by the priest. Let us apply the proposition. An individual is stated to be in a state of grace—that is, has confessed and been absolved; the priest tells him that his sins are forgiven, but he has to undergo a penance of 32,755 years! To be sure, he has an easy method of escaping from even double the penance by an indulgence on the terms prescribed by Sixtus IV. The proposition would rather startle the penitent. But what is to be said of the last extract from the ritual above quoted? has that any reference to the sacrament of penance? An indulgence, therefore, is not necessarily connected with the sacrament of penance.

III. Again, we are told that the benefit of the indulgence, like that of absolution, entirely depends upon the disposition of the sinner. The real doctrine of Romish absolution does not depend on the disposition of the sinner. The priest represents Jesus Christ in the confessional, and is supposed to know the mind of the penitent. When he absolves, his words are, "I absolve thee;" not, "if truly penitent I absolve thee." He acts *judicially*. The sentence, according to Romish theory, is irrevocable; yet the recipient may still not really be in a proper disposition. God alone knoweth the heart. If there is any condition or uncertainty, then the priest does not represent Christ, for Christ could not be deceived, and he could not delegate his functions to so fallible a representative. But let us test this proposition also. It is quite a common thing to see appended to indulgences—"These indulgences are also applicable to the faithful departed," or "to souls in purgatory." What does this mean but that, when we obtain an indulgence or pardon for having done some notorious act in the eyes of the church of Rome, and having obtained, say 10,000 years' pardon, we have the option of applying all or part of these years to the souls of persons whom we may name, supposed to be in purgatory. For instance, in a little tract now on sale, called "Devotions of the Scapular," in page 24, indulgences are given to the wearer of the scapular; and we are told that "these indulgences are also applicable to the souls in purgatory by a constitution of Clement X." We are quite aware of what some assert, that it is by "suffrage" only that indulgences are applicable to the dead—that is, by the united voice given in public prayer—another of the "technicalities" of Romanism. Indulgences nevertheless are, in one way or another, applicable to the dead. How will the objector apply his proposition, that the indulgence entirely depends upon the disposition of the sinner, when the supposed recipient is dead and gone, and, for anything we know to the contrary, has no *disposition* one way or the other? Therefore the benefit of the indulgence does not depend on the disposition of the supposed recipient.

IV. Again, when we assert that indulgences are bartered for money at the present day, it is indignantly denied. We, nevertheless, assert that it is an almost every day practice, even in this country. Buying and selling is a mutual exchange of some commodity for money. Here is a devout Romanist in a state of grace—he has gone through the prescribed forms, he has confessed, attended masses, has said the prescribed number of prayers before an image, or the prescribed number of Aves and Pater Nosters, but still he has not got the indulgence. This can be obtained; yes, even a *plenary indulgence*, that is, a forgiveness of all punishment due for past sins up to that day, for £20, or by paying £1 1s. annually. We find this advertised, almost weekly, in the Romish papers, the *Tablet* and the *Weekly*

Register. The following is from the papers of the 24th September and 1st October, 1861:—

"The Rev. Mother Superior of the Female Orphanage at Norwood offers to present each perpetual or life subscriber to the institution with a copy in *fac-simile* of the rescript of his holiness Pius IX., containing the written signature of the holy father, and granting a plenary indulgence to the benefactors of the Orphans of Our Blessed Lady."

In other words, to every annual subscriber of £1 1s., or a life subscriber of £20 (for these figures are actually given), is guaranteed by the pope a plenary indulgence; so that the happy possessor, if he die forthwith, is supposed to have given even purgatory the "go by," and to have a passport to heaven direct!

While it must be admitted that this is a clear case of bargain and sale, we doubt whether the signatures of the so-called "Vicar of Christ" will be honoured at the gates of that "heavenly Jerusalem which is above," though the receipt for the due payment of the subscription be duly certified by the "Rev. Mother Superior." Of course the sale is denied. The mother only "offers to present;" in fact, the indulgence is *given away.* These "technical" words mean nothing. But take another case. Dr. Wiseman, writing to his clergy, desirous of making a collection for the "Poor School Committee Festival," says, "You will inform them (the people) of the plenary indulgence which they will gain on the following Sunday by giving alms to this pious work, and going to confession *or* communion on that day, or within eight days after. See Directory, p. 146."[1] On consulting the directory indicated, we find, "*and* communion,"

[1] "*Catholic Standard*," now "*Weekly Register*," June 8, 1850, No. 35, p. 3

that is, communion added to confession; and the grant is made perpetual, in favour of this committee, by the pope. Of course it will be asserted that the plenary indulgence is also given in consideration of the "confession or communion," and not for the subscription; but the rescript of his holiness says, " and subscribe to the fund" in question. There can be no mistake. You give the money, and I will give you the indulgence. This we call buying and selling. Such acts are of daily occurrence.

V. We have stated that indulgences were the subject of barter or sale. That money is an element in the transaction, we have proved. What, then, is given in exchange? The theory is simply as follows. There is supposed to exist an inexhaustible store of the superabundant merits of Christ, of the blessed Virgin, and other departed saints. Of Christ, they say, one drop of his blood was sufficient to wash away all the sins of the world; but he gave his life for us, and therefore there is a vast surplus of saving material at the disposal of the church; and, added to this, saints who have departed this life have acquired more merit than was sufficient to save themselves; the surplus of this is also, in like manner, placed at the same disposal. This accumulation is called the "treasure of the church," and the pope, for the time being, has the distribution of it. The document by which he transfers a stated portion of this treasure to the fortunate recipient is called an indulgence. These used to be documents regularly drawn up in legal form, signed and sealed.[1] The reverend mother superior of the convent of Norwood, as we have shown, has at her disposal the distribution of such documents. The purchaser, in exchange for

[1] For examples and *fac-similes*, see Mendham's "*Spiritual Venality of Rome.*" London, 1832.

his money, has transferred to him, certified by this document, a given quantity of these merits from the bank of "celestial treasure" to make up the deficiency that may exist in himself, so that, by transferring the same to his own account he, *pro tanto*, cancels a debt of punishment due to his sins, by which means he is supposed to have satisfied the wrath of God for the sins committed. He has often the option given him of transferring a portion for the benefit of a friend or relative supposed to be suffering in purgatory. If it be a limited indulgence, then he escapes, say forty years' punishment; or, as we have seen, perhaps receives even 32,755 years' pardon. The theory is rather startling, and we may add, so monstrous and difficult of belief, that we are not surprised to find the whole system repudiated. Such a step is convenient, and even at times absolutely necessary. We will give an instance of such repudiation. Veron wrote a book professedly to dispel "popular errors and misstatements" with reference to Romish doctrines. It has been translated by father Waterworth,[1] and published for the object of softening down genuine Romanism, and making it palatable to English tastes. This monstrous doctrine, as before defined, is wholly repudiated. He writes (p. 52):—

"With regard to the power of granting indulgences, it is not of faith that there is in the church a power to grant such indulgences as actually will remit at the tribunal of God, either in this life or in the life to come, the temporal punishment which may remain due after our sins have been pardoned; or, in other words, it is not an article of Catholic faith that the church can grant an indulgence, the direct effect of which shall be the remission of the temporal punishment which is due to the justice of God, and which would otherwise have to be undergone either in this life or in purgatory."

[1] Birmingham, 1833.

And Veron alleges that—

"There are Catholic writers who deny in plain and undoubted terms that indulgences are of any use to the dead." "The grant of indulgences is an exercise of jurisdiction. Now, as the pope has not been appointed judge over the souls in purgatory, he has no jurisdiction over them." "Even our *private suffrages* in favour of the dead are far from being necessarily beneficial to them; how much more doubt must there be as to the effect of indulgences" (pp. 57, 58).

Again, he says (p. 45) :—

"It is not an article of faith that there is in the church a treasure composed of the satisfaction of the saints; and consequently, it is not of faith that indulgences, whether in favour of the living or the dead, are granted, by making them partakers of that treasure."

In pages 46 and 47, the following passages are found:—

"The treasure of the church is not formed of satisfactions of the saints: and an indulgence is not an application of any of these satisfactions towards the remission of the temporal punishment due to sin." "The existence of a treasure in the church, composed of the satisfactions of the saints, is not to be admitted as an article of faith."

All this is very reasonable, plain, and straightforward. We do not deny the necessity of the repudiation; but is Veron's dilution the doctrine of his church? It is not, as the following extracts prove. Our first extract is the definition of an indulgence as given in a book published by "R. Grace and Son," 45, Capel-street, Dublin (the authorized or recognised publishers of papal books), entitled "Indulgences granted by Sovereign Pontiffs to the Faithful, collected by a member of the Sacred Congregation of Indulgences in Rome, translated into English with the permission of superiors." As this book appears to be for all time, it bears no date, but is now on sale. In page 5, we read :—

"An indulgence is the remission of the temporal punishment which generally remains due to sins already forgiven, in the sacrament of penance, as to the guilt and eternal punishment. This remission is made by the application of the merits and satisfactions which are contained in the treasures of the church. These treasures are the accumulation of the spiritual goods arising from the infinite merits and satisfaction of Jesus Christ, with the superabundant merits and satisfaction of the holy martyrs, and of the other saints, which ultimately derive their efficacy from the merits and satisfactions of Christ, who is the only Mediator of redemption. These CELESTIAL TREASURES, as they are called by the Council of Trent, are committed by the Divine bounty to the dispensation of the church, the sacred spouse of Christ, and are the ground and matter of indulgences. They are *infinite* in reference to the merits of Christ, and *cannot, therefore, be ever exhausted.*"

Dens, in the place before quoted, informs us that—

"This treasure is the *foundation* or *matter* of indulgences, and is that infinite treasure made up in part from the satisfactions of Christ, so as never to be exhausted; and it daily receives the superabundant satisfactions of pious men."[1]

Now, let us take the opinion of an illustrious doctor and canonized saint, Thomas Aquinas. He is quoted as "the Mighty Schoolman," "the Seraphic Doctor," and "the Blessed Thomas;" and, on the 17th March in each year, Romanists are taught to pray thus:—

"O God, who dost enlighten thy church by the wonderful erudition of the blessed Thomas thy confessor, and makest it fruitful by thy holy operation, grant to us, we beseech thee, to embrace with our understanding what he taught, and to fulfil, by our imitation, what he did through the Lord."[2]

This seraphic doctor taught—

"That there actually exists an immense treasure of merit

[1] Dens' Theologia, tom. vi. p. 417. No. 30, Tract. de Indulg. Dublin, 1832.
[2] Missal for the Use of the Laity, p. 560. London, 1810.

composed of the pious deeds and virtuous actions which the saints had performed beyond what was necessary for their own salvation, and which is, therefore, applicable to the benefit of others; that the guardian and dispenser of this precious treasure is the Roman pontiff; and that, of consequence, he is empowered to assign to such as he thinks proper a portion of this inexhaustible source of merit proportioned to *their* respective guilt, and sufficient to deliver them from the punishment due to their crimes."[1]

These superabundant merits Cardinal Bellarmine terms "Thesaurus Ecclesiæ," or "the Treasure of the Church."[2]

But, to go to a higher authority, Pope Leo X., who issued a special bull on the subject of indulgences. The following is a literal translation of part of the document which relates to this subject :—

"The Roman church, whom other churches are bound to follow as their mother, hath taught that the Roman pontiff, the successor of Peter in regard to the keys, and the vicar of Jesus Christ upon earth, possessing the power of the keys, by which power all hindrances are removed out of the way of the faithful —that is to say, the guilt of actual sins by the sacrament of penance, and the temporal punishment due to those sins according to the Divine justice by the ecclesiastical indulgence; that the Roman pontiff may, for reasonable cause, by his apostolic authority, grant indulgence out of the superabundant merits of Christ and the saints, to the faithful who are united to Christ by charity, as well for the living as for the dead; and that in thus dispensing the treasure of the merits of Jesus Christ and the saints, he either confers the indulgence by way of absolution, or transfers it by the method of suffrage. Wherefore all persons, whether living or dead, who really obtain an indulgence of this kind, are delivered from so much temporal punish-

[1] Quoted by Mosheim in his Eccl. Hist. cent. xii. pt. ii., cap. iii. sec. 3.
[2] Bell. de Indulg., sec. iii. p. 657, tom. iii. Prag. 1751, and lib. De Purg. 8.

ment due, according to Divine justice, to their actual sins, as is equivalent to the value of the indulgence bestowed and received."[1]

But this is not all; for this same pope, in this same bull, denounces by an excommunication all who deny this doctrine. And to come more to our own time, Leo XII., in 1825, in his bull for the observance of the jubilee of that year, said—

"We have resolved, by virtue of the authority given to us from heaven, fully to unlock that sacred treasure composed of the merits, sufferings, and virtues of Christ our Lord and of his Virgin mother, and of all the Saints, which the Author of human salvation has entrusted to our dispensation. To you, therefore, venerable brethren, patriarchs, primates, archbishops, bishops, it belongs to explain with perspicuity the power of indulgences; what is their efficacy in the remission, not only of the canonical penance, but also of the temporal punishment due to the Divine justice for past sin; and what succour is afforded out of this heavenly treasure, from the merits of Christ and his saints, to such as have departed real penitents in God's love, yet before they had duly satisfied, by fruits worthy of penance for sins of commission and omission, and are now purifying in the fire of purgatory, that an entrance may be opened for them into that eternal country where nothing defiled is admitted."[2]

[1] "Monument. ad Historiam Concilii Tridentini." Judoci Le Plat. 4to. tom. ii. pp. 21, 24. Lovanii, 1782.

[2] Laity's Directory for 1825. Keating and Brown, London. It is worthy of remark that Leo XII. struck a medal to commemorate this jubilee, bearing on one side his own image, on the other that of the church of Rome, symbolized as a *Woman*, holding in her right hand a *cup*, with the inscription around her, *Sedet super universum*, which may be rendered "the whole world is her seat." (See Elliott's "Horæ," vol. iv. p. 30. London, 1851.) The mystical Babylon of the Apocalypse is represented as having a cup in her hand (Rev. xvii. 4) full of abominations. This *Queen* is supposed to rule over all nations. We know the queen of Babylon was worshipped as Rhea (*Chronicon Paschale*, vol. i. p. 65. Bonn, 1852), the great mother of the gods (Hesiod, *Theogonia*, v. 453, p. 36. Oxford, 1737), whose cup was brimful of abominations of the most atrocious character, and this apocalyptical

Here, then, we have Romish divines expressing opinions on the same doctrine diametrically opposed to each other. We Protestants can afford to look on this *Bellum papale*, or war of opinions, with a smile, and suggest to our Romish brethren that, when they have agreed among themselves on their own doctrine, it will be time enough for them to prove us to be heretics for not believing as they do.

As a matter of *doctrine* or *faith*, the creed of the church of Rome simply says, " I also affirm that the power of indulgences was left by Christ in the church, and that the *use* of them is most wholesome to Christian people." The Trent Council does not give any definition, but adds "that moderation should be shown in granting indulgences, according to ancient and approved custom of the Church, lest by too much laxity ecclesiastical discipline be weakened." Now we maintain, that, while the church of Rome has wandered from the ancient custom, the statements last given embrace the " custom " of the church of Rome of the present day, whatever Veron or any other Romanist, who is ashamed of the practical teaching of his church, may state to the contrary. As has been already said, we have nothing to do with the fallibility or infallibility of popes, or the variation of opinions existing in the so-called centre of unity. The definition given is the accepted and practical teaching of the church of Rome at the present day, however monstrous, however degrading, however anti-Scriptural it may be, and certainly is.

emblem of the harlot with the cup in her hand was embodied in the symbols of idolatry derived from ancient Babylon as they were exhibited in Greece, for thus was the Greek Venus originally represented. See Kitto's Bible Cyclopædia, which gives an engraving of the woman with cup from Babylon. Pausanias describes a heathen goddess with a cup in her right hand, lib. i. *Attica*, cap. xxxiii. p. 81. Leipsic, 1696.

K

VI. Intimately connected with the subject of indulgences is the issue by popes of "jubilees." A jubilee is thus defined:—

"A jubilee signifies a plenary indulgence in its most ample form, granted at different periods by the sovereign pontiff to those who, either residing in the city of Rome or visiting it, perform there the visitations of the churches and other prescribed works of piety, prayer, fasting, and alms-deeds, with confession and communion, which are always enjoined for the giving of these indulgences, in order to facilitate the return of sinners to God by the last-mentioned exercise of religion."[1]

Boniface VIII., in A.D. 1300, was the first pope who took upon himself to proclaim a jubilee, though not under that name. His predecessors, Calixtus II., Eugenius III., and Clement III., had reaped such rich harvests by the issue of simple indulgences, that this more daring pope went a step further, probably to see how far he could impose on the credulity of mankind, knowing that if he succeeded a rich harvest would be certain. To make the "outpouring" of the treasure of the church more precious, Boniface proclaimed that a jubilee should occur but once in a century. So jealous was he of this privilege that he closed his bull thus:—

"Let no man dare to infringe this bull of our constitution, which if he presume to attempt, let him know he shall incur the indignation of Almighty God, and of Peter and Paul, etc."[2]

---

[1] "Instructions and Devotions for the Forty Hours' Adoration ordered in the Churches during the Jubilee of 1852. Published with the approbation of the most Rev. Dr. Cullen." Duffy, Dublin, 1852.

[2] "Nulli hominum liceat hanc paginam nostræ constitutionis.... infringere, siquis attentare præsumpserit indignationem omnipotentis Dei.... noverit se incursurum." Corpus, Juris. Canon. lib. v. tit. 9, c. 1, vol. ii. p. 315. Paris, 1612; and for the Bull of Clement VI. ibid. p. 317.

Forty years, however, had scarcely elapsed, when Clement VI., A.D. 1343, burned with a desire to benefit mankind and to reap the advantage to be gained by the exchange of earthly treasures for heavenly. He therefore reduced the period to fifty years, and imposed the very same curse, and in the same words as his predecessor, on those who violated his decree. It was this pope who invented the name of "Jubilee." Fifty years was a convenient division of time; but Urban VI., in 1389, notwithstanding the aforesaid prohibition and threatened indignation, having also a keen eye to the commercial value of the commodity placed at his disposal, soon found an excuse for issuing another jubilee: he reduced the period to 33 years, that being the age of our Saviour. Such was his excuse. Paul II., A.D. 1464, was not to be outdone by his predecessors: he braved the tempest also, and disinterestedly reduced the period to 25 years, thus placing the benefit within the reach of each generation,—that was his excuse: while the present pope, in the exercise of that benevolent spirit which we are told he enjoys in a superabundant degree, reduced the period to six years! He issued a jubilee in November, 1851, and again another in September, 1857. And why not (if there is any practical good in a jubilee) once a year, or even oftener?

On announcing the fact of this last jubilee to his flock, the gentleman who claims to be "bishop of Shrewsbury" used these words:—

"You will probably have heard from your brethren of some of the other dioceses, that the holy father has vouchsafed to open again the spiritual treasury of the church, and to grant a jubilee to the whole world."[1]

[1] "*The Weekly Register*" for May 1, 1858.

The pecuniary profit to Rome by these jubilees was enormous, as they brought together in that city an immense number of the *devout* (?), to gain the benefit of the plenary indulgence, who paid ready cash in exchange.[1] People came professedly to have their sins wiped away; but, if we are to credit the Roman Catholic historian, Fleury, another effect was produced. He tells us that Alexander VI. proclaimed a jubilee in A.D. 1500; and although the numbers in attendance were not so numerous as on former occasions, on account of the wars which then troubled Italy, yet "license and disorder reigned at Rome beyond any other place in the world. Crime was on the throne; and never, perhaps, had so monstrous a corruption of morals been seen, especially among the clergy."[2]

It will complete our definition if we here add the terms on which the benefit of the last jubilee might be gained.

[1] "The Bishops," says Mosheim, "when they wanted money for their private pleasures, or for the exigences of the church, granted to their flock the power of purchasing the remission of the penalties imposed upon transgressors, by a sum of money, which was to be applied to certain religious purposes; or, in other words, they purchased Indulgences, which became an inexhaustible source of opulence to the episcopal orders, and enabled them, as is well known, to form and execute the most difficult schemes for the enlargement of their authority, and to erect a multitude of sacred edifices which augmented considerably the external pomp and splendour of the church. To justify, therefore, these scandalous measures of the pontiffs, a most monstrous and absurd doctrine was now invented by St. Thomas in the following century (the thirteenth), and which contained, among others, the following enormities:—'That there actually existed an immense treasure of merit composed of the pious deeds and virtuous actions which the saints had performed beyond what was necessary for their own salvation, and which were therefore applicable to the benefit of others; that the guardian and dispenser of this precious treasure was the Roman pontiff; and that, of consequence, he was empowered to assign to such as he thought proper a portion of this inexhaustible source of merit, suitable to their respective guilt, and sufficient to deliver them from the punishment due to their crimes! It is a most deplorable mark of the power of superstition, that a doctrine, so absurd in its nature, and so pernicious in its effects, should yet be retained and defended by the church of Rome."—Mosheim, Eccl. Hist. Cent. xii. cap. iii. sec. 3. London, 1825. See also Neander's Church History, vol. vii. p. 485. London, 1852.

[2] Fleury's Eccl. History, tom. xxiv. p. 399. Paris, 1769.

Under date of 2nd February, 1858, Dr. Wiseman issued what he called a "Lenten Indult and Proclamation," which appeared in all the Romish journals of the week, declaring "the conditions for gaining the jubilee," which are stated to be as follows :—

"1st. A contrite and sincere confession of sin, and sacramental absolution.

"2nd. The worthy and devout receiving of the blessed Eucharist.

"3rd. A visit to three churches, or three visits to one.

"4th. At each visit to pray for a short space for the exaltation and prosperity of holy mother church and of the apostolic see: for the *uprooting* of heresy; and for the peace and concord of Christian princes, and the peace and unity of the whole Christian people.

"5th. To give first an alms to the poor, and second, to contribute towards 'the propagation of the faith,' for which distinct object an alms-chest, legibly labelled, and pointed out by the priest reading this pastoral, shall be set aside in each church.

"6th. To fast one day.

"On observance of these conditions, the Holy Father grants the most plenary indulgence, in form of jubilee, *applicable to the faithful departed.*"

Now, we challenge the whole of these conditions, and declare them to be an imposition and a cheat.

As to the first condition—the sin of the penitent must be first absolved by confession and absolution. If it be asserted that a sincere and true repentance (technically called *contrition*) is demanded as an element, then we neither require confession to the priest, nor his absolution to wipe away the sin, nor the indulgence to remit the punishment due to the sin supposed to be forgiven or absolved; for the Trent Council declared—" that perfect contrition reconciles a man to God before the sacrament of penance is received;" and the Trent Catechism puts it clearer, thus:

"Contrition can never be rejected by God, never prove unacceptable to him; nay more, as soon as we have conceived this contrition in our hearts our sins are forgiven. 'I said I will confess my injustice to the Lord, and thou hast forgiven the wickedness of my sin.'"[1]

If God forgives the sin, he, being a just God, also remits the punishment. This no Romanist will deny, and in that case the indulgence is useless. If, on the other hand, a priest tells us that he has power, by means of confession, to absolve the sinner of his sin, when the repentance is imperfect, which he does pretend to have, then he takes upon himself the authority and prerogative to admit into the kingdom of heaven those whom God would exclude; or, in other words, to forgive the sin which God himself has not forgiven. In either case, therefore, the application of the indulgence, even in a time of jubilee, can have no effect on the condition stated by Dr. Wiseman.

Again, as to the other conditions. We will place against Dr. Wiseman's theory the *dictum* of other Romanists. Dr. Murray, an Irish papal archbishop, deposed on oath before a committee of the House of Commons, that in Veron's "*Rule of Catholic Faith*," from which we have already quoted several passages, "was to be found (among other books) the most authentic exposition of the faith of the Catholic church."[2] Dr. Wiseman makes the reception dependent on the performance of certain specified acts, and the contribution

---

[1] Catech. Concl. Trent. Professor Donovan's Translation, p. 269. Dublin, 1829. And Council of Trent, Sess. xiv. chap. 4.
[2] Digest of Evidence, etc., on the State of Ireland, March 22, 1825. Commons' Report, p. 225. Phelan and O'Sullivan. p. 171. London, 1826.

of funds to the coffers of the church to propagate the Romish faith. Veron repudiates this system: he says (p. 61) :—

"No jubilee or indulgence granted by the pope or by a council, whether plenary or otherwise, and confined to a special number of years; or particular, that is, granted for particular reasons, or depending on the performance of certain specified works, is an article of faith; or, in other words, the validity of no such jubilee or indulgence is of that certainty which is essential to every article of faith; whilst many of these are merely probably valid; and others, which have a certain currency, having no other object but sordid gain, are scandalous, and, as such, consequently are by all means to be done away with.—Indulgences granted by popes are still less of faith."

If such be not of faith, then all the specified conditions may be rejected; and thus we can safely question Dr. Wiseman's conditions. Take away his conditions and the indulgence itself is not obtained; for, according to his theory, all the conditions must be fulfilled, including the subscription of money, which, according to Veron, is scandalous. If our position be questioned, we require that Veron's theory, backed by the authority of Archbishop Murray, should first be proved erroneous.

VII. We call in question, in the next place, all the foundations on which the doctrine of indulgences is built, namely—

1. That punishment does remain due after the forgiveness of sin.

If the sin be forgiven, why is not the penalty remitted? What authority have priests for saying that the two do not go together? We do not ask the *reason* for upholding their system, for that is obvious. The two processes have their advantages: the confession gives a moral influence; the barter for indulgences gives a material advantage to the priest. He has a double hold on the deluded votary, controlling both his conscience and his purse.

The punishments usually inflicted are prayers, fastings, and almsdeeds. These are, or should be, acts of religious devotion; and if done for sordid motives, or as a punishment or penance, they cannot be pleasing in the sight of God. Acts of devotion cannot be considered punishments; and if not punishments, what is the value of the indulgence?

2. That there is a purgatory.

This doctrine we have proved to be a modern invention. Fisher, the celebrated Romish bishop of Rochester (A.D. 1504), wrote:—

"It is not sufficiently manifest from whom indulgences had their original. Of purgatory there is very little or no mention among the ancient fathers:—but *after* purgatory began to terrify the world, after men had for some time trembled at the torments thereof, indulgences began to be in request. As long as purgatory was not cared for, there was no man sought for pardons; for the whole price of pardons hangs on purgatory. Take away purgatory, and what shall we need of pardons?"[1]

But, even supposing there is a purgatory, Veron says that it is not of faith, that is, it may be disbelieved "that the remission of punishment is caused by the application of our satisfaction to the souls in purgatory."[2] The principal value of indulgences, according to Fisher, depends on the

[1] "...Quam diu nulla fuerat de purgatorio cura, nemo quæsivit indulgentias. Nam ex illo pendet omnis indulgentiarum existimatio—Cœperunt igitur indulgentiæ, postquam ad purgatorii cruciatus aliquandiu trepidatum erat." Jon. Ruffens, Epis. art. 18, Assert. Lutheran. Confut. fol. 132. Colon, 1624, and fol. iii.2. Antw. 1523.

[2] Birmingham, 1833. "*The Catholic Rule of Faith,*" p. 69.

existence of purgatory. We leave our readers to reconcile the teaching of Veron and Fisher as best they can.

3. That there are merits and works of supererogation.

If there are no such merits, then there can be no indulgences. Veron, as we have seen, declares that the existence of such merits is not an article of faith. We, on the authority of Scripture, deny their existence. We are saved by the mercy and grace of God, not by our merits; for, "if the righteous scarcely be saved," what will there be to spare of *their* merits for the ungodly?

4. That these merits, if they exist, can be transferred by a priest for the benefit of the living or the dead.

Though specially and emphatically asserted by the Roman priesthood in the affirmative, Hilary, bishop of Poictiers, accounted a canonized saint by the Roman church, laid it down "that no man, after this life, can be helped or delivered by the good works or merits of others, because every man must necessarily provide oil for his own lamp."[1] And where is the authority for the assumption of this power? Where is the evidence of the alleged results? Nowhere. We have seen that it is not of faith that merits or satisfactions can be transferred to the dead; and Veron says that "it is not a doctrine of the Catholic church [that is, it may be disbelieved or rejected] that the just man can merit for others, in any of the various meanings of the word merit, not even by merit of congruity; or obtain by his merit the conversion of a sinner, or any other grace whatever."[2] Now if this be so, the whole groundwork of indulgences fails.

[1] "Alienis operibus ac meritis neminem adjuvandum, quia unicuique lampadi suæ emere oleum fit necesse." Hilary, Comment. in Matt. canon. 27, p. 591. Paris, 1631.
[2] Birmingham, 1833. "*The Catholic Rule of Faith,*" p. 34.

VIII. We deny the antiquity of the doctrine as now taught.

We admit that, in the third century, it was a custom to enjoin mortifications and severities on those who had been found guilty of ecclesiastical offences. These have since been called penances. These punishments the bishops of the church had power, but as a matter of discipline only, to mitigate or relax: this mitigation was called a pardon or indulgence. The "lapsed," during the persecutions, more particularly, had to undergo these *canonical* punishments. Martyrs, or those confined in prison for the faith, frequently interceded for a mitigation of the punishment; and the bishops remitted them on this ground, on condition that the offenders gave adequate proof of repentance; and the lapsed were received again into communion with the church. There is not the faintest resemblance in all this to the modern doctrine of indulgence. Dr. Wiseman alleges that "there are the strongest reasons to believe that, in most cases, absolution preceded the allotment of penance, or at least that it was granted during the time of its performance."[1] There is not the slightest ground for this assertion: we deny the allegation and demand the proof.

Alphonsus à Castro, the celebrated Franciscan friar and archbishop (A.D. 1550), after admitting that there was no subject on which the Scriptures had expressed less, or of which the ancient fathers had written less, than that of indulgences, added—"and it seems the use of them came but lately into the church;"[2] and the famous Cardinal Cajetan said "there is no authority of Scripture, or ancient

---

[1] Lectures. London, 1851. Vol. ii. p. 76. Lecture XI. "Indulgences."
[2] ...Harum usus in ecclesiam videtur sero receptus. Alph. contra hæres. viii. Verbo Indulgentia, p. 115. Paris, 1543.

fathers, Greek or Latin, that brings them [indulgences] to our knowledge." [1] He could trace the origin no further back than Gregory I. (A.D. 601), who instituted the Indulgences of Stations; and he adds, "After him some popes granted indulgences very imprudently and to no purpose." This is letting them off very easily, and we shall do so in the same spirit by giving them credit for good intentions, admitting, with those quoted by Thomas Aquinas,[2] who said that an ecclesiastical indulgence of itself could remit no punishment, either in the judgment of the church or in the judgment of God; but that it was a kind of pious fraud, whereby the church, by promising such remission, might allure men to the devout performance of good works.

CHAPTER XII.

TRADITION.

"He [Ignatius, A.D. 70] exhorted them [the churches] to adhere firmly to the Tradition of the Apostles, which, for the sake of greater security, he deemed it necessary to attest, by committing to writing."—EUSEBIUS, lib. iii. cap. 36. Paris, 1678.

WE have now passed in review some of the leading doctrines taught by the modern church of Rome, and have shown them to be of human invention. Though some of these

---

1 "...Verum quia nulla Scripturæ sacræ, nulla priscorum doctorum Græcorum aut Latinorum authoritas scripta, hunc ad nostram deduxit notitiam, etc." Thom. de Vio Cajetan Opusc. Tract. 15. De Indulg. cap. i. tom. i. p. 129. August, Taurin, 1582.

2 "...Errant, qui dicunt indulgentias tantum valere, quantum fides, et devotio recipientis exiget: et ecclesiam ideo sic eas pronunciare, ut quadam *piâ fraude* homines ad bene faciendum alliciat." Thom. Summæ Theol. Supp. Tert. pars. quæst. xxv. art. iv. 4to. Colon. 1620; and Greg. de Valent. de Indulg. c. 2, p. 1784. Paris, 1609.

may be old, they are not old enough to sustain the character of being apostolic, nor even sanctioned by what is called apostolic tradition. This brings us to consider our last head—namely, the doctrine of tradition.

The Council of Trent, by the first decree at its fourth session—having stated that "having constantly in view the removal of error and the preservation of the purity of the gospel in the church, which gospel, promised before by the prophets in the sacred Scripture, was first orally published by our Lord Jesus Christ, the Son of God, who afterward commanded it to be preached by his apostles to every creature, as the source of all saving truth and discipline"—declared, that "this truth and discipline are contained both in written books, and in unwritten traditions, which have come down to us either received by the apostles from the lips of Christ himself, or transmitted by the hands of the same apostles, under the dictation of the Holy Spirit." It further declared, that, "following the example of the orthodox Fathers, the council doth receive and reverence, with equal sentiments of piety and veneration, all the books as well of the Old as of the New Testament; and also the aforesaid traditions, pertaining both to faith and manners, whether received from Christ himself or dictated by the Holy Spirit, and preserved in the Catholic church by continual succession." And it is important to observe that, "lest any doubt should arise respecting the sacred books which are received by the council," it "judged proper" to set out a list of such books, but it does not set out what are the points of faith handed down by "continual succession," as forming the unwritten tradition. The object of this omission is apparent; for what cannot be proved by Scripture finds shelter under the dark mantle of tradition. As the Romish bishop, Canus, ingenuously observed, "Tradition is not only of greater force than the Scriptures, but almost all disputations with heretics are to be referred to traditions." [1] The all-importance of traditions to the Romish church is summed up in the following passage from a work of a popular writer of his day, Costerus. Expatiating on the excellence and importance of tradition, he says:—

"The excellency of the unwritten word doth far surpass the Scripture, which the apostles left us in parchments; the one is written by the finger of God, the other by the pen of the apostles. The Scripture is a dead letter, written on paper or parchment, which may be razed or wrested at pleasure; but tradition is written in men's hearts, which cannot be altered. The Scripture is like a scabbard which will receive any sword, either leaden, or wooden, or brazen, and suffereth itself to be drawn by any interpretation. Tradition retains the true sword in the scabbard; that is, the true sense of the Scripture in the sheath of the letter. The Scriptures do not contain clearly all the mysteries of religion, for they were not given to that end to prescribe an absolute form of faith; but tradition contains in it all truth, it comprehends all the mysteries of faith, and all the estate of the Christian religion, and resolves all doubts which may arise concerning faith; and from hence it will follow that tradition is the interpreter of all Scriptures, the judge of all controversies, the remover of all errors, and from whose judgment we ought not to appeal to any other judge; yea, rather, all judges are bound to regard and follow this judgment."

The importance of the doctrine, therefore, is undeniable. But to return to the Trent decree, on which we have to make three observations:—

---

[1] Mel. Canus Loc. Theol. 3, cap. iii. p. 156. Colon. 1605.
[2] Coster. Eucharist. cap. i. p. 44. Colon. 1606. Quoted by Sir H. Lynd. *Via Devia*, sec. viii.

1. The admission of unwritten tradition, as of authority in points of faith, tends decidedly to the establishment of error instead of its removal; and to the corruption of the gospel instead of, as is erroneously asserted, the preservation of its purity.

2. That it is notoriously untrue that the framers of the above decree did follow the example of the "orthodox Fathers." We challenge the production of any one of the orthodox Fathers who held unwritten tradition with "equal sentiments of piety and veneration" as the written word on points of *faith*.

3. If Romanists will produce to us any unwritten tradition received from Christ, or dictated by the Holy Spirit, and preserved in the church by continual succession, on some reliable evidence of its authenticity, we will receive it.

The Trent decree asserts, as a matter of fact, that the example of the orthodox Fathers was followed in framing the foregoing declaration of faith. It is admitted, however, that [1] "it is no article of Catholic Faith that the church cannot err in *matters of fact* relating to faith, or in matters of speculation, or civil policy depending on mere human judgment or testimony." According to Dr. Wiseman, in order to arrive at a judicious decision on this "historical inquiry," all "human prudence" must be used to arrive at the fact. Alleged matters of fact may, therefore, be disbelieved without the charge of heresy; and it is incumbent on those who allege a matter, as a fact, to prove it to be so. The very essence of tradition is, or ought to be, based on fact. That fact should be so patent as to recommend itself to our belief in a most undoubted and palpable manner. It

---

[1] Kirk and Berington's "*Faith of Catholics*," Prop. xi. p. 477. London, 1846.

is alleged, however, (as we shall presently see), that these traditions are now recorded in writing. The alleged facts can, therefore, if true, be put beyond doubt by adequate proof. While, then, we are ready to admit all those doctrines which can be proved to have been received from Christ himself, or dictated by the Holy Spirit, and preserved in the Christian church, we emphatically deny that the characteristics of Romanism come within this definition of tradition.

Again, it is important to observe, that had the doctrine of tradition been admitted by the Fathers, and handed down " from hand to hand," as alleged, to the time when the doctors of Trent met (April, 1546), the council would have had simply to declare the teaching of the church on this head, and there would have been no question; but it was far otherwise, for Cardinal Pallavicino and Father Paul Sarpi, who wrote histories of the Trent Council, testified that, when the question of tradition came to be discussed, there were as many opinions as tongues.[1]

If, then, the question whether tradition was to be held in the same reverence as the Scriptures formed the subject of hot debate, (the doctrine itself being proposed only on the authority of tradition), on what principle can we be asked to accept propositions as points of faith which professedly are only based on tradition? Romanists tell us that there is in the church an authority, in matters of doctrine, of equal value with the Scriptures—namely, tradition. We assert, without fear of contradiction, that it was at the Council of Trent, A.D. 1546, that oral tradition was FOR THE FIRST TIME declared to be of equal authority with the Scriptures,

---

[1] "Tot sententias quot linguas tunc fuisse comperio." Pallav. lib. ii. c. 2. Romæ, 1656. Sarpi, lib. ii. s. 45, 47. Gen. 1629.

and that they both were to be received with *equal* sentiments of piety and reverence.

Rome does not disguise the fact that she teaches points of doctrine as articles of faith, which are not to be found in the Holy Scriptures. Melchior Canus, who was summoned by Paul III. to the Council of Trent, testified that "many things belong to the doctrine and faith of Christians which are not contained either plainly or obscurely in Holy Scripture;"[1] and Dominic Banhes said: "Not all things that belong to the Catholic faith are contained in the canonical books, either clearly or obscurely."—"All things necessary to salvation have not been committed to the Scriptures."[2]

To explain exactly what tradition means, we adopt the definitions given by Dr. Wiseman, in his own words, in his lectures on "The Doctrine and Practices of the Roman Catholic Church."[3] He admits the Scriptures to be the revealed word of God, which he calls the written word;"[4] but the apostles, he says, did not consider the Scriptures as the sole foundation on which they built the church. They employed, in fact, two codes—the written and the unwritten. He says:[5]—

"An authority to teach was communicated to the apostles, and by them to their successors, together with an unwritten code; so that what was afterwards written by them was but a fixing and recording of *part* of that which was already in possession of the church."

---

[1] Mel. Canus de Loc. Theol. lib. iii. c. 3, Opera, tom. i. p. 198. Matrit. 1785. He says that this has been proved by Innocent III. in his treatise *De Celebratione*.

[2] In Secundum Secundæ, S. Thomæ, q. i. Art. x. Concl. ii. col. 519, Venice, 1587. Ibid. Concl. v. col. 542, quoted by Scudamore. *England and Rome*, p. 326. London, 1855.

[3] Lectures. London, 1851.

[4] Lecture III. pp. 58, 60.

[5] Lecture V. pp. 128, 130.

But this unwritten word he asserts to be a "body of doctrines which, in consequence of express declarations in the written word, we believe not to have been committed, in the first instance, to writing, but delivered by Christ to his apostles, and by the apostles to their successors;"[1] and he says further,—" I have more than once commented on the incorrectness of that method of arguing which demands that we prove every one of our doctrines individually from the Scriptures." He maintains that "many of these truths were committed to traditional keeping;"[2] but he desires to guard us from falling into the popular error of supposing that these traditions are not fixed and certain: in fact, that they are not now reduced to writing. The cardinal overlooks the fact that he assumes the very point he has to prove, namely, that there was a precise time when they were first committed to writing. Were they so committed by the apostles? or by whom?

"By the term unwritten word (he says) it is not to be understood that these articles of faith or traditions are nowhere recorded. Because, on the contrary, suppose a difficulty to arise regarding any doctrine, so that men should differ, and not know what precisely to believe, and that the church thought it prudent or necessary to define what is to be held, the method pursued would be to examine most accurately the writings of the fathers of the church, to ascertain what, in different countries and in different ages, was by them held; and then collecting the suffrages of all the world and of all times—not, indeed, to create new articles of faith, but to define what has always been the faith of the Catholic church. It is conducted in every instance as a matter of historical inquiry, and all human prudence is used to arrive at a judicious decision."[3]

The investigation, therefore, resolves itself into an histori-

[1] Lecture III. p. 60.   [2] Lecture XI. vol. ii. p. 53.
Lecture III. vol. i. p. 61.

cal inquiry, in which any person extraordinarily gifted with patience, and with a knowledge of the dead languages, can arrive at a decision as to what was, or what was not, of faith in the early church, as well as Dr. Wiseman or any other Romish priest. We maintain that this very investigation will result, and has resulted, in the demonstration that the peculiar doctrines of Romanism, now forming the standard creed of the papal church, formed no part of any accepted creed or article of faith of the Christian church for the first five centuries. In no point of the Romish faith does this stand out in more bold relief than in the dogma now under consideration. While it is admitted that certain ceremonies were at an early date introduced into Christian worship, from which doctrines were subsequently deduced, and were imposed on Christians under the assumed authority of the church by interested ecclesiastics, we nevertheless maintain that these several innovations were without the sanction of Scripture, and had only the authority of doubtful and unauthoritative *tradition* to support them. All the Romish traditions were introduced subsequently to the days of the apostles. Step by step, little by little, custom became rooted in the system, and eventually took the form of doctrine, and was finally imposed as such, until we find the mass of corruptions of preceding ages heaped together, sanctioned and codified, as it were, by the doctors of Trent. And, in 1564, for the first time, twelve articles in addition to the old creed were put forward, embracing these novelties, and enforced under pain of eternal damnation. One of these articles alone is sufficiently sweeping, but rather vague. We are required to accept *all* things taught and defined not only by the Council of Trent, but by all other General Councils! The church that requires this, actually has not yet authoritatively defined which of the councils are or are not to be considered general. Romanists are not even agreed as to which parts of these councils are to be admitted and which to be rejected. But there is a more formidable difficulty. Cardinal Bellarmine says that "the books of councils being negligently kept, abound with many errors!"[1] And as to the testimony of the fathers to whom Dr. Wiseman would send us, no authoritative list of their works has been published by his church, nor will she vouch for the accuracy or authenticity of any of them; nor will it be denied that the writings of many of the fathers have been grossly corrupted, amended, and expurgated, when it suited the views of the church for the time being.

We are, in precise terms, referred to written documents by which the truth and source of tradition are established. If the text of these written documents is admitted to be corrupt, what reliance can be placed on them as affording the evidence sought to be adduced? But if these same writings are placed before us as evidence against Protestantism, then it is quite legitimate for us to adduce them in evidence to overthrow the theory advanced by Dr. Wiseman. We assert, then, that, if a careful examination be made of the earliest records that can be produced, we shall find that practices were, from time to time, introduced into the church, and their use sanctioned only on the authority of *tradition*, but that to establish points of doctrine, the sacred Scriptures were *alone appealed to as of authority.* Nay, further, when the early Christians applied the term *tradition* to points of doctrine, they expressly referred to the traditions handed down by the apostles *in their writings.* In arguing

[1] "Libri conciliorum negligenter conservati sunt, et multis vitiis scatent." Bell. de Concil., lib. i. c. 2, sect. 1. Prag. 1721.

with the heretics of his day (A.D. 140), Irenæus applied this word tradition to those doctrines which Romanists themselves admit to be clearly taught by the Scriptures. He declared that "the Scriptures are perfect as having been dictated by the Word of God and his Holy Spirit." [1]

And he says:—

"For we have become acquainted with the dispensation of our salvation through no other men than those through whom the gospel has come to us; which indeed they then preached, but afterwards, by the will of God, delivered to us in the Scriptures to be the foundation and pillar of our faith." [2]

And, in fact, this same father accused the heretics of his day of using, on this very subject, the argument invariably advanced by Romanists of the present day, against Protestants:—

"When they (the heretics) are confuted out of the Scriptures they turn round and accuse the Scriptures themselves, as if they were not accurate, nor of authority, and because they are ambiguous, and because the truth cannot be discovered by those who are ignorant of the tradition, for that the truth was not delivered in writing, but orally." [3]

And while Tertullian (A.D. 194) set great value on usage, custom, and tradition, which he admitted not to be authorized by Scripture, on questions of doctrine he looked

---

[1] "Scripturæ quidem perfectæ sunt, quippe à Verbo et Spiritu ejus dictæ," Iren. cont. hæres. lib. ii. c. 47, p. 173. London, 1522; and Edit. Grabe, 1853; and c. 25. p. 117. Edit. Basil, 1526.

[2] "Non enim per alios dispositionem salutis nostræ cognovimus, quam per eos per quos evangelium pervenit ad nos; quod quidem tunc præconiaverunt, posteà verò per Dei voluntatem in Scripturis nobis tradiderunt fundamentum et columnam fidei nostræ futurum." Iren. Advers. hæres. lib. iii. c. 1, p. 198. Oxon. 1702; and p. 117. Basil, 1526.

[3] (Hæretici) "quum enim ex Scripturis arguuntur, in accusationem convertuntur ipsarum Scripturarum, quasi non recte habeant, neque sint ex authoritate, et quia variè sint dictæ, et quia non possit ex his inveniri veritas ab his qui nesciunt traditionem, non enim per literas traditam illam, sed per vivam vocem." Iren. cont. hæres. lib. iii. c. 2. in Init. same edition; and p. 140. Edit. Basil, 1526.

to the Scriptures alone as of authority. In arguing with the heretics, he demanded from them proofs from Scripture—" If it is not written, let them fear the curse allotted to such as add or diminish." [1] Suicer, the eminent professor of Greek, whose works are almost indispensable to the study of the Fathers, furnishes examples of the fact that the word παραδοσις, *traditio*—tradition—was used as "identical with the written word."

The passages from the early Christian fathers, which insist on the Scriptures as alone of authority in matters of doctrine, are so numerous and so well known, that it is at the present day almost labour and time lost to repeat them: they are to be found in almost every Protestant controversial work. We will, nevertheless, transcribe two or three of these, merely as illustrations. What could be more striking than the words delivered at the first General Council of Nice (A.D. 325) by Eusebius, bishop of Cæsarea, in the name of the three hundred and eighteen bishops then assembled? "Believe the things that are written: the things that are not written, neither think upon nor inquire into." [2] And Gregory, bishop of Nyssa (A.D. 379), said, "Let a man be persuaded of the truth of that alone which has the seal of the written testimony." [3] And Cyril, bishop of Jerusalem (A.D. 386), places the matter very clearly before us. He said:—

"Not even the least of the Divine and holy mysteries of the faith ought to be handed down without the Divine Scriptures.

---

[1] "... Si non est scriptum, timeat *væ* illud, adjicientibus aut detrahentibus destinatum." Tert. contra Hermog. p. 272. Paris, 1580; and cap. xxii. vol. ii. p. 111. Edit. Semler. Halæ. Magd. 1773.

[2] "τοῖς γεγραμμένοις πιστευε, τὰ μὴ γεγραμμένα μὴ ἐννόει μηδὲ ζήτει."—Euseb. ad Philosp. in Gelas. Cyzic. Comment. Act. Conc. Nic. P. 2, c. xix. p. 185. Edit. Balf.

[3] "Ἐν τούτῳ μόνῳ τὴν ἀλήθειαν τιθέσθω, ᾧ σφραγὶς ἐπέστι τῆς γραφικῆς μαρτυρίας." —Greg. Nyss. Dialog. de Anima et Resurrect. tom. i. p. 639. Edit Græcolat.

Do not simply give faith to me while I am speaking these things to you, except you have the proof of what I say from the holy word. For the security and preservation of our faith are not supported by ingenuity of speech, but by the proofs of the sacred Scriptures." [1]

Such passages might be multiplied. They all tend to prove that the modern practice of placing tradition on a level with Scriptures to establish a point of faith, was then considered most heretical. Indeed, one father, Theophilus, bishop of Alexandria (A.D. 412), emphatically said, "It is the part of a devilish spirit to follow the sophisms of human falsehoods, and to think anything to be divine that is not authorized by the Holy Scriptures." [2]

The doctrine of tradition cannot, however, be dispensed with; for, as we have seen, it is freely admitted that Romanists do hold doctrines which are not proved by Scripture. All these are most conveniently classed under the head of apostolical traditions. The assertion that they are such is easily made, and reliance is placed on the difficulty of disproof. Logic and fair dealing require that the affirmative be established. No one should be called upon to prove a negative. We will, however, endeavour to accomplish this task in the following manner. We shall take each successive age, and note down, in chronological order, clear and undisputed historical facts, which will show the origin, progress, and full development of each of the modern popish

---

[1] " Δεῖ γαρ, περι τῶν θείων καὶ ἁγίων τῆς πιστεως μυστηρίων, μηδὲ το τυχὸν ἄνευ τῶν θείων παρα διδοσθαι γραφῶν μηδὲ ἁπλῶς πιθανότητι καὶ λογων κατασκευαῖς παραφερεσθαι μηδὲ ἐμοὶ τῷ ταυτά σοι λέγοντι ἁπλῶς πιστευσῃς, ἐὰν τὴν ἀπόδειξιν—τῶν καταγγελλομένων ἀπὸ τῶν θείων μὴ λαβῃς γραφῶν. ἡ σωτερία γὰρ αὕτη τῆς πίστεως ἡμων, οὐκ ἐξ εὑρεσιλογιας, αλλὰ ἐξ ἀποδείξεως των θείων ἐστι γραφῶν."—Cyril Hiers. Catech. iv. sect. 17, p. 108. Monac. 1848.

[2] "Dæmoniaci spiritus esset instinctus, sophismata humanarum mentium sequi, et aliquid extra Scripturarum auctoritatem putare divinum." Theophil. Alex. (A.D. 402) Op. Epist. Paschal. i. s. 6, in Biblioth. Vet. Petrum, tom. vii. p. 617. Edit. Galland.

dogmas against which we protest. We maintain that, previously to the dates recorded, no evidence can be adduced from any authentic records to show that the doctrine referred to existed as an article of faith.

The inquiry we are about to enter upon is as interesting as it is curious. It is a common device of Romanists, when it is alleged that their *peculiar* doctrines are new, to inquire, in turn, *first*, when and how the innovation came about; and, *secondly*, why and how it came to pass that the fact of the innovation was not detected and remedied at the time. As to the latter question, were it a part of the inquiry, we could show a regular succession of witnesses who have, from the time of the apostles to the date of the Reformation, borne testimony to the truth, and directly or indirectly, or in anticipation, protested against each error and heresy. The former question we now propose to answer.

PART II.

CHRONOLOGICAL ARRANGEMENT.

CHRONOLOGICAL ARRANGEMENT.

"Where is your religion? Where is the reverence due to your fathers? You have renounced your ancestors, in your manners, your living, your teaching, your manner of thinking, finally, in your very language. You are constantly applauding antiquity, and yet daily live in novelties. Thus it appears that, whilst you depart from the good institutions of your ancestors, you keep and retain those which you ought not to do, and those which you ought to retain you do not."—*Tertullian.*[1]

THE APOSTOLIC AGE.

THE foundation of the Christian religion is JESUS CHRIST. What he did and taught must be our rule. We only know of him and his precepts from the testimony of those who have *recorded* his acts and teaching, as eye and ear witnesses, or, as in the case of St. Luke, from the testimony of those who had the advantage of a personal intercourse with our Saviour. When the apostles whom God had singled out to build his church upon Christ, the only Foundation, were removed from their labours, they left us, in *writing*, an inspired book, to guide us in the right way, and teach us the saving truths entrusted to them by their Divine Master. They acknowledged no object of adoration but God, no intercessor but Christ, no expiatory sacrifice but his death, no other way of justification but through FAITH

---

[1] " Ubi religio? ubi veneratio majoribus debita a vobis? habitu, victu, instructu, censu, ipso denique sermone proavis renuntiastis. Laudatis semper antiquitatem, et nove de die vivitis. Per quod ostenditur, dum'a bonis majorum institutis deceditis, ea vos retinere et custodire quæ non debuistis, cum quæ debuistis non custoditis."—*Apolog. adv. gentes.*, cap. vi. p. 20, vol. v. Halæ Magd. 1773.

in their blessed Redeemer. We read of no altar at the supper, nor image in temples, no universal bishop in the church, no souls in purgatory, nothing of a queen in heaven, nor merits of saints, nor pompous ceremonies. The greatest ornaments of the church were simplicity of doctrine and sanctity of life.

Any deviation from the written and inspired word of God must be based on human invention—and what is human is fallible. What has been added to the Word is "wood, hay, and stubble." The introduction of Jewish and heathen ceremonies by the early converts to Christianity, the pomp of paganism, the ignorance of the people, and the connivance or craft of those who would be teachers, gradually obscured the word of God, under the guise of tradition. Innovations were introduced by degrees; and, step by step, we find consummated in the sixteenth century, that huge deformity called POPERY.

In the following pages, the gradual development of papal errors and corruptions will be traced in chronological order. It will be seen how, age after age, a succession of unscriptural novelties crept in, and were by degrees incorporated with the faith of the primitive church, till at length the heterogeneous mass of truth and error which makes up the creed of Rome was sanctioned and authorized by the council of Trent.

THE SECOND CENTURY.

THE characteristic of the apostolic age was simplicity. Justyn Martyr (A.D. 130) has left us a record of the service and worship of that day. He thus describes it:—

"On the day that is called Sunday there is an assembly, in the same place, of those who dwell in towns or in the country; and the histories of the apostles and the writings of the prophets are read, whilst the time permits; then the reading ceasing, the president verbally admonishes and exhorts the imitation of these good things. Then we all rise in common and offer prayers, bread and wine and water are offered, and the president in like manner offers prayers and thanksgivings, as far as it is in his power to do so, and the people joyfully cry out, saying—Amen. And the distribution and the communication is to each of those who have returned thanks, and it is sent by the deacons to those who are not present. And this food is called by us the Eucharist. And in all that we offer we bless the Maker of all things by his Son Jesus Christ and by the Holy Spirit. Of those who are rich and willing, each according to his own pleasure, contributes; and what is thus collected is put away by the president, and he assists the orphans and widows, and those who through sickness or any other cause are destitute."[1]

Such was the simplicity of worship in those early days; but even here we trace an innovation, in the addition of water to the wine, not sanctioned by the sacramental institution or apostolic ordinance.[2]

---

[1] Second Apology for Christians, p. 97. Paris, 1615.
[2] According to Polydore Vergil, this custom was introduced by Alexander I., bishop of Rome, A.D. 109. Polydore Vergil, De Invent. Rer., B. v. c. vii. p. 108. Langley's Edition, London, 1551. Polydore Vergil was a member of the Roman church, a man of great learning and genius of the 15th century. He was sent into this country by Pope Alexander II. to collect the papal tribute. The work from which we quote, and to which we shall have frequently to refer, is the "De Inventionibus Rerum." This honest writer could not be tolerated, so his book was ordered to be corrected, and we find it accordingly expurgated in several places, both in the Expurgatory Belgic Index, and that of Madrid; and Possevine tells us in his "Apparatus Sacer," a catalogue of ecclesiastical books (tom. ii. p. 294; Cologne, 1607), that the edition which Pope Gregory XIII. commanded to be purged at Rome, 1576, might be read, which varies considerably from the edition published by Robert Stephen; printed at Paris, 1528. For further information see "Defence of Sir H. Lynd's," "*Via Tuta.*" London, 1850, pp. 96, 97.

A.D. 110 (*circa*).—It has been seen that the celebration of the Lord's Supper formed an important part of the worship of the primitive church. The Jews, when they made their solemn appearances before God, took offerings with them, usually the produce of the earth, in token of their grateful acknowledgment of daily mercies. The early Christians, who were mostly Jews by birth, retained this custom; and, at the public assemblies, brought with them bread and wine, fruits, corn, and grain. These, when consecrated by prayer, seem to have been used in part for the communion, and the rest distributed to the poor, etc.[1] The gifts thus brought retained the name of offerings, and from this simple beginning we can trace the complicated superstitions of the mass. From these offerings the eucharist was called an oblation, afterwards a sacrifice, *gratulatory* and not *expiatory*. It was the offering of the first fruits of the earth, not of the body of Christ—though this furnished a pretence for changing the supper into a sacrifice, by reason of the several attendant circumstances connected with the services, as hereafter stated [A.D. 787].

A.D. 113.—Platina, in his Lives of the Popes, attributes the introduction of the use of *holy water* to Alexander I.[2] (A.D. 108—117). The authority for this statement is a decretal epistle of doubtful authenticity, to say the least of it. But even if introduced, the practice was condemned by some of the subsequent Fathers as a pagan custom. The emperor Julian, to spite the Christians, ordered the provisions in the markets to be sprinkled with *holy water* from

---

[1] See Pfaff. *Dissert. de Oblat. et Consec. Eucharistæ;* in his Stigmata Dissert. Theologia. Stut., 1720.

[2] In the *Clementine Constitutions* the authorship of Holy Water is attributed to St. Matthew. Lib. viii. c. xxix, in Labb. Concil. Tom. i. col. 494. Lutet. Paris, 1671.

the heathen temples, on purpose, as Middleton observes, either to starve them, or force them to eat what they esteemed polluted. The use of holy water by the heathens at the entrance of their temples, to sprinkle themselves with, is admitted by Montfauçon and the Jesuit La Cerda—the latter, in his notes on a passage of Virgil where this practice is mentioned, says—" Hence was derived the custom of holy church, to provide purifying or holy water at the entrance of their churches." The modern priests use the same "aspergillium," or sprinkler, which was used by pagan priests for the same purpose, as seen on ancient bas-reliefs and coins. The Indians, the Brahmins, etc., also use holy water in sprinkling their houses, etc., and believe that they can thereby wipe out their sins.[1]

But the abuse of this custom was not until some centuries after. (See *post*, A.D. 852.)

Whatever might have been the first intention of the originators of the custom it is very certain that the present use is mingled with the grossest superstitions. Marsilius Columna, archbishop of Salerno, attributes to the use of holy water seven spiritual virtues: 1. To frighten away devils; 2. To remit venial sins; 3. To cure distractions; 4. To elevate the mind; 5. To dispose it to devotion; 6. To obtain grace; 7. To prepare for the sacrament. As to corporal gifts: 1. To cure barrenness; 2. To multiply

[1] " La purification du corps, quelque génante qu'elle puisse être, est bien plus aisée que cette de l'ame. Il falloit conserver l'usage de celui-ci et c'est ce qui fit instituer l'usage de *l'eau lustrale* que la Religione Chretienne a abolie dans la suit pour lui substituer *l'Eau benite*. Les Prêtres et le Peuple prenoient de cette eau lustrale, quand ils entroient dans les Temples pour faire leurs sacrifices. Ceux d'entre les Chrétiens qui ont retenu l'usage de l'Eau benits lui attribuent plusieurs qualités qui approche beaucoup des miracles. Les Indiens ont aussi leur *Eau lustrale*. Ils arrosent tous les matins le devant de leurs maisons avec de l'urine de vache, et prétendent s'attirer par ce moien la benediction des Dieux. Ils croient encore que cette a la force d'effacer entierement leurs péches." Picard's Cérémonies et Coûtumes Religieuse, vol. i. p. xviii. note *b*. Amsterdam, 1723.

goods; 3. To procure health; 4. To purge the air from pestilential vapours.[1] There are other virtues attributed to holy water that are not fit to be spoken of to modest ears.[2] While we feel humbled that any who call themselves Christians should be slaves to such degrading superstitions, we feel thankful that Protestantism is a foil to such priestcraft.

Even at this early period, divers heresies existed in the church, such as the Valentinian, the Gnostic, the Encratite. These heretics declared against marriage and forbade eating flesh. The Montanists were likewise enemies to marriage, especially of the clergy. Almost all the present papal heresies existed in some form or other during these early periods, either among the pagans or Jews, or one or other of the heretical sects. We shall see how and when they were successively engrafted on Christianity. Cardinal Baronius, in his Annals, under the year 740, says that—"It is allowable for the church to transfer to pious uses those ceremonies which the pagans employed impiously to superstitious worship, after they had been purified by consecration: for the devil is the more mortified to see those things returned to the service of Jesus Christ, which were instituted for his own."[3]

A.D. 140.—Telesphorus, bishop of Rome, instituted the fast of Lent upon a pretended tradition of the apostles. Fasts and festivals were practised and observed by the Jews and pagans. The admission of these into Christianity is

---

[1] Marsilius Columna. Hydragiolog. s. iii. c. ii. p. 281, etc. Rom. 1686.
[2] See Domenico Magri Notigia de vocaboli Ecclesiastici in aquâ Benedictâ, p. 41. Rom. 1669.
[3] Referring to pagan ceremonies, he says:—"Consulto introductum videtur, ut quæ erant Gentilatiæ superstitionis officia, eadem veri Dei cultui sanctificata in veræ religionis cultum impenderentur." Baron: Annales, tom. ii. p. 384, col i. Luc. 1738.

harmless when not abused. When commanded periodically, fasts become pharisaical forms.

A.D. 160.—This was an age of violent persecutions and martyrdom. It was a custom among the Greeks to celebrate the memory of their heroes at their tombs, to excite the survivors to emulate their deeds of valour. Christians, in order to encourage each other to suffer death for the gospel, imitated this Greek custom. They gathered such of the relics of the martyrs as could be saved, and honourably buried them. An annual commemoration, called the day of their nativity, or birthday to heaven, at their tombs or at their place of martyrdom, was then celebrated on the days of their death.[1] At their assemblies, after prayers and exposition of the Scriptures, they rehearsed in order the names of the martyrs and their deeds. Then were thanksgivings to God offered up for giving them victory. The proceedings terminated with the celebration of the eucharist. The intent of these meetings was obviously to teach that those who died in Christ lived with the Lord, and in the memory of the church, and to excite survivors to constancy and faith. This is recorded by the ecclesiastical historian, Eusebius.[2] "There (namely, where their bones were deposited), if it be possible, meeting together in joy and gladness, the Lord grant us to celebrate the birthday of this martyrdom, both in memory of those who have wrestled before us, and for the exercise and preparation of those that come after." No religious worship was rendered to

[1] Tertullian De Cor. Militis, Edit. Roth. 1662, p. 289; and see De la Cerda, Soc. Jesu, in loc. Tert. Oper. Paris, 1624, p. 657; and Priorius in loc. Tert. Oper. p. 102. Paris, 1664. And see the Epistle of the Church of Smyrna to Philomelius in Eusebius' Eccl. Hist. lib. iv. c. xv.
[2] Eusebius' Eccl. Hist. lib. v. c. ix., and lib. iv. c. xv. Paris, 1659, p. 135; and Edit. R. Stephani. Paris, 1554, and lib. xiii., c. xi. de Præp. Evang.

the martyrs themselves; for Eusebius, in the treatise last referred to, thus expresses himself, touching these ceremonies — "We are taught to worship God only, and to honour those blessed powers that are about him, with such honour as is fit and agreeable to their estate and condition." And again, "To God only will we give the worship due unto his name, and him only do we religiously worship and adore."[1] From this harmless, nay, laudable, custom, arose prayers for the dead, intercession of the departed, and ultimately the sacrifice of the mass.

THE THIRD CENTURY.

A.D. 200. — Offerings now began to be presented at the celebrations in memory of martyrs; the action, however, still being one of commemoration only. Hence arose the custom of offerings for the dead. These offerings were generally made by the parents of the deceased.[2] The gifts were distributed to the poor. From this arose saints'-days. The transition was easy to *prayers* for the dead; and this was the first great innovation in Christianity. It is important to observe that it is clearly admitted by Tertullian, a writer of this age, that this practice was founded on custom and not on Scripture,[3] and therefore was called a tradition, and like all traditions

[1] And see Euseb. de Præp., Evang. lib. iv. c. x. pp. 88, '89. Edit. Stephani, Paris, 1544; and lib. iv. c. xxi. p. 101.
[2] Neander, in his *Church History*, vol. iii. pp. 469, 470, London, 1851, works out this part of our subject with great precision, and adds references to the early writers of this and subsequent periods.
[3] Tertullian. De Cor. Militis. cap. iii. p. 121. D. Paris, 1634.

liable to abuse. It must be clearly noted that, though some Christians did now begin to pray for the dead, it was not that they should be freed from purgatory or its pains. It was a common belief that souls did not enjoy the beatific vision until the day of resurrection and the last judgment; but there is no trace of a belief at this period that they were in a place of torment.[1] They prayed for the consummation of their glory, and that they themselves might join the departed in the resurrection of the just — a custom having no sanction in Scripture, but still differing widely from the modern practice and intention of praying for the dead.

A.D. 240.—The next step in advance was a mistaken zeal of martyrs and others in the prospect of death. They began to make mutual agreements with each other, to the effect that he who should first depart should remember the survivor, and implore God on his behalf when in the next world.[2] Here we have the beginning of intercession of saints, but it was the departed for the living.

A.D. 250.—About this time, and for some time after, the bishop of Rome took upon himself to interfere in

---

[1] "Sixtus Sennensis says, and he says very truly, that Justin Martyr, Tertullian, Victorinus Martyr, Prudentius, St. Chrysostom, Arethas, Enthymius, and St. Bernard (lib. vi., Bibl. Sanct. Annot. 345), did all affirm, that before the day of judgment the souls of men all slept in secret receptacles, reserved, until the sentence of the great day, and that before then no man receives according to his works done in this life. We do not interpose in this opinion to say that it is true or false, probable or improbable; for these Fathers intended it not as a matter of faith, or necessary belief, so far as we find; but we observe from hence, that, if their opinion be true, then the doctrine of purgatory is false; if it be not true, yet the doctrine of purgatory, which is inconsistent with this so generally received opinion of the Fathers, is at least new, no Catholic doctrine, nor believed in the primitive church; and therefore the Roman writers are much troubled to excuse the Fathers in this article, and to reconcile them to some seeming concord with their new doctrine." Jeremy Taylor's Works "*Dissuasive from Popery*," c. i., sec. iv. Edit. by Heber, vol. x. p. 149. London, 1839.

[2] Cyprian. Ep. ad Cornel. Ep. 57, p. 96. Edit. Paris, 1726.

matters which had been adjudged or determined by the bishop of Africa. Cyprian, bishop of Carthage, opposed this newly assumed power, and denied the right of the bishop of Rome to intermeddle with the decisions of other bishops in their own sees. He wrote to the bishop of Rome, and told him that "it was decreed by the African bishops that every case was to be heard where the crime was committed."[1] These interferences continued for some time, and were always resisted, until the Council of Melevi, in Numidia (A.D. 415), passed a decree, signed by sixty bishops, among whom was St. Augustine, prohibiting all appeals to any other tribunal than the primate of the province where the subject matter arose.[2]

A.D. 257.—"The hallowing of priests' vestures and altar cloths, with other ornaments of churches, and the diversities of vestures of sundry orders, was taken out of the Hebrew priesthood and used in our church first by Stephen, the first bishop of Rome of that name. For, at the beginning, priests in their massing used rather inward virtues of soul than outward apparel of the body, which is rather a glorious gaze than any godly edifying."[3]

A.D. 260.—By reason of the persecutions of this age some began to seek the deserts, and a monastic life. Paul was the first hermit who fled from Alexandria into the desert, on account of the persecutions in the time of the emperor Valerian. Fleury, the celebrated Roman Catholic

---

[1] Ep. ad Cornel. p. 136. Oxon, 1682. Paris edit., 1836, p. 73, Ep. 59.

[2] Can. xxii. "Item placuit ut presbyteri, diaconi, vel cæteri inferiores clerici, in causis quas habuerint, si de judiciis episcoporum suorum questi fuerint, vicini episcopi eis audiant, et inter eos quicquid est, finiant . . . . Quod si ab eis provocandum putaverint, non provocent nisi ad Africana concilia, vel ad primates provinciarum suarum. Ad transmarina autem qui putaverit appellandum, a nullo infra Africam in communionem suscipiatur." Mansi's Councils, tom. iv. p. 507. Venetiis, 1785.

[3] Polydore Vergil, b. vi. c. viii. p. 126. London, 1551.

ecclesiastical historian, canonist, and confessor of Louis XV. A.D. 1716, from whose ecclesiastical history we shall have frequent occasion to quote, says,[1] " Monasticism was introduced into favour mainly by the influence of Athanasius (A.D. 370) ; but, in the year 341, the profession of a monk was despised at Rome as a novelty." And Polydore Vergil says, "The institution of this state of things came, I grant, of a good zeal to godliness ; but the evil perverter of all good things did so empoison the hearts of them that followed, that they had more trust in their monks than faith in Christ's blood ; and then every man began new rules of monks to be their own saviours, and went so superstitiously to work, that it was out of rule and abominable in the sight of God."[2]

The Christians being now much mixed with pagans, and suffering from their taunts and persecutions, made themselves known to each other by making the sign of a cross on the forehead, in token that they were not ashamed of the cross of Christ. It was a kind of badge of their profession, and a silent calling on the name of Christ. There was no virtue attributed to the action, but a profession made of Christ, whose name was tacitly invoked. In modern times, this original custom has been perverted. It is now supposed that the signing of the cross drives away evil spirits. What was at first harmless, has degenerated into a superstition.

[1] "St. Athanase pouvait vingt-trois ans quand il vint à Rome, il commença à y faire connoître la profession monastique, principalement par l'écrit qu'il avoit composé de la vie de St. Antoine, quoique ce saint vécût encore. Jusque-là cette profession étoit méprisée comme nouvelle ; elle étoit même inconnue aux dames Romaines." Fleury, Histoire Ecclesiastique. Paris, 1722—1734; tom. iii. pp. 340, 341, and Fleury, tom. iii. p. 283. Paris, edit., 1760—1774.
[2] Polydore Vergil, b. vii. c. i. p. 131. London, 1551.

It was about this period that a custom became prevalent from which the modern theory of Indulgence has been derived. Christians who had been convicted of crimes were required to make confession of them publicly before the whole congregation, to implore pardon, and to undergo whatever punishment the church thought fit to impose on them. This was done as well for example as to prevent reproach to the Christian religion amongst infidels. These punishments were not supposed to be satisfactions to God. Such an idea cannot be traced in any of the writers of the age who mention the practice. At the latter end of the third century, when many had lapsed through fear of persecution, the punishment and period of probation became more severe and lengthened before they were readmitted. Sometimes the period was protracted for years together. Hence arose the custom of prescribing times or periods—five, ten, or more years—of penance: but, lest the penitent should lose heart, or be driven to despair, the bishops took upon themselves, under certain circumstances, to mitigate the period of punishment. This act was termed a relaxation or remission. It was not till long after this that the term *indulgence* was substituted, and when introduced, it was in quite another sense to its modern use. It signified only a discharge, or a mitigation, of ecclesiastical censures and penalties inflicted by the church, and not a remission of the penalty due to God's justice for the sin of the penitent which had been forgiven, which is the modern theory. But the transition from one to the other can well be comprehended, when we have craft and avarice on the one side, and superstition and ignorance on the other.

A.D. 290.—As to divers orders of the priesthood, Polydore Vergil says—

"The bishops of Rome, following the shadows of the old abrogated law of the Hebrews, have ordained a swarm of divers other orders, as porters or sextons, readers, exorcists, acolytes, sub-deacons, deacons, priests, bishops, archbishops, as a certain degree, one above another. Caius (A.D. 290), bishop of Rome, did begin the orders first; yet some say Hygenius (A.D. 140) ordained those degrees long before Caius' time. Hygenius might be the first deviser of them, and afterward Caius accomplished the work and brought it to a final consummation." [1]

THE FOURTH CENTURY.

A.D. 300.—The Emperor Constantine becoming a Christian, the church, now emancipated from persecutions, began to assume a pageantry and splendour ill-suited to the simplicity of its founders. We trace now more frequently the terms sacrifice and altar, though still used in a different sense to their modern application.[2] Freedom from persecution gave opportunities of collecting the relics of martyrs. These were now re-interred under the communion-table. This custom was of decidedly pagan origin. A similar custom among the Athenians is related by Plutarch in his life of

---

[1] B. iv. c. iv. p. 83. London, 1551.
[2] When the word "sacrifice" was used by the Fathers, it was not in the sense in which it is now used; and this is evident from the fact that they used the same term as applied to "baptism," as admitted by Melchior Canus. He said :—"But you demand what cause had *many of the ancient Fathers* that they called baptism a sacrifice, and therefore said there remained no sacrifice for sin, because baptism cannot be repeated. Truly, because in baptism we die together with Christ, and by this sacrament the sacrifice of the cross is applied unto us to the full remission of sin, hence they call baptism metaphorically a sacrifice." (Canus Loc. Theol. lib. xii. fol. 424—426. Louvan. 1569.) And for the same purpose did they call the Sacrament of the Lord's Supper a sacrifice, metaphorically being a *memorial* of the sacrifice on the cross. Here we may appropriately refer the reader to the passage from Peter Lombard, quoted *ante*, p. 50.

Theseus; and, as they did of old with their heroes, so the modern Romanists deposit relics of the so-called saints, with processions and sacrifices. The building of churches led to superstitious consecrations, and other ceremonies. Eusebius informs us that, "this emperor, to make the Christian religion more plausible to the Gentiles, adopted the exterior ornaments which they used in their religion." The consecration of (temples) churches, with superstitious ceremonies, is decidedly of pagan origin; the vestal virgins sprinkled the ground with lustral water. This and many similar ceremonies were now adopted.

A.D. 325.—A General Council, the first of Nice, met at this date, and settled certain points of discipline. It was determined that the bishop of each metropolitan church should rule the district attached to that church, and be independent, in his ecclesiastical jurisdiction, of any other bishop.[1] Rome, however, in consequence of being the seat of empire, had a precedence of honour, but not of ecclesiastical rank. The bishop of Constantinople, by conciliar decree, enjoyed the same *primacy* and ecclesiastical prerogatives with the bishop of Rome.[2]

---

[1] "Τὰ ἀρχαῖα ἔθη κρατείτω, τὰ ἐν Αἰγύπτῳ καὶ Λιβύῃ καὶ Πενταπόλει, ὥστε τὸν Ἀλεξανδρείας ἐπίσκοπον πάντων ἔχειν τὴν ἐξουσίαν, ἐπειδὴ καὶ τῷ ἐν Ῥώμῃ ἐπισκόπῳ τοῦτο συνηθές ἐστιν. Ὁμοίως δὲ καὶ κατὰ τὴν Ἀντιόχειαν, καὶ ἐν ταῖς ἄλλαις ἐπαρχίαις τὰ πρεσβαῖα σώζεσθαι ταῖς ἐκκλησίαις." κ. τ. λ.—See the 6th canon of the first Council of Nice. Labb. et Coss. tom. ii. col. 32. Paris, 1671.

[2] "Πανταχοῦ τοῖς τῶν ἁγίων πατέρων ὅροις ἑπόμενοι, καὶ τὸν ἀρτίως ἀναγνωσθέντα κανόνα τῶν ρν΄. Θεοφιλεστάτων ἐπισκόπων γνωρίζοντες, τὰ αὐτὰ καὶ ἡμεῖς ὁρίζομεν καὶ ψηφιζόμεθα περὶ τῶν πρεσβείων τῆς ἁγιωτάτης ἐκκλησίας Κωνσταντινουπόλεως, νέας Ῥώμης· καὶ γὰρ τῷ θρόνῳ τῆς πρεσβυτέρας Ῥώμης, διὰ τὸ βασιλεύειν τὴν πόλιν ἐκείνην, οἱ πατέρες εἰκότως ἀποδεδώκασι τὰ πρεσβεῖα. Καὶ τῷ αὐτῷ σκοπῷ κινούμενοι οἱ ρν΄. Θεοφιλέστατοι ἐπίσκοποι, τὰ ἴσα πρεσβεῖα ἀπένειμαν τῷ τῆς νέας Ῥώμης ἁγιωτάτῳ θρόνῳ, εὐλόγως κρίναντες, τὴν βασιλείᾳ καὶ συγκλήτῳ τιμηθεῖσαν πόλιν καὶ τῶν ἴσων ἀπολαύουσαν πρεσβείων τῇ πρεσβυτέρᾳ βασιλίδι Ῥώμῃ, καὶ ἐν τοῖς ἐκκλησιαστικοῖς, ὡς ἐκείνην, μεγαλύνεσθαι πράγμασι, δευτέραν μετ' ἐκείνην ὑπάρχουσαν. κ. τ. λ."—Council Chalced. can. 28; ibid. tom. iv. col. 769. Paris, 1671.

This decree is important, for not only did it declare the rights of the see of Constantinople, but it expressly points out the nature of the precedency enjoyed by Rome, a precedency arising from the fact of Rome having been the seat of empire; this precedency was now shared by Constantinople for the same reason. The 28th canon is as follows:—

"We everywhere following the decrees of the holy Fathers, and acknowledging the canon which has just been read of the 150 bishops most dear to God [namely the sixth canon of Nice], do also ourselves decree and vote the same things concerning the precedency of the most holy church of Constantinople, New Rome; for the Fathers, with reason, gave precedency to the throne of Old Rome, *because it was the imperial city;* and the 150 bishops, beloved of God, moved by the same consideration, awarded *equal precedency* to the most holy throne of New Rome, reasonably judging that a city which is honoured with the government and senate should enjoy equal rank with the ancient queen, Rome, and, like her, be magnified in ecclesiastical matters, having the second place after her."

It was at this council that the question of the celibacy of ecclesiastical persons was seriously mooted. Marriage was then allowed to all, though it had been previously the subject of discussion.[1] Ecclesiastics, on taking their charge, stated whether they would refrain from marrying or not; and if they answered that they would refrain, they were

[1] The Council of Elvira in Spain, A.D. 305, was the first to announce the law that the clergy of the first three grades should abstain from all marriage intercourse, or be deposed. (Neander's "Church History," vol. iii. p. 208. London, 1851.) The other orders were left to the free choice of each individual. By the Council of Neo-Cæsarea (A.D. 314), presbyters were not allowed to marry; and it enjoined the degradation of priests who married after ordination. (Labb. et Coss. Concil. tom. i. col. 1479. Paris, 1671.) And the Council of Ancyra, held shortly previous, but in the same year, by the 10th canon allowed those persons who, at the time of their being made deacons, declared their intentions to marry, to do so, and to

not allowed to marry, otherwise they were allowed. The question first arose in consequence of the persecutions of the times and the poverty of the church. At the Synod of Nice, however, it was debated whether celibacy should be compulsory. Bishop Paphnutius protested against a law being passed on the subject, on the ground that such a prohibition would produce great immorality, and was contrary to Scripture.[1] It was ultimately decreed that such as were received already into the number of the clergy, being as yet unmarried, should not be allowed to marry; but the custom was not universally received, for we find after this that the bishops Hilary, Gregory Nyssen, Gregory Nazianzen, and Basil, were all married men. Synesius, in the fifth century, when made bishop of Ptolemais in Pentapolis, was also a married man. This, however, was the first step towards the establishment of this unnatural and anti-Christian doctrine, or rather discipline, of compulsory celibacy. Even so late as A.D. 692, at the Sixth General Council, it was decreed by the thirteenth canon, that they should be deposed who should presume to deprive deacons and priests, after the receiving of orders, of the company of their lawful wives, and that they who, after the taking of orders, under the pretence of greater holiness, should put away their wives,

---

remain in the ministry: those who did not so declare their purpose, but were ordained professing continence, to be deposed if they afterwards married. (Labb. et Coss. Concil. tom. i. col. 1456, and Neander, as above, p. 209.) The Council of Gangra (*circa.* A.D. 380) by the 4th canon decreed, "If any one shall contend against a *married presbyter*, that it is not fitting to communicate in the oblation when he celebrates the holy offices, let him be accursed." (Labb. Concl. ii. p. 419. Paris, 1671.) This is directly contradicted by the decree of the 2nd Lateran (A.D. 1139), 7th canon, which decrees, "We command that no one hear the masses of those whom he may know to be married." (Labb. Concl. vol. x. p. 999.)

[1] Sozomen. Hist. Eccles. lib. i. cap. xxiii. p. 41. Cantab. 1720. Socrates, Hist. Eccles. lib. i. cap. xi. p. 39. Cantab. 1720.

should be deposed and properly excommunicated.[1] In fact, the Roman canon law did admit that the marriage of the clergy is not prohibited by the law, the gospel, or the apostles, but that it is strictly prohibited by the church.[2]

Celibacy was most esteemed amongst the heathen philosophers; and Jerome, in his second book against Jovinian, relates some curious customs practised by the Athenian and Egyptian priests. Josephus and Pliny also inform us of the customs of the Jewish church with respect to this subject.

Constantine, in the commemoration of the Passion, now first ordered Friday to be held as a solemn fast.

A.D. 347.—The Council of Sardis is supposed by the fifth canon to have ordered that if a bishop, condemned in his own province, should choose to be judged by the bishop of Rome, and desire him to appoint some of his presbyters to judge him in his name, together with the bishops, the bishop of Rome may grant him his request. Dr. Barrow, in his treatise on the Pope's Supremacy, has advanced very good reasons for supposing that the canon is spurious, it being wholly unknown to those who at the time would have made good use of the precedent, if then existing; but in any case the Sardic was a provincial council, and its decrees were not confirmed or recognised. This direction was clearly contrary to a decree

---

[1] Si quis ergo fuerit ausus præter apostolicos canones incitatus aliquem eorum qui sunt in sacris, presbyterorum, inquimus, vel diaconorum, vel hypodiaconorum, conjunctione cum legitimâ uxore et consuetudine privare, deponatur. Similiter et si quis presbyter vel diaconus suam uxorem prætali prætextu ejecerit, segregatur et si perseveret, deponatur. Can. xiii. Concl. in Trullo. A.D. 692. col. 947. E. tom. xi. Mansi. Florentiæ, 1765, and Surius Concl. tom. ii. p. 1042. Col. Agrip. 1567.

[2] Ante, quam evangelium claresceret, multa permittebantur, quæ tempore perfectioris disciplinæ penitus sunt eliminata. Copula namque sacerdotalis vel consanguineorum nec legali, nec evangelica, vel apostolica auctoritate prohibetur, ecclesiastica tamen lege penitus interdicitur." Decreti Secunda Pars. Cause xxvi. Q. ii. c. i. fol. 884.

passed at the Council of Antioch six years before, which referred all such cases to the neighbouring bishops, whose judgment, if unanimous, was to be irreversible,[1] and it directly contradicts the sixth canon of the Council of Nice.[2]

A.D. 350.—About this date we have to record the derivation of an important term in the Latin church, the sense of which has been perverted from its original meaning. After the sermon, the eucharist was celebrated. At this period there were three classes of persons who were not permitted to partake of this sacrament—the *Catechumens,* or those under instruction; the *Penitents,* not as yet received into the church; and *Demoniacs,* or those supposed to be possessed with devils. The sermon being ended, the deacon intimated to these that they should withdraw, dismissing them with these words, "*Ite, missa est,*" a valedictory expression, or solemn leave-taking of them, which did not apply to the ceremony which followed. In succeeding ages, these words began to be contracted into *Mass,* and the eucharist, which followed, was called from thence *The Mass.*[3]

Even this is of pagan origin. In the work by which Apuleius, a Platonic philosopher of the second century, made himself best known, entitled "De Asino Aureo,"

---

[1] Labb. et Coss. Concl. Synod. Ant. c. 16. tom. ii. p. 1674. Paris, 1671; and see Syn. Ant. c. 9. Ibid. tom. ii. p. 584.

[2] Ibid. tom. ii. col. 32, fol. 1675. Paris, 1671. See ibid. tom. iii. p. 1675. Venet, 1728. Concl. Afric. ad Papam. Celest.

[3] Neander, in his *Church History,* gives this as the origin of the term. See vol. iii. p. 461, *note.* London, 1851. Cardinal Baronius (Annales, ann. Eccl. 34. No. 59. tom. i. p. 136. Lucæ, 1738), and Cardinal Tollett (Instit. Sacerdot. lib. ii. c. iv. Lugd. 1614), and see Bellarmine (Lib. i. de Missa, cap. i. tom. iii. p. 710. Paris, 1608), pretend that the word is derived from the Hebrew word *Missah.* But the learned Jesuit Azorius (Instit. Moral. lib. x. c. 18. tom. i. pp. 989, 990) opposes this speculation, stating that the word is rather a Latin than a Hebrew word.

The Golden Ass, we read that, in imitation of an old ceremony among the Greeks, when the worship of Isis was concluded, the people were dismissed by two Greek words, signifying their discharge. The pagan Romans, when their devotions were over, discharged the people with the words, " Ite Missio est." This, by corruption, passed into *Massa.* Polydore Vergil says :—

"When mass is ended, the deacon, turning to the people, sayeth, *Ite missa est,* which words are borrowed from the rite of the pagans, and signifieth that then the company may be dismissed. It was used in the sacrifices of *Isis,* that when the observances were duly and fully performed and accomplished, then the minister of religion should give warning or a watchword what time they should lawfully depart. And of this springs our custom of singing *Ite missa est* for a certain signification that the full service was finished."[1]

A.D. 366.—Fleury affixes this date as the real commencement of the appellate authority or jurisdiction of the bishop of Rome; he says that the emperor Valentinian ordered that the bishop of Rome, with his colleagues, should examine the causes of other bishops.[2]

The decree empowered (in matters not canonical) the metropolitans to judge the inferior clergy, and the bishop of Rome to judge the metropolitans; but this only extended the jurisdiction of Rome westward. This privilege was conceded to Damasus, whose election was by no means canonical.[3] At a council subsequently held at Rome, A.D.

[1] Book v. c. ix. p. 110. Edit. London, 1551.
[2] "Dès le commencement de ce schisme, Valentinien ordonna que l'évêque de Rome examineroit, les causes des autres évêques, avec ses collegues, et en general il ordonna par une loi, que dans les causes de la foi, ou de l'ordre ecclesiastique, le juge devoit être d'une dignité égale ; c'est-a-dire, que les évêques seroient jugez par des évêques et non par des laïques." Fleury, Eccl. Hist. tom. iv. p. 146. Paris, 1724, and tom. iv. p. 154. Paris, 1760.
[3] A double election of bishops was made, Damasus placing himself at the head of his party, clergy'and laymen, who, armed with clubs, swords and axes,

378, Damasus addressed a memorial to the emperor Gratian, to confirm the above decree, the object of which was to shift the clergy from civil to ecclesiastical jurisdiction, or to the emperor himself; but it is important to note that they accepted the boon as an indulgence, or concession from the emperor. The notion of "divine right," now so confidently appealed to, was not then introduced. The "exemption" did not extend to criminal cases. It was from these small beginnings, concessions made by temporal princes, that the huge ecclesiastical fabric and papal hierarchy was ultimately constructed.

The preference given to the see of Rome arose from the splendour and importance of the city, and the magnificence and luxury, even at this early age, of the bishop of that see. Fleury gives the words of a pagan historian of the day, who said that he was not at all surprised to see the strifes to attain the see, when he considered the splendour of Rome, where the chief bishop is enriched by offerings from ladies, and that they drove in chariots, clothed splendidly, lived well, their tables surpassing even those of kings. This author jokingly said to Damasus, "Make me bishop of Rome, and I will become Christian."[1]

A.D. 370.—This age was famous for orators. They displayed their talents on the occasions of celebrating the

attacked his opponent, Urinus. The affray resulted in a massacre of 160 persons, including women. Fleury, Ecc. Hist. vol. iv. pp. 145, 146. Paris, 1724.

[1] "Ammian Marcellin auteur paien, qui vivit alors, rapportant cette histoire, [namely, the strife for the seat of bishop of Rome] blâme egalement l'animosité des deux partis, et ajoûte. 'Quand je considere la splendeur de Rome, je ne nie pas que ceux qui desirent cette place, ne doivent faire tous leurs efforts pour y arriver, puis qu'elle leur procure un établissement sûr, où ils sont enrichis des offrandes des dames, ils sortent dans des chariots, vêtus splendidement, et font si bonne chere, que leurs tables surpassent celles des rois,—il disoit par plaisanterie au même pape Damase, Faites moi évêque de Rome, et aussi-tôt je serai chretien." Fleury, Eccl. Hist. vol. iv. p. 146. Paris, 1724.

memorial of saints, and in funeral orations, by reciting their virtues. To give effect to their eloquence, they began to apostrophize the departed. Gregory Nazianzen, in the first oration, exclaimed, " Hear likewise, thou soul of great Constantine, *if thou hast any understanding in these things.*"[1] And so the same orator, in the second oration, equally addressed his speech to the soul of Julian the apostate, which he believed to be in hell. These apostrophes were figures of rhetoric: the sentiments offered were no enunciation of doctrine, and were very different from the modern custom of invocation of saints. There is no doubt that a way was thereby opened for the introduction of the more modern heresy; for thenceforward, little by little, people began to address their requests to saints departed; but it was not until long after, that invocation of saints was introduced into the church service as a recognised practice.

Invocating angels became common in the province of Phrygia. Oratories of St. Michael were erected. This heresy was at once condemned by the Council of Laodicea, held about this time, A.D. 368. The 35th canon is as follows: " It does not behove Christians to leave the church of God and go and invoke angels, and make assemblies, which things are forbidden. If, therefore, any one be detected idling in their secret idolatry, let him be accursed, because he has forsaken our Lord Jesus Christ the Son of God, and gone to idolatry." It may be urged by the advo-

---

[1] Vol. i. p. 78. Paris, 1778. Benedictine Edition. The editor's note on this is as follows, "'If the dead are sensible of anything.' Thus Isocrates, in the same words, but somewhat more fully, 'If there is any perception of what is going on here.'" See the note of Greek Scholiast (Schol. Græc. in priorem, Nazianzeni Invectivam, p. 2. Edit. Etonens), "He speaks according to the manner of Isocrates, that is to say, 'If thou hast the power of hearing the things that are here.'"

cates of saint worship that "idolatry" alone is condemned, but in passing such a decree the council would have made some reservation for a legitimate innovation, had such been the custom of the church in those days.[1]

A.D. 380.—*Praying for the dead* appears now to have come into more general practice. Eusebius tells us, that on the death of Constantine they prayed for his soul; but it must be noted, that the intent of these prayers was very different from the modern custom; for the writers of this age testify that, in the same prayers were included those whom the modern church of Rome would exclude, namely, those supposed to be in hell; as also those who, it is now supposed, do not require such prayers, but, on the contrary, are *prayed to,* namely, patriarchs, prophets, evangelists, apostles, martyrs, and the Virgin Mary.[2] Here we have the foundation on which the modern custom is based, which, however, is inseparable from the doctrine of purgatory, not then developed.

From a passage in Epiphanius,[3] we must presume that, at this time, some desired to introduce paintings in churches; for he records the fact, that on finding in a certain village, in Palestine, at the entrance of a church, a painted cloth representing Christ, he cut it down.[4]

---

[1] "Ὅτι οὐ δεῖ Χριστιανοὺς ἐγκαταλείπειν τὴν ἐκκλησίαν τοῦ θεοῦ, καὶ ἀπιέναι, καὶ ἀγγέλους ὀνομάζειν, καὶ συνάξεις ποιεῖν· ἅπερ ἀπηγόρευται. Εἴ τις οὖν εὑρεθῇ ταύτῃ τῇ κεκρυμμένῃ εἰδωλολατρείᾳ σχολάζων, ἔστω ἀνάθεμα, ὅτι ἐγκατέλιπε τὸν Κύριον ἡμῶν Ἰησοῦν Χριστὸν, τὸν υἱὸν τοῦ θεοῦ, καὶ εἰδωλολατρείᾳ προσῆλθεν."—Labb. et Coss. Concil. Laodic. c. 35. tom. i. col. 1503. Paris, 1671.

[2] The references here might be numerous. See Cyril's Catech. xxiii. Mystag. v. n. ix. x. p. 328. Paris, 1720. Chrysost. Hom. xxix. in Acts. ix. Liturg. Oper. tom. xii. p. 1011. Paris, 1838. And admitted by Dr. Wiseman in his Moorfields Lectures, Lecture xi. p. 66, note. London, 1851.

[3] Epiph. Epist. ad Joan. Hierosolym. Hieron. tom. i. p. 251. Colon. 1682.

[4] The authenticity of this epistle has been questioned by Bellarmine; but it has been vindicated by the learned critic, Rivet, in his Crit. Sacer. b. iii. c. 26, Epiph. Epist. ad Johan. Hieros. tom. ii. p. 317. Edit. 1682.

A.D. 386.—If the document be not a forgery (which, however, it is thought to be), Siricius, bishop of Rome, was the first, by decree, to prohibit the clergy within his jurisdiction from marrying. The previous Council of Ancyra (A.D. 314) did not prohibit the marriage of the clergy; but the tenth canon expressly allowed those persons who, at the time of their being made deacons, declared their intention to marry, to do so, and to remain in the ministry; but those who did not declare their purpose, but were ordained, professing that they would live a single life, were to be deposed if they afterwards married.[1] Socrates, the ecclesiastical historian of the fifth century, designated this as a "new law."[2] He ought rather to have said that it was a revival of an old pagan custom. The ancient Egyptian priests were prohibited from marrying. It was a Manichean heresy.[3] It was not until A.D. 950 that the decree was observed in every Christian church: for throughout the provinces of Europe many ecclesiastics were married. Athanasius (A.D. 340), writing to Bishop Dracontius, told him "that in his days many monks were parents of children, and bishops were likewise fathers."[4] Gratian does not hesitate to testify that many bishops of Rome were priests' sons. He names popes Damasus, Hosius, Boniface, Agapetus, Theodorus, Silverius, Felix, Gelasius, as all being popes and sons of priests, some even of bishops, and he adds, "there were many others also to be found who were begotten of priests, and governed in the apostolic see."[5]

[1] Labb. et Coss. Concl. Gen. Concl. Ancyra, can. x. tom. i. col. 1456. Paris, 1671.
[2] Socrates' Hist. Eccles. lib. i. c. ii. Bib. Max. Patr. tom. vii.
[3] See Aug. Ep. 74. p. 848. tom. 2. Paris, 1679.
[4] Athanas. ad Dracontium, p. 739, tom. i. Heidel. 1601.
[5] "Complures etiam alii inveniantur, qui de sacerdotibus nati, Apostolicæ sedi præfuerunt." Grat. Par. 1, Dist. 56, c. 3, p. 291, tom. i. Lug. 1671.

Roman bishops, descended from ecclesiastical parents, were married during their clerkships; as were Boniface I., Felix III., Gelasius I., etc. Even so late as A.D. 1068, we find that at a council held in Barcelona, by the Legate Cardinal Hugo, it was unanimously agreed that the clergy should not be married, "as had hitherto been permitted."[1] The decree was authoritatively enforced in 1074, under Hildebrand (see *post*, A.D. 1074), and renewed by the twenty-first canon of the first Lateran Council, A.D. 1123,[2] and also by the sixth and seventh canons of the second Lateran Council (A.D. 1139). The latter canon forbade any one to hear mass celebrated by a married priest,[3] which canon, by the way, is in direct contradiction to the fourth canon of the Council of Gangra (A.D. 325, or, as some say, 380).[4]

There were many unscriptural and superstitious customs practised at this period, under the pretended authority of tradition; and so great was the corruption of the age, even at this early period of the church, that Cyprian exclaimed that "the church of God, and spouse of Christ, was fallen into this bad state, that, to celebrate the heavenly mysteries, light borrowed discipline even from darkness itself, and Christians do the very same things that antichrists do."[5] And, in the succeeding century, Augustine complained that such was the accumulation of ceremonial observances, that the condition of the Jews under the servile yoke of the law, was more supportable than that of Christians under the gospel.[6]

---

[1] See Landon's Manual of Councils, p. 56. London, 1846.
[2] Lab. et Coss. Concl. tom. x. col. 899. Paris, 1671.
[3] Ibid. col. 1003.
[4] See *ante*, p. 170.
[5] Cyprian, Epist. Pomp. Ep. lxxiv. 224. Leipsic edit. 1838.
[6] Aug. Epist. ad Januar. 55, sec. 35, vol. ii. p. 142. Paris, 1700.

A.D. 390.—A remarkable occurrence took place this year as recorded by the historians Socrates and Sozomen,[1] with reference to *private confession*. Confession of sins was in the early church made publicly before the whole congregation. The penitent was, after a public confession and performance of penance, readmitted into the communion of the church. About the year 250, during and after the Decian persecution, the numbers of penitents returning to the faith was so great, that the bishops could not attend to them all, and the public confession was scandalous; accordingly a new officer was created as " penitentiary presbyter," to whom all who desired to be admitted to public penance for private sins should first confess their sins to this officer, and afterwards, if not too scandalous for public ears, confess them in public. This was also necessary, as some public confessions entailed other and palpable inconveniences. This was the first institution of the penitentiary priest. In this year (A.D. 390) the office was suppressed, and with it private confession abolished. This occurred at Constantinople by order of Nectarius, bishop of that city, and the example was followed all over the East. The circumstance came about by reason of a scandalous occurrence happening to a lady of distinction after confession, the crime having been committed in the church itself. The misbehaviour of one priest was visited on all the clergy, and set the whole city in an uproar; and, to appease the tumult, Nectarius not only deprived the offending deacon of his office, but also removed the penitentiary, and with it all private confessions; and the more effectually to prevent for the future the scandal, inseparable, as it appears,

---

[1] Socrates, lib. 5, c. 19. Soz. l. 7. c. 16.

from the system, abolished that office, and, to use the words of Nectarius above referred to, "leaving any man free to partake of the holy mysteries according to the direction of his own conscience," thus abolishing the custom of private, or as it is now called *auricular confession*. This was deemed then a human institution, and the confession and penance enjoined were left optional to the people. Private confession to a priest is now made compulsory on every member of the Romish church.

A.D. 397.—The Council of Carthage, held this year under Aurelius the bishop, by the twenty-ninth canon, ordered that mass [if we may give it that name at this early period] should be said fasting.[1]

THE FIFTH CENTURY.

A.D. 400.—From A.D. 230 to this period, many different speculations were broached as to the state of souls after death. Origen (A.D. 230), a Greek father, seems to have been the first to pave the way for the reception of purgatory. His idea was, that the faithful, as well as unbelievers, would pass through a fire which was to consume the world on the last day, after the resurrection, when all, even the devil himself, would be eventually saved. This speculation, however, was condemned by a general council of the

[1] Labb. et. Coss. Concl. Carth. can. xxix. tom. ii. col. 1165. Paris, 1671.

FIFTH CENTURY. 181

church.¹ The theory led to many other speculations as to the existence of a purgatory. And about this time, St. Augustine, though he condemned Origen's theory, put forward his own speculations. Some such thing as a purgatorial fire, he said, might be probable,² but he did not treat it as a matter of accepted faith or doctrine; this is certain. There was enough material here, however, out of which to construct a doctrine, which, in course of time, came to maturity.

It was at the Council of Toledo (A.D. 400) that the bishop of Rome was for the first time spoken of simply by the title of "Pope."³ But it was not until much later (A.D. 1073) that the title was assumed exclusively by the bishop of Rome.

A.D. 417.—The custom of hallowing paschal candles on Easter eve was commanded by Zosimus, and ordered to be practised in every church.⁴

A.D. 419.—Boniface, when he found himself seated on the papal throne, affected to be shocked at the scandals witnessed at the elections of bishops of Rome. In order to prevent cabals and intrigues on similar occasions to the scandal of the Christian religion, from which he himself had not been free, he petitioned the Emperor Honorius to pass a law to restrain the ambition and intrigues of aspirants to the papacy. Accordingly, Honorius made a decree to the effect that, when two rival candidates were chosen, neither was to hold the dignity, but the people and clergy were to proceed

---

1 By the General Council held at Constantinople, A.D. 553. See Bals. apud Beveridge. Synod. tom. i. p. 150. Oxon, 1672. Augustine lib. de Hæres. c. xliii. tom. viii. p. 10, Benedictine Edition. Paris, 1685.
2 Augustine, Enchiridion de Fide, Spe, et Caritate, tom. iv. p. 222. Paris, 1685.
3 See Landon's Manual of Council. London, 1846, p. 578.
4 Polydore Vergil, b. vi. c. v. p. 120. London, 1551.

to a new election.¹ This is the first instance in history, says Bower, in his History of the Popes, of princes intermeddling in the election of the bishop of Rome, a necessity imposed on the Roman church on account of the many disorders of which the clergy and people were guilty in those elections. The emperors reserved a right of confirmation, which they exercised for many years after. A notable example is in the case of Gregory I., who, when elected, wrote to the emperor, entreating him not to confirm his appointment.

A.D. 431.—The first law was passed this year granting asylum in churches to fugitives.²

Mr. Elliott, in his Horæ Apocalypticæ,³ assigns this as the date when the bishop of Rome distinctly assumed the "keys" as a symbol of ecclesiastical power. The use of the keys as symbolical of the papal power is, like many other similar customs, curiously connected with pagan mythology. The key was a symbol of two well-known pagan divinities of Rome. Janus bore a key,⁴ as did also Cybele. It was only in the second century before the Christian era that the worship of Cybele, under that name, was introduced into Rome; but the same goddess, under the name of Cardea, with the "power of the key," was worshipped in Rome, with Janus, many years before.⁵ Hence, perhaps, the two keys that the pope emblazons on his arms, as the ensigns of his spiritual authority. The device was familiar to the Romans, and came home to their ideas of such sovereignty. As the statue of Jupiter is now

---

1 See F. Pagi's Crit. Hist. in Annal. Baroni. ad ann. 419.
2 Cod. Theodosius, lib. ix. Tit. 45, l. 4, vol. iii. Lips. 1736. Neander's Church Hist. vol. iii. p. 206. London, 1851. See *post*, A.D. 620.
3 Vol. iii. p. 139. London, 1851.
4 See Ovid's "Fasti," vol. iii. l. 101. p. 346. Opera, Leyden, 1661.
5 Tooke's "Pantheon," "Cybele," p. 153. London, 1806.

worshipped at Rome as the veritable image of Peter, so the keys of Janus and Cybele have for ages been devoutly believed to represent the keys of the same apostle.

A.D. 434.—This year is referred to for proof that the bishop of Rome exercised a supreme authority over the church, as to the right of calling councils. With this view, a long letter from Sixtus III. to the Eastern bishops, as establishing several of the papal prerogatives, is quoted by Bellarmine[1] and others to prove that councils ought to be called by none but the pope. Sixtus is represented as saying, "The emperor Valentinian has summoned a council by our authority." It has been clearly proved, however, that the letter is wholly made up of passages borrowed from the Eighth Council of Toledo, from Gregory I., from Felix III., from Adrian, and from the Theodosian and Justinian codes; and, therefore, evidently spurious, and the passage in question forged, in order to introduce a sentence supposed to have been passed by the emperor Valentinian. A charge of immorality has been invented against Sixtus, who is supposed to have written the letter on the occasion of his having cleared himself before a council; but the Acts of that council are so manifestly fabulous, that even Binius and Baronius have been forced to give them up, though the emperor, whom the Acts suppose to have assisted at the council, is said to have referred the pronouncing of the sentence to the pope himself, "because the Judge of all ought to be judged by none." There can be no doubt that it was in order to establish this maxim that the Acts of this council were forged, as well as those

---

[1] Bell. de Concl. lib. 2, c. 12.

of the alleged previous council of Sinuessa (A.D. 303), which is supposed to have condemned Marcelinus, and which, at the expense of this man's reputation, is cited to exalt the see of Rome. No writers earlier than Anastasius, librarian of the Vatican, who flourished in the ninth century, and the historian Platina, who died A.D. 1481, have treated the charge against Sixtus as a serious fact. This letter, with other palpable forgeries, was for a long time received as genuine, but is now wholly renounced. If the Roman system be of God, and the Roman church founded on a rock, against which the gates of hell shall never prevail, surely falsehood, fraud, and forgeries were not required to prop it up. To the Acts of the council referred to are added those of the judgment, supposed to have been given at Rome, on the occasion of an appeal made to that see by one Polychronius, said to have been bishop of Jerusalem, and to have appealed from the judgment of his colleagues in the east to that of the bishop of Rome. This judgment also has been for a long time held up as genuine, to prove that eastern bishops appealed to the bishop of Rome. Nicholas I., in the ninth century, appealed to these Acts as genuine, in a letter which he wrote to the emperor Michael. But that they are mere forgeries is palpable on the face of them. One is almost ashamed to waste time in confuting them, but, in a chronological table like the present, it is necessary to do so, as showing the growth of Romanism, and to expose the rottenness of its foundation, though antiquity is confidently appealed to in its support. The judgment is supposed to have been given while the emperor Valentinian was the seventh time consul with Avienus, that is, no fewer than eleven years after the death of

Sixtus III.! Besides, it is manifest from the acts of the councils of Ephesus (A.D. 431) and Chalcedon (A.D. 451), that Juvenalis assisted at both as bishop of Jerusalem; and the first of these two councils was held a year before the election of Sixtus III., and the latter eleven years after his death (Sixtus became bishop of Rome A.D. 432, and died A.D. 440); so that Polychronius was not bishop of Jerusalem in his time. Indeed it may be questioned whether there ever was a bishop of Jerusalem bearing that name: it cannot be found in any catalogues of the bishops of that city that have been handed down to us.[1]

A.D. 450. — Leo I. seems to have been the first bishop of Rome who interfered with the election of bishops of other dioceses. He is reported to have interposed in the institution of Anatolius, " by the favour of whose assent he obtained the bishopric of Constantinople;"[2] and he is stated to have confirmed Maximus of Antioch, and Donatus, an African bishop. But, on the other hand, other bishops arrogated the same privilege—for instance, Lucifer, a Sardinian bishop, ordained Paulinus, bishop of Antioch; Theophilus, of Alexandria, ordained Chrysostom; Eustatheus, of Antioch, ordained Evagrius, bishop of Constantinople, etc.; and Acacius and Patrophilus expelled Maximus, and instituted Cyril, bishop of Jerusalem, in his room. All these acts, and many more that might be cited, were done without any reference to the bishop of Rome.

The bishop of Rome [Leo] now boldly assumed an authority never before acted upon by any of his predecessors, declaring that the supreme authority over *Western churches* rested in him as bishop of Rome. " In the chair

---

[1] See Bower's History of the Popes, vol. ii. pp. 5, 6. London, 1750.
[2] Labb. et. Coss, Concl. tom. iv. col. 847. Paris, 1671.

of Peter (he said) dwelleth the ever living power, the superabundant authority." The circumstances attending this assumption of authority are important to be noted, as it obtained the sanction of the emperor. Hilary, metropolitan bishop of Arles, took upon himself the right of ordaining all Gallican bishops. Leo was jealous of this authority being vested in a rival. He bestirred himself, and began by bringing false accusations against Hilary (see his 9th and 10th Epistles), and eventually appealed to Valentinian III., at this time emperor of the West, a weak prince, who was no match for a man of Leo's craft, address, and ambition. Leo represented Hilary as a disturber of the peace, a rebel against the apostolic see, and even against his Majesty. The emperor was induced to issue the famous rescript, vesting in the bishop of Rome an absolute and uncontrolled authority over the Gallican churches and bishops. This rescript was addressed to Aetius, general of the Roman forces in Gaul, under pretence of maintaining peace and tranquillity in the church, and in it he calls Hilary a traitor and an enemy both to the church and state. This document was no doubt dictated by Leo himself. It is set out in full by Baronius in his Annals (Ann. 445); we transcribe the following passage to illustrate the nature of the power now first usurped by the bishop of Rome:—

" In order, therefore, to prevent even the least disturbance in the churches, and that discipline may not thereby be infringed, we decree that, hereafter and for ever, not only no Gallic bishops, but no bishop of any other province, be permitted, in contradiction to ancient custom, to do anything without the authority of the venerable pope of the eternal city; but, on the contrary, to them and to all men, let whatsoever the authority of the holy see hath ordained, or doth or shall ordain, be as law; so that any bishop being summoned to the judgment seat of the Roman pontiff, be thereunto *compelled by the governor of the province."*

Thus was the secular arm brought to bear to enforce ecclesiastical usurpation. Hilary, and with him other Gallican bishops, opposed to the last this papal encroachment, and would never acknowledge the authority of the bishop of Rome. Notwithstanding Hilary's alleged traitorous conduct and repudiation of one of the alleged fundamentals of the church of Christ, "the sum and substance of Christianity," as Bellarmine has it, this same Hilary is claimed by the modern church of Rome as a canonized saint, standing side by side with his opponent and oppressor, Leo! The framer of this edict did not hesitate to record a deliberate untruth when "ancient custom" was alleged as authority. No such authority can be adduced,[1] and even Leo himself did not for long after the event above alluded to, claim the authority of ordaining bishops all over the Western provinces, for in his eighty-ninth epistle, addressed to the bishops of Gaul, he expressly disclaimed the authority. "We do not (he said) arrogate to ourselves a power of ordaining in your provinces;"[2] and this would warrant us in suspecting that the edict itself is, to a great extent, spurious. But it must be specially noted as a fact that, while Leo placed himself at the head of the Western bishops, he admitted the superior

[1] It was only a few years previous to this, A.D. 421, that the Emperor Theodosius referred the dispute of the election of Perigenes to the See of Patræ in Achaia, one of the provinces of Illyricum, to the bishop of that diocese after he had consulted the bishop of Constantinople. See Cod. Theod. l. 45. de Episcop. l. 6.

[2] "Non enim nobis ordiuationes vestrarum provinciarum defendimus." P. Leo. Ep. 89, quoted by Barrow. See "On the Pope's Supremacy," p. 343. Revised Edit. London, 1849.

authority of the State, appealing on all occasions to the emperor as his superior in ecclesiastical matters, under whose authority alone, since the first Christian emperor, all the early General Councils were convoked, who, as Eusebius expresses the sentiment of those days (referring to Constantine), " as a common bishop appointed by God, did summon synods of God's ministers." [1]

A.D. 460.—Leo I., bishop of Rome, ordered the observance of four fasts, namely, Lent, Whitsuntide, the seventh and tenth months.

A.D. 470.—The first recorded act we can find of the invocation of a saint, is when the body of Chrysostom was transported to Constantinople. The Emperor Theodosius knelt down before it, praying it to forgive his parents, who had persecuted it while living. But this superstition was rebuked by the Fathers of this age.

Nicephorus, in his Ecclesiastical History, informs us, that one Peter Gnapheous, patriarch of Antioch, A.D. 470, was the first who introduced invocation of saints into the prayers of the church, and ordered that " the Mother of God" should be named in every prayer. But this man was infected with the Eutychian heresy, for which cause he was condemned by the Fourth General Council. A superstition, which was hitherto only private, became public; the commemoration of the saints was changed into invocation; preachers, instead of addressing their discourse to the living, to excite them to imitate the actions of their dead, began now to direct their prayers to the dead on behalf of the living. But, as yet, the custom was restricted to a sect of the Greeks; the Latins did not receive it for 120 years after.

---

[1] " Οἷά τις κοινὸς Ἐπίσκοπος ἐκ θεοῦ καθιστάμενος συνόδους τῶν τοῦ θεοῦ λειτουργῶν συνεκρότει."—Euseb. de Vit. Const. I. 44, p. 524. Cantab. 1720.

A.D. 492.—Another innovation was at this time attempted to be introduced, but checked. In the celebration of the eucharist, a custom had arisen of soaking or dipping the bread for those who would not drink wine. Julius, bishop of Rome, in A.D. 340, condemned this custom; notwithstanding which, the practice was subsequently re-introduced in the Romish church. About A.D. 440, the Manichees, who held wine in abhorrence, attempted to introduce the custom of taking the communion under one species only, namely, the bread. Leo (A.D. 450)[1] and Gelasius (A.D. 492),[2] both bishops of Rome, condemned in express terms this heresy, and ordered that the communion should be received entire, as instituted by our Lord, or not at all.

The words of Gelasius are so precise and so contradictory to the modern Romish teaching, that we have only to quote them to convict the Roman church of imposing on Christians a doctrine most emphatically condemned by a bishop of their own church. His words are—

"We find that some, having received a portion of the holy body only, do abstain from the cup of the holy blood, who, doubtless (because they are bound by I know not what superstition), *should receive the whole sacrament, or be driven from the whole;* for the dividing of one and the same mystery cannot be done without sacrilege."[2]

As connected with the eucharist, we cannot pass over this period without recording the deliberate opinion of this

[1] Leon. Mag. Oper. Lut. 1623, col. 108, Serm. iv. de Quadrag.
[2] Comperimus quod quidam, sumpta tantummodo corporis sacri portione, a calice cruoris abstineant; qui proculdubio (quoniam nescio quâ superstitione docentur obstringi) aut integra sacramenta percipiant, aut ab integris arceantur; quia divisio unius ejusdemque mysterii sine grandi sacrilegio non potest provenire. Gelas. in Corp. Juris Canon.. Decret. Grat. tert. pars, de consecr. dist., ii. cap. xii. col. 1168. Ludg. 1661. And tom. i. col. 1918. Ludg. 1671.

same Gelasius, bishop of Rome, on what is now deemed a fundamental doctrine of the Roman church of the present day. We mean transubstantiation, that is, the alleged conversion of the substance and nature of the elements of bread and wine, after the consecration by the priest, into the very and real body and blood of our Saviour Jesus Christ. We place in parallel columns the dictum of Gelasius and the decree of Trent, clearly showing that transubstantiation was an invention after this date.

GELASIUS, A.D. 492.	DECREE OF TRENT, A.D. 1551.
"Certainly the sacrament of the body and blood of our Lord, which we receive, are a Divine thing; because by these we are made partakers of the Divine nature. Nevertheless, the *substance or nature* of the bread and wine cease not to exist; and, assuredly, the *image and similitude* of the body and blood of Christ are celebrated in the action of the mysteries." [1]	"By the consecration of the bread and wine, the *whole substance* of the bread is converted into the substance of the body of Christ, and the *whole substance of the wine* is converted into the substance of his blood; which conversion is suitably and properly called by the Catholic church Transubstantiation." [2]

The contradiction between the opinion of Pope Gelasius and the decree of the Trent Council, which now rules the doctrines of the church of Rome, is so obvious, that we are not surprised to find a desperate attempt made to explain away the otherwise obvious heresy of an early

---

[1] For the text see *ante*, p. 51, note.
[2] "Per consecrationem panis et vini conversionem fieri totius substantiæ panis in substantiam corporis Christi Domini nostri; et totius substantiæ vini in substantiam sanguinis ejus. Quæ conversio convenienter et proprie a sanctâ catholicâ ecclesiâ transubstantiatio est appellata." Concil. Trid. Sessio. xiii. Decret. de Sanct. Euchar. Sacramento. cap. iv. De Transubstantione.

bishop of Rome. Baronius and Bellarmine were foremost in their endeavours to explain the difficulty staring them in the face. They hit upon the expedient of declaring that some other person of the name of Gelasius, but not Gelasius the bishop, was the writer of the treatise in question. The Roman Catholic historian, Dupin, however, has exposed the hollowness of this " pious fraud," and proves incontestably that the work in question is the genuine production of Pope Gelasius, who was bishop of Rome A.D. 492,[1] and in this important doctrine does the church of Rome stand convicted of introducing a *novelty* in the Christian creed.

THE SIXTH CENTURY.

A.D. 500.—*Images* now began to be used in churches, but as historical memorials only, for which purpose alone they continued to be used for about one hundred years after. Even this use of images received from various bishops violent opposition. They caused them to be broken in pieces within their several dioceses.

A.D. 528.—The healing of the sick was a gift left by our Lord to the Apostles, and it died with them. Though the gift of healing had ceased, still some heretics retained the use of *Unction*, probably in imitation of the custom referred to by St. James (v. 14). Bathers on leaving the bath, and wrestlers on entering the arena, were anointed with oil. Christians, in imitation of these customs, anointed with oil those who were baptized, as being purified and

[1] *Vide* Dupin, Ecc. Hist. vol. i. p. 520. Dublin, 1723.

singled out to contend with the world. This unction formed, as yet, no part of the sacrament. The Valentinian heretics arrogated to themselves the gift of the apostles, and anointed their sick with oil on the approach of death. They pretended that this anointing, with prayers, would conduce to the salvation of the soul, not to the healing of the body. This superstition found no supporters except among this sect of heretics. Innocent I., in his letters to Decentius, bishop of Eugubium, refers to the custom of anointing the sick with oil, which was to be exercised not merely by the priesthood, but by all the faithful, and was, therefore, evidently not considered as a sacrament. The custom subsequently gained ground, and about this year (528) Felix IV., bishop of Rome, engrafted it on other Christian ceremonies, and first instituted the rite of extreme unction, by declaring that such as were *in extremis* should be anointed.[1] Ceremonies were in course of time superadded, and ultimately, but long after, extreme unction received the quality of a *sacrament*. The origin of this pretended sacrament is, in some measure, derived from paganism.

A.D. 529.—Benedict of Nursia founded the order of Benedictine monks.[2]

A.D. 535.—Agapetus I. ordained processions before the festival of Easter.

A.D. 536.—The clergy were exempted from civil jurisdiction by a decree, now for the first time made, by the emperor Justinian. But Polydore Vergil says that Caius (A.D. 290) had previously made a statute that a priest should not be convened before a temporal judge.[3]

---

[1] Polydore Vergil, b. v. c. iii. p. 102. London, 1551.
[2] Mosheim's Eccl. Hist. Cent. vi. pt. ii. p. 448, vol. i. London, 1825
[3] B. iv. c. viii. p. 93. London, 1551.

A.D. 538.—Vigilius, bishop of Rome, ordered that the priest standing at the altar should turn his face to the east, an old pagan custom; and from this there likewise arose another custom, that of placing the altar to the east of the church. Vitruvius, an eminent architect of the age of Augustus, informs us that when the pagans built their temples, they placed their choir and principal idols towards the east: "Let those (he said) who sacrifice towards the altars, look to the east part of the heavens, as also the statue which is to stand in the temple, * * for it is necessary that the altars of God be turned to the east."[1] The ancient Romans turned to the east when they sacrificed. The custom was, therefore, of pagan origin. Mosheim, in his chapter on "Rites and Ceremonies," says that "nearly all the people of the east, before the Christian era, were accustomed to worship with their faces directed towards the sun-rising: for they all believed that God, whom they supposed resembled light, or rather to be light, and whom they limited as to place, had his residence in that part of the heavens where the sun rises. When they became Christians, they rejected the erroneous belief; but the custom which originated from it, and which was very ancient and universally prevalent, they retained. Nor to this hour has it been wholly laid aside."[2] The ancient idolaters used to worship the sun, turning to the east, Ezek. viii. 16, and Deut. iv. 19. The Manichees also prayed towards the east. Leo I., bishop of Rome (A.D. 443), ordained that, in order to discern Catholics from heretics, the latter should turn towards the west to pray.[3] In the Christian temples

[1] Lib. iv. c. v. Edit. de Laet. Amst. 1649.
[2] Eccl. Hist. cent. ii. pt. ii. cap. iv. sec. 7.
[3] "Ad occidentem conversi Deum colerunt." Binius Concl. tom. i. fol. 932. Colon. 1606. And Cardinal Baronius' Annal. ann. 443, num. 5. tom. vii. p. 556.

at Antioch, in Syria, the altars were placed towards the west, and not the east.[1]

To Vigilius is also attributed the institution of the feast of the Purification of the Virgin Mary, or Candlemas. That was also of pagan origin. The pagans were accustomed, in the beginning of February, to celebrate the feast of Proserpine with burning of tapers. To make the transition more easy from paganism, they instituted on the same day a feast, and burned tapers in honour of the Virgin Mary. According to Picard, the institution of this feast is attributed to Gelasius I., A.D. 496; and the procession of wax lights, to drive away evil spirits, to Sergius I., A.D. 701.[2]

A.D. 595.—Towards the latter part of this century, John, patriarch of Constantinople, assumed the title of universal bishop. Pelagius II., and after him his successor, Gregory I., bishops of Rome, were shocked at the assumption of such a title by any individual, and denounced it in the strongest terms of reprobation. Gregory, in his letters to the emperor, said—"I confidently assert, whosoever calls himself the universal bishop, is the forerunner of Antichrist."[3] So spoke the bishop of Rome at that time. And, as a question of historical fact, he publicly asserted that none of his predecessors did ever assume the profane title of universal bishop. What would Gregory have said of his immediate successor, who assumed the same title?

Pontifex Maximus was of pagan origin. Dionysius of Halicarnassus, gives a description of the "supreme pontiff"

---

[1] Socrat. Eccl. Hist. in Euseb. lib. v. c. xxii. London, 1709.
[2] Cérémonies et Coûtumes Religieuses, vol. i. pt. ii. p. 163, notes *c* and *d*. Amsterdam, 1723.
[3] See *ante*, "Supremacy," p. 5.

of the ancient Romans, in his life of Numa Pompilius, as also does Livy. We find coins of the time of the Cæsars, on which the emperor was called "Pont. Max.," and even "Summus Sacerdos." The heathen historian, Zosimus (A.D. 426), gives the following account of the title before it was assumed by a Christian bishop. He says that, "among the Romans, the persons who had the superintendence of sacred things were the pontifices, who are termed Zephyræi, if we translate the Latin word pontifices, which means bridge-makers, into the Greek." He proceeds:—

"The origin of that appellation was this. At a period before mankind was acquainted with the mode of worshipping by statues, some images of the gods were made in Thessaly. As there were not then any temples (for the use of them was likewise unknown), they fixed up these figures of the gods on a bridge over the river Pevensa, and called those who sacrificed to the god Zephyræi, priests of the bridge, from the place where the images were first erected. Hence the Romans, deriving it from the Greeks, called their own priests Pontifices, and enacted a law that kings, for the sake of dignity, should be considered of the number. The first of the kings who enjoyed this dignity was Numa Pompilius. After him it was conferred not only upon the kings, but upon Octavianus and his successors, in the Roman empire. Upon the elevation of any one to the imperial dignity, the pontifices brought him the priestly habit, and he was immediately styled *Pontifex Maximus*, or chief priest. All former emperors, indeed, appeared gratified with the dedication, and willingly adopted the title. Even Constantine himself, when he was emperor, accepted it, although he was seduced from the path of rectitude, in regard to the sacred affairs, and had embraced the Christian faith. In like manner did all who succeeded him, till Valentinian Nolens; but when the pontifices brought the sacred robe in the accustomed manner to Gratian, he, considering it a garment unlawful for a Christian to wear, rejected the offer. When the robe was *returned* to the priests who

brought it, their chief is said to have made an observation:—
'If the emperor refuses to become pontifex, we shall soon make one.'"[1]

The title and office are, therefore, of admittedly pagan origin, and founded on a heathen ceremony.

THE SEVENTH CENTURY.

A.D. 600.—Saints (so-called) began to take the places of the "Dii minores" of the pagans, to them churches were now dedicated, and festivals and sacrificing priests appointed. Invocation of saints, which was hitherto a private superstition, now began to be publicly practised, but not yet as an acknowledged doctrine. About the same time Gregory entered the name of the Virgin Mary in the Litanies, with the *ora pro nobis*.[2]

The modern theory of invocation of saints is also clearly derived from paganism. Apuleius, to whom we have already referred, in his book, "De Deo Socratis," thus describes the pagan system:—"There are (he said) certain middle divinities, betwixt the high heavens and this lower earth, by whom our prayers and merits are carried to the gods; they are called demons in Greek; they carry up the prayers of men to the gods, and bring down the favours of the gods to men; they go and come, to carry on one side the petitions, on the other relief; they are as interpreters and salvation-carriers from the one to the other."

---

[1] Zosimus, B. iv. c. 36, p. 125. Edit. Græce et Latine, Lipsæ, 1784 (English translation).
[2] Polydore Vergil, B. viii. c. i. p. 143. London, 1551.

Is not this much the same system which is laid down by the Trent Catechism? "We ask the saints, because they have credit with God, that they may take us into their protection, to the end that they may obtain from God those things we stand in need of."[1] Different men and trades have their patron saints, and so had the pagans of old.

Purgatory began now to assume a more defined shape, though the theory as to the nature of the punishments differed from the modern teaching. It came now to be supposed that departed souls expiated their own sins (a doctrine not now admitted, for, in the popish purgatory, sins are supposed to be forgiven) in divers ways—by baths, ice, hanging in air, etc. This was Gregory's theory,[2] founded on well-known pagan fables.

The eucharist, which was hitherto a sacrament for the living, now began to be offered as a sacrifice for the dead. The offerings bestowed in memory of the piety of the departed were alms;[3] these now were called oblations, and formed part of the sacrament itself, and were offered in expiation of the sins of the departed.

On receiving the offerings made by the people, the officiating minister besought God that those fruits of charity might become acceptable to Him. The prayers or orisons offered on these occasions were retained, but instead of being rehearsed over the eleemosynary gifts of the faithful, they were now pronounced over the elements of bread and wine, designated the body of Jesus Christ.

[1] Cat. Concl. Trid. part. iv. cap. vii. Q. 3.
[2] Greg. lib. 4. Dialog. c. lv. p. 464, tom. ii. Paris, 1705.
[3] "Scultetus Medulla Theologiæ Patrum." Amstel. 1603, p. 307. On examination of Scultetus' work, the reader will be satisfied that the attempt to identify the Romish mass with the oblations or offerings of the early Christians must be abandoned by the modern Church of Rome. Scultetus was a Professor of Divinity at the University of Heidelberg (1598); see also B. Rhenan. in loc. Annot. to Tertullian. Frank. 1597, p. 43.

Gregory I. composed the office of the mass; and, according to Platina, in reducing the service to an uniformity of worship in the Western churches, the universal use of the Latin language was enjoined.

Gregory likewise introduced unction into priestly orders; and enjoined the adoption of pontifical habits; he ordained the use of incense and the relics of saints at the consecration of churches, spaces for the reception of tapers, and their being lighted in day time. He ordered pictures of the Virgin Mary to be carried about in processions, and statues to be introduced into churches for religious purposes; and, according to Polydore Vergil, first ordered that neither flesh, milk, butter, eggs, etc., should be eaten on days set apart for fasting.[1]

A.D. 604.—Sabinian, successor to Gregory, is said by Platina to have ordered that lamps should be kept perpetually burning in churches. This is still enjoined by the Roman ritual. The Egyptians, according to Herodotus, were the inventors of the custom. The pagan Romans afterwards adopted it, the office of the Vestals being to keep these lamps alight. Apuleius describes the pagan Roman processions as being attended by priests in surplices, the people in white linen vestments singing hymns, and carrying wax candles in their hands.[2] This ceremony is practised to this day in Romish countries. Lactantius often refers to the custom as a ridiculous superstition, deriding the Romans "for lighting up candles to God, as if he lived in the dark."[3]

There is supposed to be a hidden mystery in the use of

---

[1] B. vi. c. iv. p. 119. London, 1551.
[2] Apuleius, vol. i. Metam. cap. ix. pp. 1014-1016, and cap. x. pp. 1019, 1021. Leipsic, 1842.
[3] Lactantius, "Institut." lib. vi. cap. 2, p. 289. Cambridge, 1685.

these lighted tapers. Among the modern Romans, as well as the heathen, to whose religions the use is common, it has reference to some evil spirits which are supposed to be present. Among the Tungusians, near the lake Baikal, in Siberia, wax tapers are placed before the gods or idols of that country.[1] In the Molucca Islands, wax tapers are used in the worship of Nito, or devil, whom these islanders adore.[2] "In Ceylon," says the same author, "some devotees, who are not priests, erect chapels for themselves, but in each of them they are obliged to have an image of Buddha, and light up tapers or wax candles before it, and adorn it with flowers." How closely do Romanism and heathenism resemble each other! The conversions they boast of can only be a change of name.

A.D. 607.—Phocas having obtained the empire by the murder of the emperor Mauricius his predecessor, with his wife and five children, made common cause with Boniface III. against Cyriacus, bishop of Constantinople, who refused to countenance his murderous and traitorous deeds. The compact was, that Boniface should recognise Phocas as lawful emperor, and the latter should recognise the church of Rome to be the head of all churches, and the bishop of that see as sovereign and universal bishop. This spiritual title was thus given and confirmed to the bishop of Rome by imperial edict, not by Divine right. It is under this title that the succeeding bishops of Rome hold their spiritual primacy.

In the same year, Mohammed appeared in Arabia; so that the eastern and western antichrists appeared together. From this period we date the reign of Popery proper.

---

[1] See "Asiatic Journal," vol. xvii. pp. 593, 596.
[2] Hurd's "Rites and Ceremonies," p. 91, col. 1, and p. 95, col. 2

Superstition now spread rapidly, and the simplicity and purity of the Christian faith soon became almost extinct.

A.D. 610.—Boniface IV. consummated the act of pagan idolatry, by opening the Pantheon at Rome, and substituting therein images of the so-called saints, in place of the pagan deities, consecrating the place for the purpose: hence the feast of All Saints.

At this time also tonsure was introduced. The tonsure was an old pagan custom, and was in imitation of the ancient priests of Isis.[1] The tonsure was the visible inauguration of the priests of Bacchus. Herodotus mentions this tonsure:—

"The Arabians acknowledge no other gods than Bacchus and Urania [*i.e.*, the queen of heaven], and they say that their hair is cut in the same manner as Bacchus's is cut; now they cut it in a *circular form*, shaving it around the temples."[2]

The priests of Osiris, the Egyptian Bacchus, were always distinguished by the shaving of their heads.[3] The distinguishing feature of the priests of pagan Rome was the shaven head,[4] and this was equally so in China and India. Upwards of five hundred years before the Christian era, Gautama Buddha, when instituting the sect of Buddhism in India, first shaved his own head in obedience, as he pretended, to a Divine command, and was known by the title "shaved-head;" and "that he might perform the orders of Vishnu, he formed a number of disciples of shaved heads like himself."[5]

[1] Polyd. Vergil (book iv. c. x.) thinks this custom came from Egypt, where the priests were shaven in token of sorrow for the death of their god Apis.
[2] Herodotus, "Historia," lib. iii. cap. 8, p. 185. Paris, 1592.
[3] Macrobius, lib. i. c. 23, p. 189. Sanct. Colon. 1521.
[4] Tertullian, vol. ii. "Carmina," pp. 1105, 1106. Opera, Paris, 1844.
[5] See Kennedy's "Buddha" in "Ancient Hindoo Mythology," pp. 263, 264. London, 1831.

The priests and Levites were forbidden to "shave their heads in a round" (see the Hebrew, Ezek. xliv. 20, Lev. xxi. 5); modern papists, not being under the law, prefer the pagan custom. The custom of shaving the crown was adopted by the Donatists. Optatus, bishop of Mela, in Africa (A.D. 370), reproved them for this, saying—"Show where it is commanded you to shave the heads of priests; whereas, on the contrary, there are so many examples furnished to show that it ought not to be."[1] It is certain that the custom was not sanctioned, if indeed it was not condemned, at the beginning of the fourth century; for by the 55th canon of the Council of Elvira (at which nineteen bishops were present, including Hosius of Cordova, twenty-six priests assisting, besides deacons), it was declared, that priests who had only a shaven crown like idolatrous sacrificers, yet did not sacrifice to idols, after two years might receive communion.[2]

A.D. 617.—Invocation of saints generally was first used in the public liturgies in the Latin church under Boniface V.

A.D. 620.—Boniface V. confirmed the infamous law by which churches became places of refuge to all who fled thither for protection. The custom has no doubt the advantage of being very old, being of pagan origin,[3] and the Jews also encouraged it; but with this difference, that the Jewish priests extended their protection to such who had committed crimes through some unhappy accident, or

---

[1] "Docete ubi vobis mandatum est radere capita sacerdotum, cum e contra sint tot exempla proposita fieri non deberi." Optatus, lib. contra Parmenion. Oper. de Schism. Donat., fol. Paris, 1679.

[2] "Sacerdotes, qui tantum sacrificantium coronam portant, nec sacrificant idolis, placuit post biennium communionem recipere." Surius, Concil. Eliber. in can. 55. tom. i. p. 356, Colon. 1567, and Lab. et Coss. Concil. tom. i. col. 967. Paris, 1671.

[3] Mosheim's Eccl. Hist. cent. vii. part ii. p. 28. vol. ii. London, 1768.

without intention of malice; but the Romish priests threw the protection of the church over notorious criminals.[1]

A.D. 631.—The festival of the Exaltation of the Cross was instituted by the emperor Heraclius; and was subsequently established in the West by Honorius I., bishop of Rome,[2] though Polydore Vergil places the Invention and Exaltation of the Cross in the year 1260,[3] which is probably more correct.

A.D. 666.—Vitalius, bishop of Rome, was the first who ordered Divine service to be celebrated everywhere in the Latin tongue.[4] But it does not appear that this order took the form of a binding decree, since the Lateran Council, A.D. 1215 (as after observed), relaxed the custom under peculiar circumstances.

A.D. 682.—Fleury records the first instance of a council of bishops undertaking to absolve the subjects of a king from their allegiance; which assumed power soon passed into the hands of the pope.[5]

A.D. 685.—Hitherto the election of the bishop of Rome had been reserved for the confirmation of the emperor; and

---

[1] "Nous n'entrons point dans le détail des differentes ceremonies pratiquées aux autels des Catholiques; mais nous ferons seulement remarquer, que par un abus qui desbonore le Christianisme, ils servent d'asile en Italie aux plus déterminés scelerats. Il est bien vrai que cet usage est fort ancien, et que les juifs et les Païens l'ont favorisé; mais les juifs ne l'ont soufert que pour les crimes commis par malheurs et sans dessein; et le respect que l'on doit à la religion Chrétienne demanderoit qu'un abolit les mauvais usages que l'ancien paganisme y a fait glisser." Picard's "Cérémonies et Coûtumes Religieuses," p. xxix. vol. i. Amsterdam, 1723.

[2] See Baronius's Annals, ad ann. 628, and Beaumgarten "Earläuterung der Christi. Alterthümer," p. 310, quoted in Reid's edition of Mosheim's Eccl. Hist. 1852, p. 253.

[3] Polydore Vergil, B. vi. c. vii. p. 122. London, 1551.

[4] Wolphius Lect. Memorab. Centenar. Numeris Bestia Apoc. xiii. p. 149. Frankfort, 1671.

[5] "Au reste, c'est le premier exemple d'une pareille entreprise des évêques; de dispenser les sujets du serment de fidelité fait à leur prince." Fleury's Eccl. Hist. lib. xl. p. 71, tom. ix. Paris, 1703. And tom. ix. p. 71. Paris, 1769.

this rule continued in operation until the time of Pelagius II., A.D. 578. Platina, in the life of this pope, said—" Nothing was then done by the clergy in the election of a pope, unless the emperor approved the election."[1] Pelagius was chosen during the siege of Rome, but he sent Gregory, who was afterwards pope, to the emperor to excuse himself for having been elected without his confirmation. Gregory I. was also elected by the emperor's consent. The election continued to be in this form until 685, when the emperor Constantine first remitted the right in favour of Benedict II., the fact being that the emperors of the East had almost lost their influence in the West. But when the empire was established in the West under Charlemagne, Adrian I. (A.D. 795), in synod, delivered over to the emperor the right and power of electing the bishop of Rome and ordaining to this See. He, moreover, decreed that archbishops and bishops in every province should receive investiture from him; and if a bishop were not commended and invested by the emperor, he was not to be consecrated by any other; and any person acting against this decree, was to be subjected to the ban of anathema. This is testified in the Roman canon law.[2]

Louis, the son of Charlemagne, waived his right; but Lothaire, his son, resumed and acted upon it. The right was maintained until the time of Adrian III. (885). The prerogative was not given up without a struggle. The

---

[1] "Nihil a clero in eligendo pontifice actum erat nisi ejus electionem imperator approbasset." Plat. in Pelagio II. p. 81. Colon. 1568.

[2] "Hadrianus autem cum universâ synodo tradiderunt jus et potestatem eligendi pontificem, et ordinandi apostolicam sedem.—Insuper Archiepiscopos et episcopos per singulas provincias ab eo investituram accipere definivit; et nisi a rege laudetur et investiatur episcopus, a nemine consecretur; et quicunque contra hoc decretum ageret, anathematis vinculo eum innodavit." Corp. Jur. Can. vol. i. Dist. 63. cap. 22. Paris, 1695.

emperor still elected some bishops of Rome after this. Some indeed were deemed anti-popes; yet Clement II. (A.D. 1046) is reckoned a true pope, though elected by the emperor. It was not, really, until A.D. 1080, under Gregory VII., that the emperor's right was wholly superseded.[1]

THE EIGHTH CENTURY.

A.D. 700.—About this time the custom of saying private masses (that is, the priest communicating alone without the people attending) was introduced. This custom originated in the lukewarmness of the people, including the clergy, in their attendance on Divine service. Formerly, the assembly communicated every day in the week; devotion waxing cold, the communion was restricted to the sabbath and feast days, leaving the priest alone to officiate and communicate on the other days. Hence solitary masses. The capitular of Theodulf, bishop of Orleans (A.D. 787), expressly forbade private or solitary masses,[2] as did the Council of Metz, A.D. 813, and the Council of Paris, A.D. 829.[3]

---

[1] See Burnet's Vindication of the Ordinations of the Church of England, pp. 51—99. London, 1677.

[2] "Le prêtre ne célebrera point la messe seul, il faut qu'il y ait des assistans, qui puisent luy répondre quand il salue le peuple : et le Seigneur a dit qu'il seroit au milieu de deux ou trois assemblez en son nom." Fleury, Eccl. Hist. liv. 44, p. 503, tom. ix. Paris, 1703. And tom. ix. p. 459. Paris, 1769.

[3] "Aucun prêtre ne peut dire la messe seul : car comment dira-t'il ; la Seigneur soit avec vous, et le reste, qui marque des assistans ?" Fleury's Eccl. Hist. liv. xlvi. p. 144, tom. x. Paris, 1704. And Neander's Church History, vol. v. p. 188. London, 1852.

The custom seems to have been creeping in so early as the century previous; for it met the rebuke of Gregory I. He said, "The priest should never celebrate mass alone; for as the mass cannot be celebrated without the salutation of the priest and the answer of the people, it ought, consequently, by no means to be celebrated by a single individual; for there ought to be present some to whom he may speak, and who, in like manner, ought to answer him, and he must withal remember that saying of Christ, 'Where two or three are gathered together in my name, I will be present with them.'"[1] The doctors of Trent, in the sixteenth century, however, declared, in direct contradiction to these earlier decisions, that "if any one shall say that private masses, in which the priest alone doth sacramentally communicate, are unlawful, and, therefore, ought to be abrogated, let him be accursed."[2]

The roundness of the host was now insisted on by the Romish church. This shape is taken from the Egyptians. "The thin round cake occurs in all the Egyptian altars."[3] The form symbolized the sun.

A.D. 750.—Fleury, the Roman Catholic historian, tells us that the earliest instance of giving absolution to penitents immediately after confession, without waiting till their penance was fulfilled, occurred at this time in the rule established by Boniface.[4]

---

[1] "Sacerdos missam solus nequaquam celebret; quia sicut illa celebrari non potest sine salutatione sacerdotia et responsione nihilominus plebis, ita nimirum nequaquam ab uno debet celebrari, etc." Greg. in lib. Capitulari, cap. vii. apud Cassand. Liturg. 33, p. 83. Paris, 1605.

[2] "Si quis dixerit, missas in quibus solus sacerdos sacramentaliter communicat, illicitas esse, ideo que abrogandus anathema, sit." Concl. Trid. can. viii. sess. xxii. p. 150. Paris, 1832.

[3] See Wilkinson's "Egyptians," vol. v. p. 358. London, 1837—1841.

[4] ".. les canons touchant la reconciliation des pénitents, chaque prêtre aussi-tôt qu'il aura reçû leur confession, aura soin de les reconcilier par la priere, c'est à dire qu'il n'attendra pas que la pénitence soit accomplie."

A.D. 752.—Stephen II. was the first bishop of Rome who was carried in procession on men's shoulders on his election. It was a pagan Roman custom.[1]

A.D. 754.—At a council held at Constantinople, image worship was condemned.[2]

It was this council which first enjoined, under anathema, the invocation of the Virgin Mary and other saints.[3]

A.D. 763.—According to Fleury, Chrodegang, bishop of Metz, first enjoined compulsory oral confession; but this custom was restricted to his own monastery.[4]

The same bishop instituted the ecclesiastical order of Canons.[5] Nicholas II., in 1059, at a council in Rome, abrogated the ancient rules of the Canons, and substituted others in their place. Hence arose the distinction of Secular and Regular Canons. The former observed the decree of Nicholas II., the latter subjected themselves to the more

---

Fleury's Eccl. Hist. tom. ix. lib. xliii. p. 390. Paris, 1703. And tom. ix. p. 360. Paris, 1769.

[1] "Etienne II. elu pape est le premier que l'on ait porté à l'Eglise sur les épaules après son élection. Les Grands de l'ancienne Rome se faisoient porter par des esclaves dans une espece de littiere (Lectica). Il y a apparence que la coutume de porter le pape sur les épaules s'introduisit peu à peu apres la ruine du paganisme dans Rome. Pour ce qui est d'Etienne II., il paroit, par ce qu'on dit Platina, que le merite de ce pape contribua à l'honneur qu'on leur fit de porter sur les épaules." Picard, "Cérémonies et Coûtumes Religieuses." Vol. i. pt. ii. p. 50, note g. Amsterdam, 1723.

[2] Labb. et Coss. Concl. Gen., tom. vi. col. 1661. Paris, 1671.

[3] "Εἴ τις οὐχ ὁμολογεῖ τὴν ἀειπαρθένον Μαρίαν κυρίως καὶ ἀληθῶς θεοτόκον, ὑπερτέραν τε εἶναι πάσης ὁρατῆς καὶ ἀοράτου κτίσεως, καὶ μετα εἰλικρινοῦς πίστεως τὰς αὐτῆς οὐκ ἐξαιτεῖται πρεσβείας, ὡς παρρησίαν ἐχούσης πρὸς τὸν ἐξ αὐτῆς τεχθέντα Θεὸν ἡμῶν, ἀνάθεμα."—Labb. Concl. tom. vii. col. 524. Paris, 1671. "Εἴ τις...... τὰς τούτων οὐκ ἐξαιτεῖται προσευχὰς, ὡς παρρησιαν ἐχόντων ὑπὲρ τοῦ κόσμου πρεσβεύειν, κατὰ τὴν ἐκκλησιαστικὴν παράδοσιν, ἀνάθεμα."—Ibid. 528.

[4] "Il est ordonné aux cleres de se confesser à l'évêque deux fois l'année; sçavoir au commencement du carême, et depuis la mi-Aoust jusqu'au premier jour de Novembre—Celuy qui aura celé quelque peché en se confessant à l'évêque, on cherchera à se confesser à l'autres: si l'évêque le peut découvrir, il le punira de foüet ou de prison. C'est la première fois que je trouve la confession commandée." Fleury, Eccl. Hist. liv. xliii. pp. 425, 426, tom. ix. Paris, 1703.

[5] Le Beuf, Memoire sur l'Histoire d'Auxerre, tom. i. p. 174. Paris, 1743.

severe regulations of the bishop of Chartres, and were called Regular Canons of St. Augustine, professing to follow the rules of St. Augustine.[1]

A.D. 768.—Hitherto the payment of tithes was enjoined, but not compelled. King Pepin now ordered tithes to be paid by all to the clergy.[2]

A.D. 769.—At a council held at Rome, a decree was passed that images should be honoured, and the Council of Constantinople, A.D. 754, was anathematized.[3]

A.D. 787.—Previous to this date, much altercation took place as to the introduction and use of images in public worship. Irene, the empress of Constantinople, a pagan both by religion and nation, a woman of notoriously bad character, who poisoned her husband in order to establish her authority, entered into an alliance with Adrian, bishop of Rome, and convoked the so-called Seventh General Council, held at Nice. By her influence, the decree sanctioning the use of images in religious worship was passed.[4] But this decree met with decided opposition at other synodical meetings. The bishops who refused to submit to the decree were punished, persecuted, or excommunicated. It need scarcely be observed, that the use of images in religious exercises is of pagan origin. This council invented what is called a relative worship, that is, "that the honour rendered to the image is transmitted to the prototype; and he who worships the figure, worships the substance of that

---

[1] Mosheim, Eccl. Hist., cent. xi. part ii. pp. 312, 313, vol. ii. London, 1758.
[2] "C'est que les dixme n'etoient du commencement que des aumônes volontaires." Fleury, Eccl. Hist. liv. xliii. p. 455, tom. ix. Paris, 1703, and tom. ix. p. 416. Paris, 1679.
[3] Labb. et Coss. Concl. tom. vi. col. 1721. Paris, 1671.
[4] Labb. et. Coss. Concl. tom. vii. col. 899. Nicen. II. Sess. vii. action 6. Paris, 1671, and Surius Council, tom. iii. p. 150. Col. Agrip. 1567.

which is represented by it."¹ And although this council asserted, with the usual bold assumption and effrontery ever assumed by the Roman church, that this institution was established by "the holy fathers, and the tradition of the Catholic church, which from one end of the earth to the other had embraced the gospel," we have shown in our chapter on Images, that the doctrine of relative worship, introduced into Christian worship at this period by the Second Council of Nice, was the identical practice the heathens adopted and defended, and was specially condemned by the Fathers Arnobius and Origen, of the third century, and Ambrose and Augustine of the fourth century.²

The modern custom of consecration of images, and lighting tapers before them, is only another retrograde step towards heathenism and paganism, these being ancient practices, as we read in the apocryphal book of Baruch (cap. vi.) of the Babylonian idolaters. It was a mark of religious veneration to kiss images (1 Kings xix. 18), as do the modern Romanists. Miracles too were attributed to images by the pagan, as now by modern Romanists. The alleged modern examples are so numerous that they need not here be repeated.

This will be a proper place to give some account of the progress of the doctrine of the alleged real or substantial presence of our Lord in the eucharist.

The sacrament of the Lord's Supper, or the celebration of the eucharist, was regarded as the most solemn act of the church. Figurative and mystical language was applied

---

¹ ... ἡ γὰρ τῆς εἰκόνος τιμὴ ἐπὶ τὸ πρωτότυπον διαβαίνει· καὶ ὁ προσκυνῶν τὴν εἰκόνα, προσκυνεῖ ἐν αὐτῇ τοῦ ἐγγραφομένου τὴν ὑπόστασιν. Οὕτω γὰρ κρατύνεται, ἡ τῶν ἁγίων πατέρων ἡμῶν διδασκαλία, εἴτουν παράδοσις. τῆς καθολικῆς ἐκκλησίας, τῆς ἀπὸ περάτων εἰς πέρατα δεξαμένης εὐαγγέλιον."—Labb. et Coss. concil. tom. vii. col. 556. Paris, 1671.

² See *ante*, pp. 81, 82.

to it, particularly by members of the Greek church; as, for instance, when Chrysostom spoke of the recipients' mouths being made red with the blood. The elements themselves took the names of the things they represented: the cup of the blood; the bread of the body of Christ. Augustine, of the fifth century, gives us several examples of this, of which illustrations will be found in a preceding page (p. 48).

While it is quite true that many of the early writers spoke of the elements as the body and blood of Christ, in terms which, when taken literally and detached from their context, might be construed as favouring the Romish doctrine; yet such an interpretation becomes wholly impossible of acceptance, when we find these same Christian writers, in succession, from the very earliest periods, speaking of the consecrated elements as similitudes, images, and types.[1]

As extravagance of speech was highest among the Greek or Eastern church, so some individuals among them, misled by these rhetorical phrases, began to teach the real substantial presence, but not as yet the transubstantiation of the elements. Such appeared to have been the doctrine of Anastatius of Mount Sinai (A.D. 680), and John, of Damascus (A.D. 740), who went still further. He denied the bread and wine to be the types of the body and blood of Christ. The council held at Constantinople (A.D. 754), which condemned image worship, checked this rising heresy in the East. It maintained that "Christ chose no other shape or type under heaven to represent his incarnation but the sacrament, which he delivered to his ministers

[1] In proof of this see the chapter on Transubstantiation, especially pp. 54, et seq.

for a type and a most effectual commemoration thereof; commanding the substance of bread and wine to be offered," and this bread they affirmed to be "a true image of his natural flesh."[1]

The Second Council of Nice (A.D. 787), which established the use of images, condemned this statement that the only true image of Christ was in the bread and wine, the type of the body and blood of Christ. They declared that Christ did not say, "Take, eat the image of my body," adding the bold assertion, that "nowhere did either our Lord, or his Apostles, or the Fathers, call the unbloody sacrifice offered up through the priest, an image, but they call it the body itself, and the blood itself."[1]

The bishops assembled at this council must have been very little informed on the subject; for Gelasius, bishop of Rome, said—"Assuredly the image and similitude of the body and blood of Christ are illustrated in the performance of the mysteries."[2] Numerous passages to a like effect may be quoted from writers of a prior and even of a subsequent date to this council.

Though this heresy was held by some in the Eastern church, it had not as yet extended to the West, as is amply testified by Bede (A.D. 720). Druthmar (A.D. 800, a scholar of Bede), Amalar of Triers (A.D. 820), and Walafrid Strabo (A.D. 860), and Elfric, the Saxon,

[1] Concl. Nicen. II. Art. vi. Labb. et Coss. tom. vii. cols. 448, 449. Paris, 1671, and Concl. Gen. tom. iii. p. 599. Romæ, 1612. The sentence of the Council of Constantinople is rehearsed after they had set down the words of our Saviour, "This do in remembrance of me,"—"Behold the whole image of that quickening body, the substance of bread."—"Ecce vivificantis illius corporis imaginem totam, panis, id est, substantiam," and see Surius. Concl. tom. iii. p. 153. Colon. 1567.

[2] .. et certe imago et similitudo corporis et sanguinis Christi in actione mysterium celebrantur. Gelas de duab. Christ. naturis. In Bib. Patr. tom. iv. p. 422. Paris, 1589. See *ante*, p. 51.

who lived at the close of the tenth century, all of whom refer to the consecrated elements as types and images.[1]

A.D. 795.—Leo III. ordered incense to be used in the Latin church in her services.[2]

The use of incense in public worship was not only a Jewish, but also a pagan custom. All the representations of heathen sacrifices on the ancient monuments have a boy in sacerdotal habits attending with an incense box, for the use of the officiating priests; and the same we see in the present day at the popish altars.

We cannot pass over the eighth century without adverting to one of the most important innovations in the papacy—namely, the assumption of temporal power by the bishop of Rome.

As yet the bishop of Rome held no temporal rule. It was not until past the middle of the eighth century that a temporal power was added to his spiritual jurisdiction. This was effected by a bargain similar to that struck with Phocas.

It is as well first to observe that, previous to the assumption of the spiritual power by the bishop of Rome, the protests of bishops Pelagius and Gregory have afforded us undeniable proofs that previous to the seventh century no single bishop, be he of the Roman or Greek church, assumed a supreme spiritual power over the whole church; so also have we a like testimony, afforded also by a bishop of Rome, that previous to the fifth century, the assumption of temporal power by the bishop of Rome was directly repudiated by Pope Gelasius. Gelasius wrote, or is believed

[1] For the original passage, see Faber's "*Difficulties of Romanism,*" b. ii. c. iv. 2nd Edit. London, 1853.
[2] Polydore Vergil, b. v. c. viii. p. 109. London, 1551.

to have written, a treatise entitled *De Anathematis Vinculo,* "on the bond or tie of the anathema." It is one of four tracts composed by him at different times, which are to be found under his name in all the orthodox editions of the councils, such as Labbeus and Mansi's editions, that of Binius, and others. It seems to have been written to explain an expression pronounced by his predecessor against one Acacius, to the effect that he never should, nor ever could, be absolved from an anathema pronounced against him. Though this part is much confused, that which follows is as plain as it is important. Gelasius in this tract, lays down a clear distinction as then existing, between the temporal and the spiritual jurisdiction of bishops and emperors or kings. He states that anciently the royalty and priesthood were often united in one and the same person, among the Jews as well as the Gentiles; but that since the coming of Christ these two dignities, and the different powers that attend them, have been vested in different persons; and from thence he concludes that neither ought to encroach on the other, but that the temporal power entire should be left to princes, and the spiritual to priests; it being no less foreign to the institution of Christ for a priest to usurp the functions of sovereignty, than it is for a sovereign to usurp those of the priesthood. This is a very clear statement, and could never have been made by a bishop of Rome had he held the modern notions of the present possessor of the papal See, who declares that the temporal is inseparable from and is necessary to the spiritual rule.[1] It is not, however, our task to reconcile Roman inconsistencies.

---

[1] This declaration is so important that we give the original. We cannot here enter into an examination whether the production is a genuine tract from the pen of Gelasius; it is sufficient for our purpose that it is attributed

We have seen that the spiritual supremacy owed its origin to a murderer; the temporal owes its origin to an usurper.

Pepin, the son of Charles Martel, aspired to the throne of France, then occupied by Childeric III. He consulted Zachary, bishop of Rome, and desired to know if it were lawful to depose the then lawful ruler. Zachary wanted this daring soldier's help to protect himself from the Greeks and Lombards; the result was an unholy compact, or alliance, between them. Childeric was deposed by Pepin, and the kingdom transferred to the latter. The bishop of Rome formally recognised the act. Stephen, the second successor of Zachary, went to France again to solicit Pepin's aid against the Lombards; and in 754, solemnly confirmed the decision of his predecessor, absolved Pepin from his oath of allegiance to Childeric, and crowned him king in his stead. In return, by force of arms, Pepin handed over to the see of Rome the exarchate of Ravenna and other provinces.[1] Thus was the bishop of Rome now, for

to him by the canonists of the church of Rome, and is inserted by them among others attributed to Gelasius:—

"Quamvis enim membra ipsius, id est, veri regis atque pontificis, secundum participationem naturæ, magnifice utrumque in sacrâ generositate sumpsisse dicantur, ut simul regale genus et sacerdotale subsistant: attamen Christus memor fragilitatis humanæ, quod suorum saluti congrueret, dispensatione magnifica temperans, sic actionibus propriis dignitatibusque distinctis officia potestatis utriusque discrevit, suos volens medicinali humilitate salvari non humana superbia rursus intercipi; ut et Christiani imperatores pro æternâ vitâ pontificibus indigerent, et pontifices pro temporalium cursu rerum imperialibus dispositionibus uterentur, quatenus spiritalis actio a carnalibus distaret incursibus: et ideo militans Deo, minime se negotiis sæcularibus implicaret: ac vicissim non ille rebus divinis præsidere videretur, qui esset negotiis sæcularibus implicatus, ut et modestia utriusque ordinis curaretur, ne extolleretur utroque suffultus, et competens qualitatibus actionum specialiter professio aptaretur. Quibus omnibus rite collectis, satis evidenter ostenditur, a sæculari potestate nec ligari prorsus nec solvi posset pontificem," etc. Sacro. Conc. Coll. tom. viii. cols. 93, 94, Mansi (edit. Florent. 1762); and Binius, Concil. tom. ii. par. i. p. 487. Colon. 1618.

1 "Le roy en fit une donation à Saint Pierre, à l'Eglise Romaine et à tous

the first time, raised to the rank of a temporal prince. Gregory (A.D. 741), the predecessor of Zachary, had already offered to withdraw his allegiance from the emperor and give it to Charles Martel, if he would deliver the city from the Lombards. This scheme did not succeed; but his successor, Zachary, carried out the negotiations with Pepin, as above stated.

Charlemagne, the son of Pepin (A.D. 774), not only confirmed the grant made by his father, but added other Italian provinces to the see of Rome. In return for Charlemagne's donation, the bishop of Rome gave him the title of "The Most Christian King," and by his help made Charlemagne emperor of all the West.[1]

The bishop of Rome (as yet he was not pope) having attained to this high degree by fraud, a further fraud was now perpetrated by the appearance of the infamous and notorious forgeries known as the decretal epistles of the early popes. These decretals were put forward to confirm their spiritual and temporal power. Binius, archbishop of Cologne, who, in 1608, published a collection of councils, while endeavour-

---

les papes à perpetuité.—Il mit ainsi le pape en possession de toutes ces villes au nombre de vingt-deux : sçavoir, Ravenne, Rimini, Pesaro, Fano, Cesene, Sinigaille, Jesi, Forlimpopoli, Forli, Castrocaro, Monte-Feltro, Acerragio, que l'on ne connoit plus, Mont-Lucari, que l'on croit être, Vocera, Serravole, S. Marini, Bobio, Urbin, Caglio, Luceoli prés de Candiano, Eugubio, Comaichio, et Narni. C'est le dénombrement qu'on fait Anastase. Et voilà le premier fondement de la seigneurie temporelle de l'Eglise Romaine." Fleury, Hist. Eccl. liv. xliii. An. 755. cap. xviii. p. 382, 383. tom. ix. Paris, 1703.

[1] "In 755, King Pepin confirmed to the holy see, in the person of Stephen II., the Exarchate of Ravenna, and part of the Romagna now wrested from it; and in 774, Charlemagne confirmed his father's gift, and added to it the provinces of Perugia and Spoleto, which are now sought to be revolutionized, that so a title of a thousand years' possession (which few, if any other, of European dynasties can pretend to) may, by a stroke of the pen, or a slash of the sword, be cancelled or rent." Dr. Wiseman's London Pastoral for 1860. See *Tablet* for April 21st, 1860, p. 243, col. iv. The wily doctor uses the word "confirmed," whereas Pepin "gave," not "confirmed," these provinces to the bishop of Rome. Lower down he calls it a "gift."

ing to sustain the genuineness of these epistles, admitted that "most of these letters of the popes were written about the primacy of Peter; the dominion of the Roman church; the ordination of bishops; that priests are not to be injured, nor accused, nor deposed; and about appeals being made to the apostolic see."

These documents were first published by Autgarius, bishop of Mentz, in France, about the year 836. They were never heard of before. These forgeries, for nearly 700 years, deceived the world, and had their desired effect.[1] The frauds were exposed at the time of the Reformation, and are now admitted even by Romanists to be forgeries. But the popes had the advantage of 700 years, during which period their temporal and spiritual supremacy, founded on these forged documents, was firmly believed to be derived from St. Peter himself, and thus the belief became grafted into the Roman system.[2]

THE NINTH CENTURY.

A.D. 818.—We have traced the rise and progress in the East of the heresy of the alleged substantial presence of Christ in the eucharist. It had now spread to the West. Paschase Radbert advanced the following doctrine:—

---

[1] See Fleury's Eccl. Hist. vol. ix. liv. 44, p. 500, *et seq.* Paris, 1703, and tom. ix. p. 456. Paris, 1769, where the proofs of their being forgeries are set out.

[2] For a short, popular description of these forgeries, see Neander's Church History, vol. vi. p. 1, *et seq.*; and Life and Times of Charlemagne; Religious Tract Society.

"That the body of Christ in the eucharist is the same body as that which was born of the Virgin, which suffered upon the cross, and which was raised from the grave."[1] This theory, hitherto unknown in the West, was immediately opposed. In 825, Rabanus, archbishop of Mentz, in his epistle to Heribald, specially condemned this new theory, as then lately introduced. His words are:—

"Lately, indeed, some individuals, not thinking rightly concerning the sacrament of the body and blood of the Lord, have said, 'that that very body and blood of the Lord which was born from the Virgin Mary, in which the Lord himself suffered upon the cross, and in which he rose again from the sepulchre, is the same as that which is received from the altar.' In opposition to which error, as far as lay in our power, writing to the abbot Egilus, we propounded what ought truly to be believed concerning the body itself."[2]

He then proceeded to give a spiritual interpretation deduced from our Lord's words in St. John's Gospel, ch. vi., as being applied to the Lord's Supper. The theory then lately introduced by some individuals, and condemned by this archbishop, is exactly the same theory now taught by the church of Rome. The Trent Catechism informs us that the *body* contained in the sacrament is identical "with the true body of Christ, the same body which was born of the Virgin Mary, and sits at the right hand of the Father."[3]

---

[1] Paschas. Radbert de Sacram. Euchar. cap. iii. p. 19. Colon. 1551.
[2] "Nam quidam, nuper de ipso sacramento corporis, et sanguinis domini non recte sentientes dixerunt: 'hoc ipsum corpus et sanguinem domini; quod de Maria Virgine natum est, et in quo ipse dominus passus est in cruce et resurrexit de sepulchro, idem esse quod sumiter de altari.' Cui errori, quantum potuimus, ad Egilum abbatem scribentes, de corpore ipso quid vere credendum sit, aperuimus." Raban Archiepis. Mogunt. Epist. ad Heribald. Episc. Antissiodor. de Euchar. c. xxxiii. ad calc. Reginou. Abbat. Pruniens. Libr. II. de Eccles. Disciplin. et Relig. Christian. p. 516. Stephan. Baluz. Tutel. Paris, 1671.
[3] Catech. Concl. Trent, p. 221. Donovan's Translation, Dublin, 1829.

This teaching, as we have seen, was only introduced in the ninth century. The doctrine was considered so offensive and so novel that this archbishop not only wrote to the abbot Egilus, but also to Heribald, to whom he declares that the theory was then only lately introduced.

The Western church, however, now took the infection, and it created some excitement; so much so that the emperor Charles was induced to take the opinion of Bertram, a monk of the abbey of Corbie. In reply to the emperor's demand, he wrote a treatise on the body and blood of Christ, wherein he not only repudiated the idea advanced by Radbert, word for word, but also declared that "the bread and wine are the body and blood of Christ *figuratively*."[1]

A.D. 845.—According to the acknowledgment of Alexander of Hales, who was styled from his skill the "irrefragable doctor" (A.D. 1230), *confirmation* was instituted as a sacrament in the Meldesium (Meaux) Council of this date.[2] This was only a provincial council. *Confirmation* was admitted by the church of Rome authoritatively as a sacrament in 1547, at the seventh session of the Council of Trent.

A.D. 850.—At a synod in Pavia, the custom of priestly unction, especially in mortal sickness, was sanctioned, and was placed in the same rank with the other sacraments.[3]

---

[1] The whole of this reply is such a complete refutation of the modern Roman theory that we have added, in Appendix A, the entire passage with the translation, to which we desire particular attention. Bertram. Preshyt. de Corp. et Sanguin. Domin. pp. 180—222. Colon. 1551, or sec. lxxxix. Oxon. 1838.

[2] "Institutum fuit hoc sacramentum spiritus sancti instinctu in concilio Meldensi." Alex. Ales. op. omn. vol. iv. p. 109. Venet. 1575.

[3] Neander's Church History, vol. vi. p. 146. London, 1852.

218   THE NOVELTIES OF ROMANISM.

A.D. 852.—The Capitular of Hincmar (an eminent bishop of France) directed holy water to be sprinkled on the people, houses, cattle, and the food of men and beasts.[1] (See *ante*, A.D. 113.)

A.D. 855.—The feast of the Assumption of the Virgin Mary has no warranty in any ancient document.[2] Leo. IV. now firmly established the festival, and added the octave to invest it with greater dignity.[3]

A.D. 869.—Hitherto the sacred Scriptures were alone of authority in the church. The Fourth Council of Constantinople (A.D. 869), by the first canon, first passed a decree recognising *tradition;* but it was not an *oral tradition*, as subsequently relied on by the Council of Trent, but a tradition preserved in the records of the church by the writings of a continual succession of witnesses in the church, capable therefore of proof; nor did this council place this tradition on an equal footing with the sacred Scriptures, as the Council of Trent subsequently did, but as a "secondary oracle" only. It was left for the Council of Trent, in 1546, to consummate the corruption by converting the written to an oral tradition, and placing the latter on the same footing as the Scriptures. The decree in question is as follows:—

"Therefore we profess to preserve and keep the rules which have been delivered to the holy Catholic apostolic church, as well

---

[1] "Tous les dimanches chaque prêtre avant la messe fera de l'eau benite, dont on aspergera le peuple entrant dans l'église; et ceux qui voudront en emporteront, pour en asperger leurs maisons, leurs terres, leurs bestiaux, la nourriture des hommes et des bêtes." Fleury's Eccl. Hist., Lib. 44, p. 541. Paris, 1704; and in tom. x. p. 462. Paris, 1769.

[2] The various spurious documents cited by Romanists to prove the antiquity of this festival are ably exposed by the Rev. Mr. Tyler in his "Worship of the Virgin Mary," part ii. c. ii. London, 1851.

[3] "Il instituа l'octave de l'assomption de le Sainte Vierge, qui ne se celebroit point encore à Rome." Fleury, Eccl. Hist. lib. xlix. p. 598, tom. x. Paris, 1704, and Tom. x. p. 502. Paris, 1769.

NINTH CENTURY.

by the holy and most illustrious apostles, as by the universal as well as local councils of the orthodox, or even by any divinely speaking father and master of the church; governing by these both our own life and manners, and canonically decreeing that both the whole list of the priesthood, and also all who are counted under the name of Christian, are subjected to the pains and condemnations, and on the other hand, to the approbations and justifications which have been set forth and defined by them. To hold the traditions which we have received, whether by word or by epistle of the saints who have shone heretofore, is the plain admonition of the great apostle Paul."[1]

A.D. 884.—Adrian III., bishop of Rome, was the first who advised the canonization of saints; but the authoritative confirmation by decree was of later date, under Alexander III. (A.D. 1160). The first act of canonization is supposed to have taken place in A.D. 933, under John XV. The happy individual was Uldaric, bishop of Augsburg, who died about twenty years before.[2] Ferraris,[3] however, says it

---

[1] .. Canon I. "Igitur regulas, quæ sanctæ Catbolicæ ac apostolicæ ecclesiæ, tam a sanctis famosissimis Apostolis, quam ab orthodoxorum universalibus, necnon et localibus conciliis, vel etiam a quolibet diloque patri ac magistro ecclesiæ traditæ sunt, servare ac custodire profitemur; his et propriam vitam, et mores regentes, et omnem sacerdotii catalogum, seu et omnes qui Christiano censentur vocabulo, pænis et damnationibus, et è diverso receptionibus, ac justificationibus quæ perillas prolatæ sunt et definitæ subjici canonice decernentes; tenere quippe traditiones, quas accepimis, sive per sermonem sive per epistolam sanctorum qui antea fulserunt, Paulus admonet aperte magnus apostolus." Labb. et Coss. Concl. tom. viii. cols. 1126, 1127. Paris, 1671.

[2] Fleury's Eccl. History, tom. xii. p. 275.

[3] "Hinc non certo constat, quisnam fuerit primus summus pontifex, qui solemniter canonizationem sanctorum celebraverit. Nam multi tenent, quod prima canonizatio solemniter celebrata fuerit a Leone III., A.D. 804." Ferraris, "Biblioth. Prompt., Veneratio Sanctorum," tom. vii. sec. xix. Francof. 1781. And Picard says:—"On ne voit point d'exemple d'une Canonization solennelle avant celle de St. Suibert, que le Pape Leon III. canonisa au commencement de neuvième siécle mais quelques-uns attribuent au Pape Adrien la premiere canonisation solennelle, et quelques autres prétendent que S. Udalric canonisé en 993 par le Pape Jean XIV. ou XV. est le premier St. canonisé en ceremonie. Il en a même qui donne au Pape Alexander III. la gloire de cette institution." "Cérémonies et Coûtumes Religieuses." Picard, tom. i. part ii. p. 143. Amsterdam, 1723.

is not certain who was the first that celebrated the canonization of a saint, and adds, that many believed that it was by Leo. III., A.D. 804.

Neander, in his "Church History,"[1] notes this last-mentioned period as the proper date for ascertaining the authoritative introduction of invocation of saints, which was then recognised by the bull of Pope John XV.

THE TENTH CENTURY.

A.D. 956.—Octavian was made bishop at the age of eighteen under the title of John XII. We note this as being the first authentic instance of the adoption of a new name by the bishop of Rome. It then became, and is now, the custom for popes to change their names on their election. Adrian VI. (A.D. 1522), a Dutchman, refused to follow this rule. According to Polydore Vergil,[2] Sergius I. (A.D. 701) first ordained that the bishop of Rome might change his name on election, after the example of Christ, who changed Simon Barjonas to Peter. Polydore Vergil on this quaintly observes, "The special prerogative and privilege of the bishop of Rome is, that he may change his name if it may seem to him not very pleasant to his ears. If he be a

---

[1] Neander, "Church History," vol. vi. p. 144. London, 1852.
[2] Book iv. c. vii. p. 91. London, 1551. Picard has the following observation on this subject:—"Sergius III. ou IV. qui s'appelloit auparavant *os porci*, est le premier des papes, qui se soit avisé de changer le nom à son exaltation au pontificat. Ses successeurs l'ont imité. D'autres croient que les papes n'ont changé de nom que depuis Jean XII., qui auparavant s'appelloit Octavien, et tient le siége pontifical en 956, long temps après Sergius II. et plusieurs années avant Sergius IV." "Cérémonies et Coûtumes Religieuses," etc., Picard, tom. i. part ii. p. 49, note *b*. Amsterdam, 1723.

malefactor, he may call his name *Bonifacius;* if he be a coward, he may be called *Leo;* a carter, *Urbanus;* and for a cruel man, *Clemens;* if not innocent, *Inuocentius;* if ungodly, *Pius.*"

A.D. 965.—John XIII.[1] baptized the great bell of St. John Lateran in Rome, naming it after himself; thence arose the custom of baptizing bells. Bellarmine[2] informs us that in these baptisms all the forms in baptizing children were used—water, oil, salt, and godfathers and godmothers. The baptized bell is dedicated to some saint, under whom they hope to obtain their demands from God, and they teach that the sound drives away devils, etc.[3] In A.D. 790, by the Capitular of Charlemagne, the baptism of bells with holy water was prohibited.[4]

THE ELEVENTH CENTURY.

A.D. 1000.—The modern form of absolution, " I absolve thee," the alleged essence of the sacrament, cannot be traced to any authentic record previous to this date. The ancient

[1] See Picard, "Cérémonies et Coûtumes Religieuses," tom. i. part ii. p. 108, note *g*.
[2] Bellarmine Disp. De Rom. Pont. lib. iv. c. xii. Prag. 1721.
[3] "On ne doit pas oublier de mettre au rang des ablutions tenues pour essentielles la benediction des cloches, telle qu'elle se pratique chez les catholiques. C'est une espéce de baptême, puis qu'on les lave avec de l'eau benite, et qu'on leur donne le nom de quelque saint, sous l'invocation duquel en les offre à Dieu, afin qu'il (le saint) les protege et qu'il aide l'Eglise à aboutir de Dieu ce qu'elle lui demande, dit le rituel d'Alet — l'ablution des cloches est accompagnée de la benediction, afin que les cloches benites sient la force de toucher les cœurs par la vertu du S. Esprit.... et quand on les sonne, elle chassent les demons," etc. Picard, "Cérémonies et Coûtumes Religieuses," vol. i. p. xix. Amsterdam, 1723.
[4] "On ne baptisera point des cloches," etc. Fleury's Eccl. Hist. tom. ix. p. 520. Paris, 1769, and tom. x. p. 573. Paris, 1703, and Harduin Concilia, tom. iv. p. 846. No. 18.

form of absolution used in the church of Rome was, "Almighty God have compassion on thee, and put away thy sins:"[1] a ministerial and not a judicial act. This was changed to the present form, "I absolve thee." Thomas Aquinas, who flourished about the middle of the thirteenth century, points out the time of this remarkable change; for he tells us that the authoritative form of absolution was found fault with by a learned man, his contemporary, asserting that thirty years were scarce passed since the supplicatory form only, "Almighty God give thee remission and forgiveness," was used by all.[2] The present authoritative form was first established in England, in 1268, when, at a council held in London under Cardinal Ottoboni, the pope's legate, all confessors were enjoined to use it.[3]

About this time, churches were first consecrated by the sprinkling of holy water, in imitation of the pagan custom of using lustral water for the same purpose.

According to Fleury, the Little Office of the Virgin was introduced about this time,[4] and was afterwards confirmed by Urban II. in the Council of Clermont, A.D. 1095.[5]

About this time also, the eucharist was changed into a so-called sacrifice; the ordination service was then also changed. Priests who were hitherto called to preach the gospel, were now ordained, according to the form prescribed in the

---

[1] "Absolutio criminum. Miseratur tui omnipotens Deus, et dimittat tibi omnia peccata tua," etc.—Confitentium Ceremoniæ Antiq. Edit. Colon. Ann. 1530.

[2] Aquin. Opus. 22, de forma absol. c. 5, quoted by Bower in his "History of the Popes," vol. ii. p. 135. London, 1750.

[3] Collier's Eccl. Hist. vol. i. p. 474. Folio Edit.

[4] "On ait aussi, que pour obtenir de Dieu un secour plus abondant en cette grande entreprise (la croisade) le pape ordonna dans le concil de Clermont que les clercs diroient le petit office de la vierge déjà introduit chez les moines par Saint Pierre Damien." Eccl. Hist. tom. xiii. p. 105. Paris, 1767, and p. 621. Paris, 1726.

[5] Mosheim's Eccl. Hist. cent. x. pt. ii. cap. iv. sec. iii.

Roman pontifical, for another purpose, namely, to sacrifice —" Receive thou power to offer sacrifice to God, and to celebrate masses as well for the living as for the dead, in the name of the Lord."[1]

A.D. 1003.—John XIV. allowed authoritatively the feast of All Souls, appointing it to be celebrated upon the morning after All Saints. This feast was instituted by Odilon, abbot of Clugny, at the latter end of the previous century. It is a commemoration of the dead by all the people. This was an ancient pagan custom. It was celebrated, according to Plutarch, in his life of Romulus, in the month of February, called the month of expiation. Modern Romanists have changed the time to November. Polydore Vergil[2] said, "The custom of performing the service for one's departed friends was long since adopted, as Cicero shows in the first oration against Anthony. Thus annual service was done—that is to say, annual sacrifices were yearly offered up in honour of the dead. * * * And there is all reason in the world to conclude that Odilon from this took the yearly celebration of the service for the dead." Romanism in this, as in so many other cases, is only the re-adoption of paganism.

A.D. 1022.—The Council of Worms, at this date, first undertook to legalize the commutation of penance for money. Fleury, the Roman Catholic historian, thus refers to the words extracted from the Decretum of Burchard, bishop of Worms :—" He that cannot fast for one day on bread and water shall sing fifty psalms on his knees in the church, and shall feed one poor man for that day, and for which period he shall take such nourishment as he likes

[1] The form prescribed by our Common Prayer Book is "authority to preach the Word of God, and to administer the Holy Sacraments."
[2] Book ix. c. x. Edit. London, 1551.

except wine, flesh, and grease. One hundred genuflexions shall be accepted instead of the fifty psalms, AND THE RICH MAY REDEEM THEMSELVES FOR MONEY." [1]

A.D. 1055.—Victor II. was the first pope who authorized what may be termed the redemption of penances. Hitherto canonical penances were relaxed by the bishop. It was now enacted that the penitent might buy off or redeem the penance by "pecuniary mulcts," or fines, under the softer expressions of alms or donations bestowed on the church. Those who had no money might redeem the same by acts of austerity, fasting, voluntary mortifications, etc., as above stated. Hence the custom of whipping proceeded, and the subsequent establishment of an order of friars called the "Batusses," who, in their nightly processions, whipped and otherwise mortified themselves. The priests of Bellona wore haircloth, and inflicted stripes on their bodies. The priests of Baal lacerated themselves. Polydore Vergil (Lib. vii., c. 6) tells us that the custom was derived from the Egyptians and Romans. He says, "Those whom you see in the public processions walk in order with their faces covered, and their shoulders torn, which they scourge with whips, as becomes true penitents, have copied after the Romans, who, when they celebrated the feast called Lupercale, marched thus naked and masked through the streets with whips. And if we must go farther to look for the origin of this verberation, I will affirm it to be derived from the Egyptians, who, as Herodotus tells us," etc. Paganism and Romanism thus go hand in hand. The Roman Breviary and Lives of the Saints are replete with the examples of the perpetration of this barbarous custom of self-flagellation.

[1] Fleury, Hist. Eccl. tom. xii. p. 413. Edit. Paris, 1769—1774, and p. 425. Edit. Paris, 1722.

A.D. 1059.—At a council held in Rome, under Nicholas II., it was declared that the bread and wine are the very body and blood of Christ; and that Christ is sensibly felt, broken, and torn by the teeth of the faithful.[1] This is not the precise doctrine of the modern Roman church, nor was the council which presented the doctrine a General Council. The above was the form of recantation which Berengarius was, for the third time, compelled to sign. Fleury, nevertheless, informs us that, though the majority of the council were against Berengarius, yet some of the members contended that the terms of Scripture were to be taken figuratively.[2]

At the same council, under Nicholas II., it was declared that if any one should be elected bishop of Rome without the unanimous and canonical consent of the cardinals, and of the other clergy and the laity, he should not be regarded as a pope, but as an intruder.[3]

A.D. 1060.—Polydore Vergil[4] says that the authority to choose the bishop of Rome belonged first to the emperor of Constantinople and the deputy of Italy, till, about A.D. 685, the emperor Constantine Pogonatus, empowered the cardinals and the people of Rome to elect him. It is quite certain that up to the time of Leo VIII., A.D. 965, the election of the bishop of Rome was vested in the clergy and people.[5] It is now in the cardinals alone.

---

[1] Cor. Juris Can. tom. i. p. 2104. Part iii. dist. ii. c. xlii. Paris, 1612. See *ante*, p. 45, for the original text.
[2] Eccl. Hist. tom. xiii. p. 289. Paris, 1726, and pp. 367, 368. Paris, 1769.
[3] Labb. et Coss. Concl. tom. ix. col. 1099. Paris, 1671.
[4] B. iv. c. vii. p. xcii. London, 1551.
[5] "Qui statim Romanorum inconstantiæ pertæsus authoritatem omnem eligendi pontificis a clero populoque Romano ad imperatorem transtulit." Platina in Vit. Leo VIII. p. 154. Coloniæ, 1568. And see Picard, "Cérémonies et Coûtumes Religieuses," etc. Tom. i. pt. ii. p. 43, note *c*. Amsterdam, 1723.

A.D. 1070.—Purgatory was now being industriously advocated by the priests; but prayers to deliver souls out of purgatory were first appointed by Odilon, abbot of Clugny, about the latter end of the previous century, by instituting a festival for that purpose.[1]

A.D. 1073.—Up to this date the title of "pope," or "papa," father, was common to all bishops. Gregory VII., in a council at Rome, decreed that there should be but one pope in the world, and that was to be himself. The title of Pope was from thenceforth assumed by the bishop of Rome exclusively among the Western bishops, though the Eastern bishops still continued to retain the title. From this date, however, the bishops of Rome only were properly called "popes."

A.D. 1074.—The compulsory celibacy of the clergy was now enforced by this same pope. The marriage of priests was not altogether forbidden till the time of Gregory VII.[2] He deprived the clergy of their lawful wives, compelled them to take a vow of continency, and excommunicated the refractory. He held a council at Rome (A.D. 1074), wherein it was declared that married priests should not be permitted to celebrate mass, or to discharge any of the superior offices of the altar.[3] At the Council of Mayence, held the following year (A.D. 1075), the decree of Gregory was published, which enjoined the archbishop, under pain of deposition, to oblige the prelates and other clergy of the province to give up either their wives or their offices. The clergy present would not submit to this decree, and opposed the archbishop, who, fearing for

---

[1] This was in A.D. 998. See Mosheim's Eccl. Hist. cent. x. pt. ii. c. iv.s. ii.
[2] Pol. Vergil, De Rer. Invent, lib. v. c. iv. p. 54. London, 1551.
[3] Labb. et Coss. concl. tom. x. col. 313. Paris, 1671.

his life, gave up the attempt, and left the enforcement of the decree to Gregory himself.¹

The first (so-called) General Council of the Roman church which authoritatively enjoined the celibacy of the clergy was the First Lateran Council (A.D. 1123), held under Calixtus II.²

On the subject of priestly celibacy, the opinion of Æneas Sylvius, who afterwards (A.D. 1458) became pope, under the name of Pius II., is noteworthy. "Perhaps (he said) it were not the worse that many priests were married, for by that means many might be saved in married priesthood which now in celibate priesthood are damned."³ Our readers will not be surprised to hear that this work has been placed in the index of prohibited books.⁴ This same Æneas Sylvius said that, "As marriage, for weighty reasons, was taken from the priests, so, upon more weighty considerations, it appears that it ought to be restored."⁵ "Take away," said St. Bernard, "from the church (*i.e.* the priesthood) honourable matrimony, and do you not fill it with keepers of concubines?" etc.⁶ Polydore Vergil⁷ cited the last quotation from Æneas Sylvius, in his book,

---

1 Labb. et Coss. concl. tom. x. col. 345. Paris, 1671.
2 Ibid. tom. x. col. 891, can. iii. The Provincial Council of Augsburg (Augustanum), A.D. 952, forbade the clergy, including bishops and sub-deacons, to marry, or to retain females in their houses. Ibid. tom. ix. col. 635. Paris, 1671.
3 Æneas Sylvius, "Commentarii de gestis Basiliensis Concilii," lib. ii. Opera, Basil, 1571.
4 See Index lib. prohib. Madrid, 1667, p. 30.
5 "Sacerdotibus magna ratione sublatae nuptiae, majori restituendae videri." Platin. in vit. Pii II. p. 328. Colon. 1611.
6 "Tolle de ecclesiâ honorabile connubium et torum immaculatum, nonne reples eam concubinariis, incestuosis, seminifluis, mollibus, masculorum concubitoribus, et omni denique genere immundorum." Bened. Serm. lxvi. in Cantica, post. init. vol. ii. p. 1. p, 555. Paris, 1839. N.B. This sermon is put among the "Opera dubia:" it is quoted as a grave assertion proved by results to be true.
7 Published in 1499, and subsequently 1528. Parisiis ex officinâ, Roberti Stephani.

"De Inventionibus Rerum," and he proved that the marriage of priests was not contrary to the law of God, that the custom continued for a long period in the church, and added, " Furthermore, whilst the priests did beget lawful sons, the church flourished with a happy offspring of men; then your popes were most holy, your bishops most innocent, and your priests and deacons most honest and chaste."[1] He gave, in the same place, also the reverse of the picture. "This I will affirm, that this enforced chastity is so far from surpassing conjugal chastity, that even the guilt of no crime ever brought greater disgrace to the holy order, greater danger to religion, or greater grief to all men, than the stain of the clergy's lust. Wherefore, it would, perhaps, be the interest as well of Christianity as of the holy order, that at least the right of public marriage were restored to the clergy, which they might rather chastely pursue without infamy, than defile themselves by such brutal lusts." As Rome cannot bear to hear the truth, the compilers of the Belgian and other Expurgatory Indices have ordered this fourth chapter of the fifth book of Polydore Vergil's work for seven consecutive pages to be expunged.

There is a curious document extant, a letter written by Udalric, or Ulrick, bishop of Augusta (A.D. 870), to pope Nicholas I. A warm dispute had arisen between the bishop and the pope on the subject of priestly marriages, the pope having censured Odo, the archbishop of Vienna, for permitting one of his subdeacons to marry. Ulrick reminded the pope that Gregory the

---

[1] "Porro, dum sacerdotes generabant legitimos filios, ecclesia felici prole virûm vigebat; tum sanctissimi erant pontifices, episcopi innocentissimi, presbyteri diaconique integerrimi castissimique." De Invent. Rerum. lib. 5, c. 4, pp. 86, 87. Ibid. c. 9. Edit. as above.

Great by a decree had deprived priests of their wives; shortly after some fishermen, instead of making a take of fish, took six thousand heads of infants which had been drowned in the ponds. When the pope heard of the scandal, the result of his decree, he immediately recalled it, and did acts of penance for the occasion he had given of so many deaths.[1] That the prohibition has led to great scandals we have, alas! too many examples; it is condemned by all good and honest men.[2]

Popery proper may now be considered in its zenith; and this period is further remarkable for the fact, that now, for the first time, the pope took upon himself to anathematize, and depose an emperor. Gregory delivered this order of deposition in presence of his council, and in the form of a solemn address to St. Peter. It was hurled against the emperor Henry. Fleury says that this was the first time that a pope had undertaken to declare such a sentence, and the whole empire was thrown into astonishment and indignation.[3]

A.D. 1090.—Chaplets and paternosters were, with the

[1] "Gregorium Magnum suo quodam decreto sacerdotibus aliquando uxores ademisse. Cum vero paulo post jussisset ex piscina sua pisces aliquot capi, piscatores pro piscibus sex millia capitum infantum suffocatorum reperisse; quam cædem infantium cum intellexit Gregorius ex occultis fornicationibus vel adulteriis sacerdotum natam esse, continuo revocavit decretum, et peccatum suum dignis pœnitentiæ fructibus purgavit, laudans apostolicum illud, 'Melius est nubere quam uri' et de suo addens, 'Melius est nubere, quam mortis occasionem præbere.'" Epist. Udalrici. apud Gerhard. Loc. Theolog. de Minist. Eccles. lect. cccxxxix. tom. vi. p. 548, 4to. Jenæ, 1619.
[2] "Les Catholiques fuit garder de celibat à leurs prêtres, et la regle de leur charge les condamne à une chastité perpetuelle. Fardeau impossible! dont la reformation des Protestants à très-bien connu le poids. Leur ecclesiastiques se marient et la religion n'est pas plus mal; bien qu'on pretende que le marriage et les soins d'un ménage et d'une famille détourne un pasteur des soin de l'Eglise. Les ecclesiastiques qui sont privés du marriage ont tres souvent des maitresses, et cela ne vaut pas mieux qu'une femme." Picard, Dissertation sur le culte religieux, p. xv. tom. i. "Cérémonies et Coûtumes Religieuses." Amsterdam, 1723.
[3] Eccl. Hist. tom. xiii. pp. 295, 301. Paris, 1769.

"Office and Hours of our Lady," invented by Peter the Hermit;[1] but the former were put in general practice at the recommendation of Dominic (A.D. 1230), and he therefore passed as the author of this species of devotion.

A.D. 1095.—It may be worth recording here, by the way, that at the Council of Clermont, held in November of this year, by Pope Urban II., at the head of thirteen archbishops and 250 bishops and abbots, by the twenty-eighth canon it was directed that all who communicated should receive the body and blood of Christ under both kinds, unless there be necessity to the contrary.[2]

A.D. 1098.—Robert, abbot of Molême, bishop of Burgundy, founded a new order of monks called Cistercians, so called from the place in which he located himself, Citeaux, or Cistercium, within the bishopric of Châlon, not far from Dijon, in France.

Bruno, an ecclesiastic of Cologne, and master of the cathedral school at Rheims in 1084, settled down at Chartreux (Cartusium), near Grenoble, and there founded the order of Carthusian monks.[3] In 1185, a Greek monk (a priest, Johannes Phocus) visited Mount Carmel, in Palestine, where he found the ruins of an old monastery, and where he also found an old priest of Calabria, one Berthold, who had, in consequence of a vision, erected on this spot a tower and small church, which he occupied, with about ten companions. Hence arose the order of the Carmelite monks.[4]

---

[1] Polydore Vergil, b. v. c. vii. p. 107. London, 1551.

[2] "Ne quis communicet de altari nisi corpus separatim et sanguinem similiter sumat, nisi per necessitatem et per cautelam." Labb. et Coss. Concl. Gen. tom. x. col. 506, can. 28. Paris, 1671.

[3] Neander's Church History, vol. vii. page 367. London, 1852.

[4] Ibid. vol. vii. p. 369.

THE TWELFTH CENTURY.

A.D. 1123.—Marriage of the presbyters, deacons, and sub-deacons was by the twenty-first canon of the First Council of Lateran prohibited. The following is the canon in question:—

"We entirely forbid the presbyters, deacons, sub-deacons, and monks to contract marriages; and we judge that marriages contracted by these sort of persons ought to be annulled, and the persons brought to repentance, according to the decision of the said canons."

A similar canon was passed by the Second Lateran Council, A.D. 1139, canon vi. and vii.[2]

A.D. 1130.—Hugo de Victore, a Parisian monk, and Peter Lombard, bishop of Paris (1140), first asserted or defined the sacraments to be seven, but this was not yet declared to be the doctrine of the Church; the determinate number of seven sacraments was mentioned for the first time in the instruction given to Otto, of Bamberg, for persons newly baptized (A.D. 1124).[3]

A.D. 1140.—The festival of the Immaculate Conception of the blessed Virgin Mary was introduced at Lyons, about this time; but was opposed by Bernard, as a novelty without the sanction of Scripture or of reason.[4]

Bernard is a canonized saint of the Roman church, and is accounted as the last of the Fathers. His opinion on doctrinal questions is greatly esteemed by Romanists of the present day. When Bernard heard of the introduction of

---

[1] Labb. et Coss. Concl. tom. x. col. 899. Paris, 1671.
[2] Ibid. tom. x. cols. 1003, 1004.
[3] Neander's Church History, vol. vii. p. 465. London, 1852.
[4] Fleury, xiv. p. 527. Paris, 1769, and p. 560. Paris, 1727.

this new festival, he wrote an epistle of protest to the church of Lyons, wherein he said : "We can never enough wonder that some of you could have the boldness to introduce a feast which the church has not the least knowledge of, which is neither supported by reason nor backed by any tradition." He asserted that the feast was founded on an "alleged revelation, which is destitute of adequate authority," and inquired, "How can it be maintained that a conception which proceeds, not from the Holy Ghost, but rather from sin, can be holy ? or how could they conjure up a holy day on account of a thing that is not holy in itself ?" And he added that this feast "either honours sin, or authorizes a false holiness."[1] It is difficult to conceive on what ground the church of Rome, after such a declaration as the above, could attempt to establish the "immaculate conception" as a doctrine. We shall below (A.D. 1476) continue this subject as more appropriate to the period when the doctrine was seriously revived.

Peter Lombard first determined the three parts of Penance—contrition, confession, and satisfaction.[2]

A.D. 1151.—Gratian's collections of ecclesiastical decrees, canons, etc., were allowed and authorized by Pope Eugene III., who commanded them to be studied in the universities

---

[1] "Unde miramur satis, quid visum fuerit hoc tempore quibusdam vestrum voluisse mutare colorem optimum, novam inducendo celebritatem, quam ritus ecclesiæ nescit, non probat ratio, non commendat antiqua traditio....Sed profertur scriptum supernæ, ut aiunt, revelationis. Ipse mihi facile persuades scriptis talibus non moveri, quibus nec ratio suppeditare, nec certa invenitur favere auctoritas....Cum hæc ita se habeant, quænam jam erit festivæ ratio conceptionis ? Quo pacto, aut sanctus asseretur conceptus, qui de Spiritu Sancto non est, ne dicam de peccato est ? Aut festus habebitur, qui minime sanctus est ? Libenter gloriosa hoc honore carebit, quo vel peccatum honorari, vel falsa videtur induci sanctitas." S. Bernard. Epist. 174, Oper. tom. i. pp. 390, 391. Paris, 1839.

[2] "Compunctio cordis, confessioris, satisfactio operis." Neander's Church History, vol. vii. p. 483. London, 1852.

and practised in the spiritual courts. This is the origin of what is called the canon law. Gratian, who arranged this new collection of ecclesiastical laws at Bologna, was a Benedictine, or, according to another account, a Camaldulensian monk.[1] Gratian's doctrine, as to the authority of this law, was—"The holy Roman church gives authority to the canons; but she is not bound by the canons, nor does she submit herself to them. As Jesus Christ, who made the law, accomplished the law to sanctify it to himself, and, afterwards, in order to show that he was its Master, dispensed with it, and freed his apostles from its bondage." The historian, Fleury, records these extravagant claims to demonstrate their falsity.[2]

A.D. 1160.—Alexander III. decreed the canonization of saints, and ordered that none should from that date be acknowledged a saint unless declared to be such by a pope.

Polydore Vergil said:—

"The fashion to deify men that had done any benefits to the commonwealth is one of the most ancient usages that I read of. For antiquity, even from the beginning, was accustomed to make gods of their kings, which, either by abundance of benefits, or notable qualities of prowess, had won the hearts of the commons. And specially the Romans did that with great pomp and circumstance, and with many observances. Of them our bishops learned, as by a pattern, their rite of canonizing saints; and the yearly sacrifices that Gregory and Felix appointed concerned nothing else but to declare that those martyrs were saints, and of the household of God. Last of all, Alexander III. ordained that no such divine solemnities should be given to any man openly, without he were canonized and admitted to be a saint by the bishop of Rome in his bull; because no man

---

[1] Neander's Church History, vol. vii. p. 282. London, 1852.
[2] Tom. xv. p. 49. Paris, 1769.

should himself choose any private saint, or commit any peculiar idolatry."[1]

Pagans were not allowed to offer up their prayers but to such as the senate, by their suffrages, had placed among the gods. Tertullian, in the thirteenth chapter of his Apology, referring to these heathen deities, said:—

"The condition of each of your gods depends upon the approbation of the senate; those are not gods whom men have not decreed to be."

Is this not exactly the case with Romish saints?

It is worthy of remark here, that, in 1165, Charlemagne was canonized as a saint by the anti-pope Pascal III., and though this canonization was made by an usurper, an anti-pope, the act has never been repudiated, and his name is still found in many calendars.[3]

This same pope (Alexander III.) is said to be the first who issued indulgences.

A.D. 1182—3.—An important innovation took place in the election of the pope (Lucius III.) Hitherto the clergy and people had a voice in the election; but now, by virtue of a decree of the Third Lateran Council (A.D. 1179), under Alexander III., the election was made by the cardinals alone.[4] It was determined that the individual chosen by two thirds of the cardinals should be lawful pope.[5]

---

[1] B. vi. c. vi. p. 122. London, 1551. See *ante*, A.D. 884, p. 140.

[2] Tertullian, "Apologeticus adversus gentes," c. xiii. vol. v. p. 38. Edit. Halæ Madg. 1783.

[3] "Ce n'est que depuis cette canonisation de Frideric Barberousse, que Charlemagne à commencé d'etre honoré comme saint, d'un culte public en quelques églises particulières, et quoique cette canonisation fut faite de l'autorité d'un antipape, les papes legitimes ne s'y sont pas opposes." Fleury, tom. xv. p. 192. Paris, 1769, and p. 219. Paris, 1719.

[4] Labb. et Coss. Concl. tom. viii. col. 1526. Paris, 1671. Fleury, vol. xv. p. 437. Paris, 1769. Mosheim's Eccl. Hist. cent. xi. pt. ii. p. 226, vol. ii. London, 1768.

[5] See Neander's Church History, vol. vii. p. 233. London, 1852.

THE THIRTEENTH CENTURY.

A.D. 1215.—Auricular confession was, by the Fourth Lateran Council, now first authoritatively required of all persons of years of discretion, under pain of mortal sin.[1] Confession was to be made at least once a year. Fleury says, "This is the first canon that I know of which has commanded general confession."[2]

We have already noted under date A.D. 329 the first introduction of secret or private confession to a priest, and the suppression of the custom, and its subsequent reintroduction, A.D. 763. We now have the custom converted into a doctrine of the Roman church. This was another reintroduction into the Christian church of the heathen custom, and in this she has followed out the Babylonian system, which required a secret confession to the priest, according to a prescribed form, of all who were admitted to the "Mysteries," and till such confession had been made, no complete initiation could take place.[3] Eusèbe Salverte[4] refers to this confession as observed in Greece, in rites that can clearly be traced to a Babylonian origin. He says:—

"All the Greeks, from Delphi to Thermophylæ, were initiated in the mysteries of the Temple of Delphi. Their silence in regard to everything they were commanded to keep secret, was secured both by the fear of the penalties threatened to a perjured revelation, and by the general confession exacted of

---
[1] Labb. et Coss. Concl. tom. xi. pt. 1. Concl. Lat. IV. Decret. xxi. cols. 171, 173. Paris, 1671, and see Neander's Church History, vol. vii. p. 491. London, 1852.
[2] Fleury's Eccl. Hist. tom. xvi. p. 375. Paris, 1769.
[3] See a very remarkable book, "The Two Babylons; or, the Papal Worship proved to be the Worship of Nimrod and his Wife," by Alexander Hislop. London and Edinburgh, 1862. Third Edition, p. 12.
[4] Des Sciences Occultes, cap. xxvi. p. 428. Paris, 1856.

the aspirants after initiation—a confession which caused them greater dread of the indiscretion of the priest, than gave him reason to dread their indiscretion."

Potter, in his " Greek Antiquities,"[1] refers to this confession in his account of the Eleusinian mysteries, though from fear of offending he clothes under the word "etcetera" the various subjects exacted from the penitent or postulant in the confessional. Thus modern Romanism vies with ancient paganism even in the obscenity which it suggests, and which is equally characteristic of the modern system.

A.D. 1215.—The Council of Trent, at the twenty-second session, declared that "although the mass do contain in it great instruction for the people, yet it doth not seem expedient to the fathers of the council that it should be everywhere celebrated in the vulgar tongue."[2] And they proceeded to decree that "whosoever shall say that the mass ought to be celebrated in the vulgar tongue only, let him be accursed."[3]

When, how, and why, this strange custom came to pass, is difficult to say; but this is the first canon on record which, so far from making the use of the vulgar tongue compulsory, anathematises those who should declare that the service should be performed in the language known to the people. We conceive the decree of Trent to be directly contradictory to the previous canon passed at the Fourth Lateran Council in A.D. 1215; and which council is

---

[1] Potter, vol. i. "Eleusinia," p. 356. Oxford, 1697.
[2] Etsi Missa magnam contineat populi fidelis eruditionem, non tamen expedire visum est patribus ut vulgari passim lingua celebraretur." Concl. Trid. Sess. xxii. c. 8, p. 156. Paris, 1832.
[3] Si quis dixerit,—lingua tantum vulgari Missam celebrari debere—anathema sit. Ibid. can. 9, de Sacrificio Missæ, p. 150. Paris, 1832.

esteemed among Romanists as a general council. The words of the ninth canon are as follows :—

"Because in most parts there are within the same state or diocese people of different languages mixed together, having under one faith various rites and customs; we distinctly charge that the bishops of these states or dioceses provide proper persons to celebrate the divine offices, and administer the sacraments of the church according to the differences of rites and languages, instructing them both by word and by example."[1]

Here, then, is a decree of a reputed general council, in a most emphatic and clear manner, directing the divine offices and sacraments of the church to be administered in the language understood by the people. We may add that the pope in his own decretals publicly declared to the same effect :—

"We command that the bishops of such cities and dioceses where nations are mingled together, provide meet men to minister the holy service according to the diversities of their manners and languages."[2]

And Cassander certified that the prayers, and especially the words of consecration, were so read by the ancient Christians that all the people might understand.[3]

That modern Romanists have changed the ancient custom,

[1] Can. IX. "Quoniam in plerisque partibus intra eamdem civitatem sive diœcesim permixti sunt populi diversarum linguarum, habentes sub una fide varios ritus et mores; districte præcipimus, ut pontifices hujusmodi civitatum sive diœcesium providebant viros idoneos, qui secundum diversitates rituum et linguarum divina officia illis celebrent, et ecclesiastica sacramenta ministrent instruendo eos verbo pariter et exemplo." Labb. et Coss. Concl. tom. xi. p. 161. Paris, 1671.
[2] Decret. Gregor. lib. 3, tit. 31, de offic. Jud. Ord. c. 14, see Cassander Liturg. p. 87. Paris, 1610.
[3] "Canonicum precem, et imprimis Dominici corpori et sanguinis consecrationem ita veteras legebunt, ut à populo intelligi, et amen declamari posset." Cassand. Liturg. c. 28, p. 17. Colon. 1558.

is therefore certain. So little do the bulk of the people understand the Latin service as it proceeds, that the people not unfrequently read other prayers while the regular service is proceeding, and this is permitted, if not encouraged by the priests.

Though the real corporeal presence of our Lord in the sacrament was insisted on as a matter of fact, it was not until the Fourth Lateran Council, under Innocent III., that the bread was declared to be transubstantiated into the body, and the wine into the blood of Christ, and thus Transubstantiation became, for the first time, an article of faith by decree of a general council; or, as Neander expresses it, was "definitely settled by the church at the Lateran Council, 1215." [1]

The canon is as follows:—

. . . . " But there is one universal church of the faithful, out of which no one at all is saved; in which Jesus Christ himself is at once priest and sacrifice: whose body and blood in the sacrament of the altar are truly contained under the species of bread and wine, which, through the Divine power, are transubstantiated—the bread into the body, and the wine into the blood, that for the fulfilment of the mystery of unity, we may receive of his that which he received of ours." [2]

In pursuance of this decree, it was ordered that all churches should be furnished with a cabinet or cupboard, in which to keep the consecrated host not used; hence the use of pixes began. Heretofore the surplus bread and wine

---

[1] Neander's Church History, vol. vii. p. 466. London, 1852.

[2] "Una vero est fidelium universalis ecclesia, extra quam nullus omnino salvatur. In qua idem ipse sacerdos et sacrificium Jesus Christus: cujus corpus et sanguis in sacramento altaris sub speciebus panis et vini veraciter continentur; transubstantiatis, pane in corpus, vino in sanguinem, potestate divinâ, ut ad perficiendum mysterium unitatis accipiamus ipsi de suo quod accepit de nostro." Labb. Concl. tom. xi. p. 143. Paris, 1671.

were either given away or burned. The host is supposed to be very God. "We command (said Innocent) that in all churches the eucharist be kept under lock and key, that it may not be touched by sacrilegious hand." Arnobius, a Christian writer of the third century, ridiculed the pagans for locking up their gods for a similar reason:—"Why keep you them locked up? Is it for fear thieves should take them away by night? If you are assured they are gods, leave to them the care of keeping themselves; leave their temples always open." [1]

A.D. 1217.—Honorius III. instituted the elevation and adoration of the host.[2] Fleury expressly states that the custom of elevating the host before the consecration of the chalice was not in use until the commencement of this century.[3] The early Christian writers repeatedly and most fully describe the way and manner of receiving the sacrament, but we find no mention whatever of the elevation or adoration of the Host. Further, "From the oldest liturgies, and the eucharistic forms in them, it appears that there was no such adoration given to the sacrament till of late, for in none of them is there any such mention, either by the priest or the people, as in the Roman missal or ritual, nor any such forms of prayer added to it, as in their breviary. Cassander, a learned Roman Catholic divine, who died A.D. 1566,[4] has collected together most of the old liturgies, and

---

[1] Arnob. Notitia Literaria, lib. vi. vol. i. Edit. Lips. 1816.
[2] "Sacerdos quilibet frequenter doceat plebem suam ut cum in celebratione missarium elevatur hostia salutaris, quilibet reverenter inclinet." See Raynaldus ad an. 1219. These words are in Honorius' Epistle to the Latin bishops of the patriarchate of Antioch, A.D. 1219.
[3] .. "Cette question n'auroit pas eu lieu si l'usage eût été dès lors d'adorer et élever l'hostie avant la consécration du calice: aussi n'ai-je trouvé jusqu'ici aucun vestige de cette cérémonie." Fleury, Eccl. Hist. vol. xv. liv. 74, p. 663, Paris, 1719; and tom. xv. p. 580. Paris, 1769.
[4] Cassandri Liturgic. oper. p. 10, etc. Paris, 1616.

endeavours, as far as he can, to show their agreement with that of the Roman church; but neither in the old Greek, nor in the old Latin ones, is there any instance to be produced of the priest's or the people's adoring the sacrament, as soon as he had consecrated it. Notwithstanding the elevation and adoration being one of the most prominent features of the modern Roman service, this last was added or brought into the Roman liturgy after the doctrine of transubstantiation was established in that church, which has produced a consequent alteration, not only in their liturgy, but even their religion in good part, and made a new sort of worship, unknown, not only in the first and best times of the church, but for above a thousand years after Christ." [1]

It should be noted that Cardinal Guido seems not to have contemplated an adoration of the host, but that on the elevation the people should pray for pardon.[2]

The ritualists Bona, Merati, Benedict XIV., Le Brun, etc., acknowledge that there is no trace of the custom of the elevation of the host, before the eleventh or twelfth century, in the West.[3]

The elevation of the host appears to have been first introduced into the diocese of Paris about A.D. 1200, by Odo de Sulli, bishop of Paris;[4] and even so late as A.D. 1536,

---

[1] See Gibson's Preservative against Popery, new Edition, p. 141, vol. x. London, 1848, and where the places alleged by Romanists out of the early Christian writers in support of the custom are examined and explained.

[2] "Bonam illic consuetudinem instituit, ut ad elevationem hostiæ omnis populus in ecclesia ad sonitum notæ veniam peteret, sicque usque ad calicis benedictionem protratus jaceret." Raynaldus, an. 1203.

[3] Bona, Rer. Liturgic. lib. ii. c. 12.—Gavanti Thesaurus a Merati—Lambertinus, de Missa, p. 115. Le Brun. Cérémonies de la Messe. tom. i. p. 469, etc. (See Palmer's Treaties of the Church of Christ, vol. i. p. 240. London, 1842.)

[4] Harduini Concilia, tom. xi. p. 1945.

the synod of Cologne explained that the people should on the elevation of the host remember the Lord's death, and return him thanks with minds raised to heaven.[1]

The veneration or adoration of the host itself was not actually enjoined until 1551, by the sixth canon of the thirteenth session of the Council of Trent. The fifth chapter declares that there is no room left for doubting that all the faithful of Christ, "according to the custom ever received in the Catholic church, exhibit in veneration the worship of Latria, which is the supreme worship due to God, to the sacrament." And the sixth canon anathematizes those who deny that the eucharist "is not to be proposed publicly to the people to be worshipped."

The custom of worshipping or praying before the elevated host, as before explained, was easily converted into an actual worship of the elements as Christ, but no fixed date can be assigned to the transition. That the elements themselves, however, were worshipped before the passing of this canon, is evident. Fisher, the Romish bishop of Rochester, A.D. 1504, said that if there was nothing more in the eucharist but bread, then the whole church for sixteen centuries had committed idolatry, for during all this time people must have been worshipping the creature in the place of the Creator.[2] We cannot, however, trace any record of the fact that the host was worshipped by the people under the sup-

---

[1] "Post elevationem consecrati corporis ac sanguinis Domini .... ab omni populo mortis Dominicæ commemoratio habenda, prostratisque humi corporibus, animis in cœlum erectis, gratiæ agendæ Christo Redemptori, qui nos sanguine suo lavit morteque redemit." Synod. Colon. an. 1536, pars. ii. can. 14, Lab. tom. xiv. Paris, 1671.
[2] "Nulli dubium esse potest, si nihil in eucharistia præter panem sit, quin tota ecclesia jam xv. annos centenarios, idololatria fuerit; ac, provide, quotquot ante nos hoc sacramento tum adoraverunt, omnes ad unum esse damnatos: nam creaturam panis adoraverint Creatoris loco." Fisher, Roffens. cont. Œcolamp. oper. p. 760. Wirceburg, 1597.

position of Christ's presence therein before Durand, bishop of Mende, who mentioned it A.D. 1286.[1] John Daille, a faithful and diligent searcher of antiquity, says that he could not find "among the interpreters of ecclesiastical offices in the Latin church, the mention of any sort of elevation before the eleventh century."[2]

A.D. 1229.—The Bible was now, for the first time, forbidden to the laity[3] by the Council of Toulouse. The decree was as follows:—"We forbid also the permitting of the laity to have the books of the Old and New Testament, unless any should wish, from a feeling of devotion, to have a psalter or breviary for Divine service. But we most strictly forbid them to have the above-mentioned books in the vulgar tongue."[4] This council was attended by the legate of the bishop of Rome, three archbishops, and several bishops and other dignitaries.[5]

A.D. 1230.—Gregory IX. added the little bell, to inform the people when to kneel down to adore the host:—

"We are informed by Alberic, in his *Chronicon ad Ann.* 1200, that the Cistercian Abbott, Guido, whom the pope had created a cardinal, and despatched as his legate to Cologne, first introduced this practice at the elevation of the host in the mass, on a signal given by a bell, for the people to prostrate themselves, and to remain in that posture until the benediction of the cup."[6]

---

[1] See his Rationale Divinorum Officium, iv. 41.
[2] Dallæus de Relig. Cult. Object, lib. 2, c. 5. Gen. 1664.
[3] Tom. xvi. p. 633.
[4] "Prohibemus etiam, ne libros Veteris Testamenti aut Novi, laici permittantur habere; nisi forte Psalterium, vel Breviarium pro divinis officiis, aut Horas Beatæ Mariæ, aliquis ex devotione, habere velit. Sed ne præmissos libros babeant in vulgari translatos, arctissimè inbibemus." Lab. et Coss. Concl. tom. xi. part 1, col. 425, Concl. Tolosanum. can. 14. Paris, 1671.
[5] For some useful information on this subject, see Massy's "Secret History of Romanism," pp. 72, 73. London, 1853.
[6] See Mosheim's Eccl. Hist. cent. xii. pt. ii. c. iv. s. ii. p. 423, note 2. Edit. London, 1852.

It appears, however, that William, bishop of Paris, about A.D. 1220, also ordered a bell to be rung at the elevation, that the people might be excited to pray, but not to worship the host.[1]

A.D. 1237.—The anthem Salve Regina was introduced by request of the preaching friars.[2]

A.D. 1238.—The patriarch of Antioch excommunicated Gregory IX., and the whole Roman church, as being stained with a constant course of simony, usury, and all kinds of crimes.[3]

A.D. 1245.—The Council of Lyons ordered that cardinals should wear red hats and scarlet cloaks, "to show the readiness with which they are prepared to shed their blood for the liberty of the church." According to Polydore Vergil, Innocent IV. (A.D. 1254), by decree, ordered cardinals to wear the red hat, and Paul II. (A.D. 1464), the scarlet robes.[4]

A.D. 1264.—Urban IV., upon the pretended revelation of a nun, instituted the festival of Corpus Christi (known in France as the Fête Dieu) and its octaves. The institution was confirmed under Clement V., at a council held at Vienna in 1311.[5] Thomas Aquinas composed the office.

The following is from Canon Wordsworth's "Tour in Italy:"—

"The history of the institution of this festival is very significant. In the thirteenth century (A.D. 1262), a time of

---

[1] "Præcipitur quod in celebratione missarum quando corpus Christi elevatur, in ipsa elevatione, vel paulo ante, campana pulsetur, sicut alias fuit statutum, ut sic mentes fidelium ad orationem excitentur." Bini. Concilia, tom. vii. pars. i. p. 536. Paris, 1636.
[2] Fleury, xvii. p. 204. Paris, 1769.
[3] Ibid. p. 225.
[4] Polydore Vergil de Invent. rer. b. iv. c. vi. p. 90. London, 1551.
[5] See Mosheim's Eccl. Hist. cent. xiii. pt. ii. c. iv. s. ii. London, 1825. Neander's Church History, vol. vii. p. 474. London, 1852.

moral-corruption and ungodliness, as Roman writers testify, a priest, who did not believe the doctrine of transubstantiation, was celebrating mass at Bolsena, in Tuscany, and saw the host trickle with blood, which is the subject of Raffaelle's frescoes in the Vatican, in the *stanza* of Heliodorus. Pope Urban IV. heard the tidings of the prodigy, and went to Bolsena, and gave orders that the corporal tinged with blood should be carried in procession to the cathedral of Orvieto, where it is still shown. In the year 1230, a holy woman, near Liège, a Cistercian nun, Santa Giuliana, had a vision, in which she beheld the moon, which, although full, seemed to have a portion of it broken off; and when she asked what was the meaning of this fragmentary appearance, she was informed that the moon represented the church, and the gap in it denoted the absence of a great solemnity which was necessary to complete its fulness; and that this solemnity was the festival of Corpus Domini.[1] It was revealed as the Divine will that a certain day in every year should be set apart for the veneration of the holy sacrament. The bishop of Liège adopted the suggestion, and it was confirmed by the apostolic legate in Belgium. Pope Urban IV., being stimulated by what had occurred in Bolsena, and desirous of providing a perpetual protest against the doctrines of Berengarius, which were then rife, carried the matter further, and decreed that the festival of the 'Corpus Domini' should be celebrated every year on the Thursday after the octave of Whit Sunday, and he gave a commission to the celebrated Thomas Aquinas (the doctor Angelicus), then at

[1] This account of the origin of the festival may be seen in a work now in the 13th edition, by Dom. Giuseppe Riva, Penitentiary of the Cathedral of Milan, A.D. 1862, p. 300.

Rome, to compose a suitable religious office for the occasion." The annual observance of the festival has received additional sanction from the Council of Trent in 1551.[1]

Thomas Aquinas likewise invented the theory of works of supererogation and celestial treasure (as explained in the chapter on Indulgences), being the supposed superabundant merits of Christ and the Saints, placed at the disposal of the pope, to be issued out by him by way of Indulgences.[2]

THE FOURTEENTH CENTURY.

A.D. 1300.—Boniface VIII. instituted the first jubilee, and ordered by bull that it should in future be solemnized once in every 100 years. This period was subsequently abridged by successive popes, as stated in the chapter on Indulgences.

Polydore Vergil says that Boniface " assigned the years according to the old feasts of Apollo and Diana, which the Roman heathens solemnized every 100 years, and that they were called 'Ludi seculares.'" These jubilees, he testifies, included " a clean remission, *a pœnâ et culpâ*, as well from the punishment as from the sin itself."[3] Cardinal Parie, referring to the jubilee, in a letter to Pope Paul II., designates it as an imitation of the " early superstition."[4]

Henry Cornelius Agrippa said that "the power of

---

[1] Sess. xiii. cap. 5.
[2] Mosheim's Eccl. Hist. cent. xii. pt. ii. c. iii. s. iii. London, 1825.
[3] B. viii. c. i. p. 144. London, 1551.
[4] "Antiquæ vanitates." See Picard's "Cérémonies et Coûtumes Religieuses," tom. i. pt. ii. p. 168. Amsterdam, 1723.

granting indulgences, extending to souls in purgatory, was first decreed by Boniface VIII."[1]

A.D. 1317.—John XXII. published what are called the Clementine Constitutions.

The same pope ordered the Ave Maria, or the words addressed by the angel Gabriel to the blessed Virgin, to be added to the prayers of Christians.

A.D. 1360.—The procession, or carrying about of the host under a canopy, was first instituted. Virgil, in his first book of the Georgics, refers to the custom of the yearly celebration of the feast of Ceres, directing the farmers to accompany the *hostia*, when carried in procession :—

"—— Annua magnæ sacra refer Cereri.
* * * * *
Terque novas circum felix eat Hostia fruges."—
B. i. 338—345.

And Ovid tells us that those who followed carried lighted tapers, and were clothed in white. And so does the Romish ritual direct "that the priest who carries it be covered with a white cope, and that all who accompany him have lighted tapers in their hands."

The Pastophoræ (initiated women in the religious processions of the ancient Egyptians) carried the god Horus in a box (pix) before them, and at stated intervals fell on their knees, and offered the idol to the adoration of the multitude. May not this have been the origin of the custom in the Latin church of carrying the wafer in a box,

---

[1] De Incertitudine et vanitate scientiarum atque artium, c. 61, p. 115. Lugd. *s.a.* [1531]. Agrippa was a physician, philosopher, and divine. He died 1535. An English translation of this book was published in London, 1684, 8vo.

with considerable ceremony, attended as it is with the adoration of the "multitude" in Romish countries?

The language of Clemens Alexandrinus [1] (who mentions the Pastophoræ [2]), with respect to the removing the veil of the box, and the directions in the Canon Missæ, are curiously similar. The words of the mass-book would seem to be almost a translation of the ὀλίγον ἐπαναστείλας τοῦ καταπετασματος, ὡς δείξων τὸν θεὸν, referred to by Clemens.

A.D. 1362.—Urban V. was the first pope who wore the triple crown. The Triregne, as the Italians call it, seems to have been of an early date, so far back, it is stated (but on no sufficient authority), as the time of Clovis the first Christian king, who sent one to Hormisdas, bishop of Rome (A.D. 520), as a pledge that he owed his kingdom, not to his sword, but to God. But this gift was not to the bishop, but to the apostle Peter alone: the crown was to be suspended before the altar, where the relics of the apostle were supposed to be deposited. The first bishop of Rome mentioned in history who was crowned, was Damasus II. Before Bishop Mark (A.D. 335) no trace exists of evidence that bishops of Rome wore any sort of crown, except what was called the martyr's crown. According to some writers, up to the time of Boniface VIII. (A.D. 1294), bishops of Rome wore a tiara closed at the top. This bishop added to this a second. The triple crown was ordered to be carried in procession, as a mark of the assumed triple jurisdiction of the bishop of Rome over the universe.[3]

[1] See the Greek Thesaurus of Stephens, Valpy's Edition, vol. i. p. clxxxiii.
[2] Pæd. 3, 2.
[3] See Picard's "Cérémonies et Coûtumes Religieuses," vol. i. pt. ii. pp. 50—52, notes *h* and *a*. Amsterdam, 1723.

A.D. 1366.—Urban V. was the first who sent to Joanna, queen of Sicily, a rose of gold in Lent, and decreed the consecration of a like toy every year upon Lent Sunday. The custom is still retained.

A.D. 1390.—The historian Platina, and Polydore Vergil, say that Boniface IX. was the first who sold Indulgences, and made merchandise of them. Polydore Vergil[1] said— "Who was the first author of them (indulgences)? I have not read in any writer, saving that Gregory proclaimed pardons as a reward of those who came to his stations. This seed sown by Gregory grew to a ripe harvest in the time of Boniface IX., who reaped the money for that chaff. For what cause, or by what authority, indulgences were first introduced into the church, has given modern divines a great deal of trouble. In a subject which is by no means clear, I think it better to use the testimony of John, bishop of Rochester [Bishop Fisher, A.D. 1504],[2] in a work he wrote against Luther. 'Many persons,' saith he, 'are inclined to place but little reliance upon indulgences, because their use seems to have come in rather late in the church.' And then he adds — 'No orthodox [Roman Catholic] doubts whether there is purgatory, concerning which, nevertheless, *there is either no mention, or the very rarest mention in ancient writers*. To this day, purgatory is not believed in by the Greek church. As long, then, as there was no anxiety concerning purgatory, no one looked for indulgences; for all the value of indulgences depends upon it. If you take away purgatory, what use will

---

[1] B. viii. c. i. p. 144. London, 1551, and p. 476. Amstel, 1671.

[2] The passage from Fisher is as follows: "Quandiu nulla fuerat de purgatorio cura, nemo quæsivit indulgentias. Nam ex illo pendet omnis indulgentiarum æstimationis; cœperunt igitur indulgentiæ, postquam ad purgatorii cruciatus aliquando trepidatum erat." Roffens. art. 18, contra Lutherum, fol. 132. Colon. 1624.

there be in indulgences? Indulgences, therefore, began when people began to entertain fears about the torments of purgatory.' These things saith the Bishop Fisher; but you, my reader, may perhaps think the subject of so great importance, that you might expect more certainty in the matter from the mouth of God."

THE FIFTEENTH CENTURY.

A.D. 1414.—It was at the Council of Constance that the laity were first, by authority of the church of Rome, deprived of the cup at the Lord's Supper. The decree admits that Christ's ordinance was in both kinds, and that the custom in the primitive church in this respect was to give both the elements to the people, "notwithstanding which" it decreed that the laity should be deprived of the cup.[1] Previous to this date, and from 1220, when the adoration of the host was instituted, the custom was introduced and partially adopted, but not universally admitted by the church of Rome.

A.D. 1438.—Though not strictly within the plan of this work, we cannot omit to record the stand made by the Gallican church against the usurpation of Rome. The

---

1 ..Hinc est, quod hoc præsens concilium sacrum generale Constantiense, in Spiritu Sancto, etc.; declarat, discernit, et diffinit, quod, licet Christus post cœnam instituerit, et suis discipulis administravit sub utraque specie panis et vini, hoc venerabile sacramentum, tamen, hoc non obstante, etc..... Et sicut consuetudo hæc ad evitandum aliqua pericula et scandala est rationabiliter introducta, quod, licet in primitiva ecclesia hujusmodi sacramentum a fidelibus sub utraque specie reciperetur; postea, etc. Labb. et Coss. Concilia, tom. xii. col. 99. Paris, 1672. See *ante*, A.D. 1095, p. 230.

Council of Bourges,[1] convoked by Charles VII., who presided, drew up the decree, containing twenty-three articles, which formed the basis of what was called the Pragmatic Sanction, when confirmed by the French Parliament, 13th July, 1439. These constitutions, which were called the rampart of the Gallican church, took away from the popes most of the power they possessed of presenting to benefices and of judging in ecclesiastical causes within the kingdom; and this independent power was retained until the concordat with Rome, made between Leo X. and King Francis I., at Bologna. The pragmatic sanction was abrogated by the pope's bull at the eleventh session of the Lateran Council, A.D. 1516.[2]

A.D. 1439.—The Council of Florence was the first council that authoritatively declared the sacraments to be seven in number.[3] This doctrine received final sanction, at a later date, at Trent.

At this Council of Florence, departed saints were, for the first time, authoritatively declared to be in a state of beatitude; and therefore now, for the first time, according to Romish theory, could be properly and lawfully invocated. The doctrine cannot bear an anterior date.[4]

Purgatory now first received the approval of a conciliar decree, but was finally confirmed at the Trent Council. The decree is as follows:—

"In the name, then, of the Holy Trinity, Father, Son, and

---

[1] Labb. et Coss. tom. xii. col. 1429. Paris, 1672.

[2] Ibid. tom. xiv. Concl. Lat. (A.D. 1512), Sess. xi. A.D. 1516. And see L'Hist. de la Prag. S. et Concordat, par Pitbon.

[3] Novæ legis septem sunt sacramenta; videlicet, baptismus, confirmatio, eucharistia, pœnitentia, extrema unctio, ordio, et matrimonium. Decretum Concl. Florent, Lab. Concilia, tom. xiii. col. 534. Paris, 1672.

[4] For the authorities, see *ante*, p. 66, the citation from Veron; p. 75, from Stapleton; and p. 99, from the Benedictine Editors of Ambrose's Works.

Holy Ghost, with the approbation of this sacred General Council of Florence, we decree also that if any true penitents shall depart this life in the love of God, before they have made satisfaction, by worthy fruits of penance, for faults of commission and omission, their souls are purified after death by the pains of purgatory; and that for their release from their pains, the suffrages of the faithful who are alive are profitable to them, to wit, the sacrifices of masses, prayers, and alms, and other works of piety which, according to the appointment of the church, are wont to be made for the faithful for other believers."[1]

We may affirm, as a fact, that the belief in A.D. 1146 was only in progression, or in process of "development;" for at this date Otho Frisigensis refers to the belief thus—"Some do affirm that there is a place of purgatory after death."[2] The doctrine was not accepted by the Greeks.[3]

The primacy of the bishop of Rome and the precedency of his see was now first defined by a so-called General Council, namely, that of Florence, held under Eugenius IV. It was thus defined at its tenth session:—

"Also we decree that the holy apostolical see and the Roman pontiff has a primacy over the whole world; and that the Roman pontiff himself is the successor of St. Peter, the prince of the apostles, and is the true vicar of Christ, and head of the whole church, and the father and teacher of all Christians; and that to him, in the person of the blessed Peter, our Lord Jesus

[1] Session xxv. In nomine igitur Sancte Trinitatis, Patris et Filii et Spiritus Sancti, hoc sacro universali approbantur Florentino Concilio: diffinimus, item, si vere pœnitentes in Dei caritate desesserint, antequam dignis pœnitentiæ fructibus de commissis satisfecerint; et omissis, eorum animas pœnis purgatoriis, post mortem purgari et ut a pœnis hujusmodi releventur, prodesse eis fidelium vivorum suffragia; missarum scilicet sacrificia, orationes et elemosynas, et alia pietatis officia, quæ a fidelibus pro aliis fidelibus fieri consueverunt, secundum ecclesiæ instituta. Lab. Conc. tom. xiii. p. 515. Paris, 1671.
[2] Chron. lib. viii. c. 26, quoted by Jeremy Taylor, "Dissuasive from Popery," c. i. s. ix. Heber's Edition, vol. x. p. 149.
[3] See *ante*, p. 104.

Christ has committed full power to feed, rule, and govern the universal church, according as is contained in the acts of general councils and in the holy canons."[1]

This declaration is ranked by Benedict XIV. in his bull dated 1742, as an "article of Catholic faith."[2]

The "acts of the General Council" and "holy canons" above referred to are mere inventions. They probably relied on the forged decretal epistles which had been embodied in the canon law.

The Greek empire was now drawing near its fall. The Emperor Palæologus, with some Greek bishops, attended this council, in the hope of obtaining aid against the Turks, and were weak enough to be prevailed upon to subscribe the above decree. But when the Greek deputies returned to Constantinople, the church there indignantly rejected all that had been done by the Greek bishops at this council; and in a council at Constantinople, held about eighteen months after the termination of the Council of Florence, the decrees of that council were declared null, and the synod itself condemned.[3] Gregory, the patriarch of Constantinople, who was inclined to the Latins, was deposed, and Athanasius chosen in his stead. The patriarchs of Alexandria, Antioch, Jerusalem, and the chief of the old patriarchs of Ephesus, Heraclea, and Cæsarea were all present at this latter council, and all concurred in the condemnation of the decrees of the Florentine Council.

[1] Lab. Concilia, tom. xiii. Concl. Florent. Sess. ⅄. col. 154, *et seq.* Paris, 1671.
[2] Bened. XIV. Bullar. tom. i. No. I. de Dog. et Ritib. sec. i. de Fide Cathol. p. 345. Mechlin, 1826.
[3] "Ἐπειδὴ ἄρα πανουργίαις καὶ φενακισμοῖς καὶ ἀνάγκαις καὶ μὴ ἐξετάσει ἀληθείας τὰ τῆς ψευδοσυνόδου ἐκείνης πέρας ἔλαβε, καὶ παρὰ τὴν ἡμετέραν διάνοιαν, ἄκυρον τὸ ἐπιτροπικὸν μενέτω."—Labb. et Coss. Concil conc. Constantin. sess. 2, tom. xiii. col. 1367. Paris, 1672.

The title "Mother Church" was not then assumed. Hitherto the title, Vicar of Christ, was a common appellation, as applied to bishops generally. The Council of Florence decreed that the title should be given to the bishop of Rome, "reserving the rights of the bishop of Constantinople." The title, however, is now assumed by the pope of Rome exclusively.

A.D. 1470.—Alane de la Roche, of the order of Jacobins, inspired, as he said, by certain visions, invented the Rosary of the Virgin Mary, subsequently authoritatively approved by Sixtus IV. Mosheim, however, places the invention of this ecclesiastical toy at an earlier date, namely, the tenth century.[1] It is a string of beads used in prayers. The same prayer is repeated a prescribed number of times, and this number is checked by the beads, every tenth bead being a large one. The word *rosary* means *remembrancer*. It appears to be derived from the Chaldee *Ro*, "thought," and *Shareb*, "director." The idea, as well as the thing itself, is of pagan origin. A certain number of prayers, it is supposed, must be gone through, and the beads bring the number in *remembrance*. A string of beads for the same purpose was used by the ancient Mexicans.[2] It is common among the Brahmins and Hindoos.[3] In Thibet it has been used in religious worship from time immemorial. Among the Tartars, the rosary of 108 beads has become a part of ceremonial dress, and there is "a small rosary of eighteen beads of inferior size, with which the Bonzes count their prayers and ejaculations, exactly as in the

---

[1] Mosheim's Eccl. Hist. cent. x. part ii. c. iv. s. iii. See Mabillon, Acta sanctor. Ord. Bened. Præf ad sæcul. x. p. lviii. etc.
[2] See Humboldt's "Mexican Researches," v. ii. p. 20. London, 1814.
[3] See Kennedy's "Ancient and Hindoo Mythology," p. 332. London, 1831.

Romish ritual."[1] So that this Romish custom, though a *novelty* among Christians, is an old heathen or pagan custom.

A.D. 1476.—Pope Sixtus IV. was the first who ordained by decree the solemnization of the feast of the Immaculate Conception of the Virgin Mary by an office or service, though it was not then a doctrine of the church.

The festival of the conception of the Virgin Mary was, as we have said, introduced at Lyons about the year 1140, but was opposed by Bernard (now a canonized saint of the Roman church) as a novelty, without the sanction of Scripture or reason. Bernard said that it was a "false, new, vain, and superstitious" idea.[2] According to Fleury, it was John Scott, commonly called Duns Scotus, at the beginning of the fourteenth century, who seriously broached the doctrine of the immaculate conception.[3]

At the thirty-sixth session of the Council of Basle, A.D. 1439—a council condemned and rejected by the church of Rome—it was declared that the doctrine which asserts that the Virgin Mary was actually subject to original sin, should be condemned; but that the doctrine that she was always free from all original and actual sin, and both holy and immaculate, should be approved, and should be held and embraced by all Catholics as being pious and agreeable to ecclesiastical worship, to the Catholic faith, to right reason, and the Scriptures, and that it should not be lawful for any one to teach or preach to the contrary.[4]

---

[1] Sir John F. Davis, "China," vol. i. p. 391. London, 1857.
[2] Fleury's Eccl. Hist. tom. xiv. lib. lxviii. p. 527. Paris, 1769, and 560, tom. xiv. Paris, 1727. "Nulla ei ratione placebit contra ecclesiæ ritum præsumpta novitas, mater temeritatis, soror superstitionis, filia levitatis." S. Bernard, Ep. 174, tom. i. col. 393. Paris, 1839, and see *ante*, p. 231.
[3] Eccl. Hist. tom. xix. p. 150. Paris, 1769.
[4] Lab. et Coss. Concl. tom. xii. cols. 622, 623. Paris, 1671.

The festival was directed to be celebrated on the 17th December. The Council of Avignon, A.D. 1457, confirmed this act of the Council of Basle, and forbade, under pain of excommunication, any one to preach anything contrary to the doctrine.[1]

The doctrine created a sore division in the church of Rome. The Dominicans following their leader, St. Thomas Aquinas, combated the new dogma most vehemently, as contrary to the Scriptures, tradition, and the faith of the church; while it was as vehemently supported by the Franciscans. The scandal became so great at each returning festival day, that Sixtus IV. (A.D. 1483) issued a bull, wherein he, of his own accord, and unsolicited, condemned those who called the doctrine a heresy, the celebration of the festival a sin, or declared that those who held the doctrine were guilty of mortal sin, and subjected those to excommunication who acted contrary to this decree. By the same bull he enacted the like penalty against those who maintained the opponents of the doctrine to be in heresy or mortal sin, declaring as a reason that "this doctrine had not yet been decided by the Roman church and the apostolic see."[2] Despite this pope's bull, the discord continued, to the great scandal of religion; and when the doctrine of "original sin" came to be argued at the Council of Trent, the Dominicans and Franciscans ranged themselves on opposite sides and re-fought the battle. The debate became so warm, that the pope ordered, through his legates, that the council should "not meddle in this matter, which might cause a schism among Catholics, but endeavour to

---

[1] Lab. et Coss. tom. xiii. col. 1403. Paris, 1671.
[2] This decree is found in the appendix of every authorized edition of the Decrees of the Council of Trent.

maintain peace between the contending parties, and to seek some means of giving them equal satisfaction; but, above all, to observe the brief of Pope Sixtus IV., which prohibited preachers from taxing the doctrine [of the immaculate conception] with heresy.[1]

The Council of Trent (A.D. 1546) expressly excluded from its decree on original sin the Virgin Mary; but declared "that the constitutions of Pope Sixtus IV., which it revives, are to be observed under the penalties contained in those constitutions." Thus, both parties claimed the victory. The theological contest raged as violently as ever. In the seventeenth century, Spain was thrown into the utmost confusion by these miserable disputes; and it was sought to bring them to a close by an appeal to the supposed infallible head of the church, who was asked to issue his bull to determine the question. "But (observes Mosheim) after the most earnest entreaties and importunities, all that could be obtained from the pontiff by the court of Spain was a declaration intimating that the opinion of the Franciscans had a high degree of probability on its side, and forbidding the Dominicans to oppose it in a public manner; but this declaration was accompanied by another, by which the Franciscans were prohibited in turn from treating as erroneous the doctrine of the Dominicans."[2]

Alexander VII., A.D. 1661, while reviving the constitution of Sixtus IV., vainly endeavoured to allay the feud; but admitted that the church had not decided the vexed question, and that he by no means desired or intended to decide it.[3]

[1] F. Paul Sarpi. Hist. Concl. Trid. lib. ii. c. 68. Geneva, 1629.
[2] Mosheim's Eccl. Hist. cent. xvii. sec. ii. part l. c. i. s. 48.
[3] Alex. Sept. An. Dom. 1661. "Mag. Bull. Romanum," tom. vi. p. 158. Edit. Luxumburghi, 1727.

Clement XI. appointed a festival in honour of the immaculate conception, to be annually celebrated by the church of Rome; but the Dominicans refused to obey this law.

Eventually Pope Pius IX. undertook to decide, as he thought, for ever, the much vexed question. On the 2nd February, 1849, he issued an "Encyclical Letter," addressed to all "patriarchs, primates, archbishops, and bishops of the whole Catholic world," exhorting each one to offer up prayers in his diocese, beseeching " of the merciful Father of light to illuminate him (the pope) with the superior brightness of his Divine Spirit, and inspire him with a breath from on high, and that, in an affair of such great importance, he might be able to take such a resolution as should most contribute as well to the glory of His holy name as to the praise of the blessed Virgin and the profit of the church militant," and desired to know their opinions on the subject. On the 24th March following, the *Tablet*, a Romish journal, announced that the pope was about to give a definitive decision on the subject, and "determine a question which for 500 years had been open, and for a portion of that time hotly debated to and fro. The Franciscans and Dominicans are now agreed, and the whole [Roman] Catholic world calls for a definite sentence from the infallible judge."

In December, 1854, the pope, in an assembly of bishops, from which all non-contents were excluded, issued his bull, declaring the doctrine as a matter of faith.[1] "Let no man (says the decree) interfere with this our declaration, pronunciation, and definition, or oppose or contradict it with presumptuous rashness. If any should presume to assail

[1] The "Univers," Paris, 20th January, 1855; the "Tablet," London, 27th January, 1855.

it, let him know that he will incur the indignation of the Omnipotent God, and of his blessed apostles Peter and Paul." Hence the *Tablet* observed, that " whosoever should thenceforth deny that the blessed Virgin was herself, by a miraculous interposition of God's providence, conceived without the stain of original sin, is to be condemned as a heretic."

Such is a brief history of the doctrine of the immaculate conception; but it is a popular fallacy to suppose that it is a doctrine of the Roman church. The pope of Rome, according to the orthodox principles of that church, cannot create doctrines of faith which have not emanated from a General Council of the church.

A.D. 1478.—The Inquisition was established in the kingdom of Castile, under Ferdinand and Isabella. We note the fact because this was an ecclesiastical institution. Fleury expressly says that it was done " by the counsel of the archbishop of Seville, and by the authority of Pope Sixtus IV."[1]

We may trace the beginning of the institution to an earlier date. At the Council of Verona, A.D. 1184, Pope Lucius III. published a constitution against alleged heretics, wherein bishops were ordered, by means of commissaries, to inform themselves of persons suspected of heresy, whether by common report or private information. Should spiritual terrors be of no avail, the offender was to be handed over to the secular power, in order that temporal punishment might be inflicted.[2] The Council of Toulouse, A.D. 1229, formally established local Inquisitions.

At the Council of Narbonne, A.D. 1235,[3] a series of

---

[1] Fleury, Eccl. Hist. Cont. tom. xxiii. p. 478. Paris, 1769.
[2] Lab. et Coss. Concl. tom. x. cols. 1737 and 1741. Paris, 1671.
[3] Ibid. tom. xi. col. 487.

oppressive and cruel regulations against alleged heretics was drawn up by the pope's command; and at the Council of Beziers, A.D. 1247, the Preaching Friars' Inquisition for the provinces of Aix, Arles, and Ebrum was established also by order of the pope. Forty-seven articles were drawn up, which, with those passed at the Council of Narbonne, formed the foundation of the rules afterwards adopted by the Inquisition.[1]

A.D. 1495.—Alexander VI. assumed a new power, namely, that of granting a dispensation to marry within a prohibited degree. He gave a dispensation to Ferdinand, the king of Naples, to marry his own niece, who was of the age of fourteen years.[2]

THE SIXTEENTH CENTURY.

A.D. 1515-17.—In these years took place the grand sale of indulgences by Pope Leo X., which was one of the immediate causes of the Reformation. This method was adopted to replenish his coffers, which were exhausted by his prodigality, or rather his extravagances; and also to complete the church of St. Peter, begun by Julius II. Fleury informs us that Leo granted indulgences on "such easy conditions, that men could hardly care at all for their salvation if they refused to gain them."[3]

A.D. 1540.—The order of the Jesuits was founded by Ignatius Loyola. Loyola was born A.D. 1491, in the pro-

---

[1] Lab. et Coss. tom. xi. col. 676.
[2] Fleury, cont. tom. xxiv. p. 226. Paris, 1769.
[3] Ibid. tom. xxv. pp. 497, 498.

vince of Guipuscoa, in Spain. He was educated for the army, but, in process of time, left the service, and entered the church. He died July, 1556. The order was confirmed by Paul III., first with limitations, and subsequently without any restrictions.

A.D. 1545.—The Council of Trent assembled, which collected in one mass former errors and superstitions, and confirmed them by conciliar decree.

A.D. 1546.—Tradition was first placed on a level with the Holy Scriptures. The doctrine is essential to the existence of the Roman system, for, under the cloak of tradition, all her innovations are attempted to be supported. They declare Scripture to be insufficient, hence the absolute necessity for tradition.

If there was one subject more than another on which the early Christian fathers especially insisted, it was the sufficiency and completeness of Scripture as a rule of faith, and the only rule, and was so held in the Roman church up to this time. Take an eminent cardinal of that church, who lived at the end of the fifteenth century. Gabriel Biel affirmed that "the Scripture alone teaches all things necessary to salvation," and instances "in the things to be done and to be avoided, to be loved and to be despised, to be believed and to be hoped for." "The will of God is to be understood by the Scriptures, and by them alone we know the whole will of God."[1] There was no room left for tradition.

The Apocryphal Books[2] were for the first time autho-

---

[1] "Et cætera nostræ saluti necessaria, quæ omnia sola docet sacra Scriptura."—"Hæc autem in sacris Scripturis discuntur, per quas solus plenam intelligere possumus Dei voluntatem." Lection. in Canon. Missæ, fo. cxlvi. p. 1, col. 2. Lugd. 1511.

[2] See *ante*, Cap. III.

ritatively recognised as part of the sacred canon of Scripture.

In June, 1546, the Council of Trent, at its fourth session, occupied itself in defining what was the doctrine of the church on the subject of original sin, justification, good works, and merit. The various opinions held by members of the Romish church up to this date render it certain that the doctrine, on any of those points, was not fixed. It is true that the priesthood, from sordid and corrupt motives, had for many years preached up merit and good works as a cause of salvation, to the almost entire exclusion of grace and faith; but still many taught the true doctrine of justification by faith. This council conveyed its opinion under different heads, embodied in sixteen chapters and thirty-three decrees, accompanied by as many anathemas, or curses, if not accepted. These decrees, however, were not passed without much unseemly brawling. The Franciscans and Dominicans were, as usual, at daggers drawn. Two venerable prelates showed their zeal in maintaining their private opinions by coming to blows, and tugging at each other's beards;[1] and Charles V. threatened to throw them all into the Adige if they could not behave better. The opinions being so various, it was necessary to frame the decrees ambiguously; and so completely had the council succeeded in mystifying the subject, that no sooner had the council ended, than Dominic à Soto, who took a leading part in the debates, published a book on justification, which was answered by Andreas Vega, who had opposed his views at the council: and each claimed the authority of the same

---

[1] "Tum vero Cavensis ut mos est, iracundiâ quam ultum ibat.—Nam in Chironensis barbam injectâ manu, multos ex eâ pilos avulsit, et confestim abscessit."—Card. Pallavicini's Hist. Concil. Trid. tom. i. p. 277. Aug. Vind. 1775.

council in support of his particular views. These discussions and debates, between different sects, continued in the Romish church for a long time after this council. We may safely assert that, previous to June, 1546, the doctrine on these subjects was not defined by the Roman church. There are, however, two points most clearly defined by this council. First, by the twenty-fourth canon on justification, he is anathematized who says that good works are the "fruits and signs of justification received, and not the cause of its increase." And second, "If any shall say the good works of a justified man are in such sort the gifts of God as not to be also the merit of the justified person; or that the justified do not really merit increase of grace and eternal life," they are equally cursed.[1] It was a great Scriptural truth uttered by St. Augustine, when he said that "all our good merits are only wrought in us by grace; and when God crowns our merits, he crowns nothing else but his own gifts."[2] So repugnant, however, was this sentiment to the interests of a corrupt and sordid church, that the passage was ordered to be expunged from his works.[3]

A.D. 1547.—The necessity of the priest's intention to give validity to a sacrament was first decreed at the seventh session of the Council of Trent.[4] The idea was not invented

---

[1] The reader is invited to consult the following texts: 1 Kings viii. 46; Rom. iii. 23; Isaiah liii. 10; Rom. iii. 22; Acts xiii. 39; Eph. ii. 8, 9; Rom. xi. 10; Luke xvii. 10; Psalm cxliii. 2; Tit. iii. 5.

[2] "Omne bonum meritum nostrum, in nobis faciat, et cum Deus coronat merita nostra, nihil aliud coronat quam munera sua."—Aug. ad Sextum. Epist. cv. tom. ii. Edit. Basil, 1529, and also p. 1116, tom. iv. part ii. Paris, 1671.

[3] "Ex Indice Augustini dele. Non merita nostra, sed dona sua Deus coronat nobis." Index Expurgatorius jussu Bernardi de Sandoval et Roxas, Madriti, 1612, et per Turretin, Genevæ, 1619.

[4] "Si quis dixerit, In ministris, dum sacramenta conficiunt et conferunt, non requiri intentionem saltem faciendi quod facit ecclesia; anathema sit." Con. Trid. Sess. VII. Decretum de Sacramentis. in genere. Can. xi. p. 77. Paris, Edit. 1848.

by the Council of Trent, but it formed no part of the doctrine of the Roman church previous to this date, as is evident by the discussions on the subject, and the opposition it received when proposed.[1] It was mentioned in the decree of Eugene at the Council of Florence, 1439.[2] It is certain that for 1200 years no trace whatever of this doctrine can be found in any ecclesiastical writer. The original introduction is attributed to the extreme ignorance of some of the priests, the service being performed in Latin, a language they did not understand; hence their unintentional mutilation of the text, not understanding the words. This gave rise to a discussion among schoolmen, whether a priest who corrupts the sacramental words in pronouncing them celebrated a valid sacrament. The opinions seemed to be that, though the priest knew nothing of what he was saying, yet if the *intention* of doing what the church did was there, it was sufficient. This appears to have been the reasoning of Pope Zachary, in his answer to Boniface,[3] about the ignorance of a priest in Bavaria, who had baptized *in nomine Patria, Filia, et Spiritua Sancta*.[4] Down to the passing of the decree at Trent (March, 1547), declaring the intention of the priest essentially necessary, it appears that all that was required was, that, provided the *intention* existed, the sacrament was valid, though the form of words was incorrect. It is, nevertheless, a fact that the church of Rome now also requires that the *form* should be strictly correct to give validity to the sacrament.

The seven (so-called) sacraments were confirmed, as an

[1] See Introduction to this work.
[2] Lab. et Coss. concl. tom. xiii. col. 535. Paris, 1672.
[3] Avent. Annal. B. l. 3, p. 297. Ingolst. 1554.
[4] See "Gibson's Preservative," vol. viii. p. 208, revised edit. London, 1848.

article of faith, at the same seventh session of the Council of Trent.[1]

This particular number was first advanced by Peter Lombard, bishop of Paris in the twelfth century, as a private opinion.[2] In 1439, the Council of Florence passed a decree on the subject; but this is denied by some to be a General Council, and many after this date disputed on the doctrine, and the matter formed the subject of serious debate, disputes, and bickerings at the seventh session of the Trent Council. The Solons of theology who formed this council sought to support their theory from analogy. They could find no better argument for their new conceit than that the number seven was a mystical number; there were seven virtues, seven capital vices, seven planets, seven defects which came from original sin; the Lord rested the seventh day; there were seven plagues in Egypt, seven candlesticks, etc.; and, therefore, there should be seven sacraments;[3] but Cardinal Bellarmine, perhaps, gives the most conclusive reason why we should adopt this number, simply because the Trent Council so decreed it.[4]

A.D. 1551.—The doctrine of Attrition was defined.[5] Gibson, in his "Preservative from Popery," says that Bishop Canus was the first that broached the doctrine—that

---

[1] "Si quis dixerit, sacramenta novæ legis non fuisse omnia a Jesu Christo, Domino nostro, instituta; aut esse plura vel pauciora quam septem; anathema sit." Conc. Trid. sess. vii. Decretum de Sacramentis, can. i. De sacramen. et genere.

[2] "Non temere quenquam reperies ante Petrum Lombardum qui certum aliquem ac definitum numerum sacramentorum statuerat." Cassauder, Consult. Art. 13, p. 951. Paris, 1616.

[3] *Vide* Father Paul Sarpi's "History of the Council of Trent," lib. iii. cap. 85, vol. i. p. 576. London, 1736.

[4] "Quod testimonium etiam si nullum habemus aliud deberet sufficere." Bell. de effect. Sacr. lib. ii. c. 25, s. 4, tom. iii. p. 109. Edit. Prag. 1721.

[5] At the xiv. Session of the Council of Trent, c. iv. See chapter on "Penance," p. 109, *ante*.

attrition, joined with the sacrament of penance, is sufficient to obtain forgiveness of sins.[1]

A.D. 1552.—At a council held at Edinburgh, by Archbishop Andrews, it was declared that the Lord's prayer might be said to the saints.[2]

A.D. 1563.—The doctrine of purgatory finally confirmed at the twenty-fifth and last session of the Council of Trent.

The Council of Trent passed, on matters of doctrine, fifteen decrees, forty-four chapters, and one hundred and thirteen canons; and it enforced these doctrines by one hundred and twenty-five anathemas or curses. This council was occupied also on internal reformation. On this head it passed one hundred and forty-eight chapters. Its sittings extended over eighteen years. The first session was held in the month of December, 1545, and the last in December, 1563.

A.D. 1564.—Until this date, all those who purely and simply subscribed to the articles of the Nicene Creed were declared members of the church of Christ, inasmuch as no new creed or symbol of faith was proposed to any one for belief as a test of his orthodoxy.

The doctors of the Trent Council, in February, 1546, at the third session, ordained that " the symbol of faith which the holy Roman church makes use of [the Nicene Creed], as being that principle wherein all who profess the faith of Christ must necessarily agree, and that firm and only foundation against which the gates of hell shall never prevail, be

---

[1] Gibson's Preservative, vol. ii. tit. viii. pp. 37, 38, folio edit. London, 1738, and vol. x. p. 235, Edit. 1848, and Melchior Canus de Loc. Theolog. Lovan. 1569. Dist. xiii. de Pœnit. art. vii. Nos. 5, 6.
[2] Bishop Skinner's Eccl. Hist. Scot. vol. ii. p. 39. London, 1788.

expressed in the very same words in which it is read in all the churches." From and after the 9th December of this year, (A.D. 1564) Pope Pius IV., by virtue of his alleged apostolic authority, and according to a resolution of the Trent Council, set forth and published a confession of faith to be received everywhere under penalties enacted by the said council. This new confession of faith consisted of the "symbol of faith" just referred to, with the addition of twelve further articles. From the last-mentioned date, therefore, a new creed was for the first time imposed upon the Christian world, to be accepted under pain of anathema. This creed embraces in a few words a great part of what has gone before; but the following are additional articles of the new faith, then for the first time introduced by this creed. (See Appendix B.)

1. Not only all apostolic and ecclesiastical traditions are to be most steadfastly admitted and embraced, but also "all other observances and constitutions" of the Romish church.

2. At the fourth session of the Council of Trent, it was decreed that no one should dare, in matters of faith and morals, to interpret the Scriptures contrary to the sense which the church hath held or doth hold.[1] Christians were now for the first time compelled to admit the Holy Scriptures according to that sense only which the church has held or does hold—a notable difference, for previously to this date, Christians might reject the interpretation of the church, but were not allowed to advance an interpretation of the Scriptures contrary to the sense of the church.

3. And so, at the same session, no person was allowed to

---

[1] "Contra eum sensum, quem tenuit et tenet sancta mater Ecclesia." Session iv. Decret. de edit. et usu sacr. librorum. "Juxta eum sensum, etc.;" Bulla super forma jura. Prof. fidei, Pii IV.

advance an interpretation of Scripture contrary to the unanimous agreement of the Fathers.[1] But now, for the first time, no Christian was permitted to understand or interpret them except according to the unanimous consent of the Fathers. That is, no interpretation must be given unless the Fathers are unanimous on that interpretation.

4. And now, for the first time, all Christians were to receive and admit, as an article of faith, "all the received and approved ceremonies of the church in the solemn administration" of all the seven sacraments, "and all other things delivered and defined by the sacred canons and Œcumenical Councils;" thus forming the entire code of decrees of councils, including ceremonies, into articles of faith.

5. And lastly, while for many centuries the pope of Rome arrogated to himself the title of "supreme bishop," all were now required, as an article of faith, to recognise the Roman church "as the mother and mistress of all churches," and to "promise obedience to the pope as successor of St. Peter and vicar of Christ." [2]

Thus was this masterpiece of Roman craft and invention consummated in the year of our Lord 1564. Whilst the

---

[1] "Contra unanimem consensum Patrum." Session iv. Ibid. et Sic Synodus in Trullo. c. xix. quam putant Constant. vi. c. Exiit, circa fin. de ver. Sig. in 6.—"Nisi juxta unanimem, etc." Bulla, etc. Pii IV.

[2] "The mother church was the church at Jerusalem, which was in existence long before the church at Rome had any being. At Jerusalem, Jesus Christ himself preached: there the apostles first planted Christianity (Acts i. 4, A.D. 33); and thence was the gospel sent forth to be preached to all nations (Luke xxiv. 47). Therefore, not Rome, but Jerusalem, should claim the presidency, and be 'the mother of all churches.' The church at Samaria was founded next to the church at Jerusalem (Acts viii., A.D. 34); and then the churches at Cyprus and Phenice, and at Antioch, by those Christians who were dispersed in consequence of the persecution which followed the martyrdom of Stephen (Acts xi. 19—21). In short, not a single writer ever affirmed that Rome is 'the mother of all churches.' On the contrary, the majority of the bishops who were convened at the second General Council of Constantinople expressly gave that appellation to Jerusalem, in their letter to Damasus, bishop of the church in Jerusalem, 'which is the mother of all the churches.'" Horne's Popery Delineated. London, 1848, pp. 211, 212.

Apostles were yet living, the evil leaven had begun to work. St. Paul, writing to the Thessalonians, warned them that "the day of Christ shall not come, except there come a falling away first, and that man of sin be revealed, the son of perdition; who opposeth and exalteth himself above all that is called God, or that is worshipped; so that he as God sitteth in the temple of God, showing himself that he is God." And he adds, "For the mystery of iniquity doth already work." In another epistle he gives as signs of the coming apostacy, "forbidding to marry, and commanding to abstain from meats, which God hath created to be received with thanksgiving."

How fully these prophetic warnings have been verified in the history of the papal Church, let the foregoing pages testify. "COME OUT OF HER, MY PEOPLE, THAT YE BE NOT PARTAKERS OF HER SINS, AND THAT YE RECEIVE NOT OF HER PLAGUES."

PART III.

THE OLD AND NEW CREEDS CONTRASTED.

THE
OLD AND NEW CREEDS CONTRASTED.

"They undermine our truths in order to build up their errors; their work rises by destruction of truth."—TERTULLIAN, "De Præs. Hær." chap. xlii. p. 55, vol. ii. Halæ. Magd. 1770.

HAVING given, in chronological order, the various "Novelties of Romanism," their rise, progress, and final adoption into the Roman church, we earnestly invite the serious consideration of Roman Catholics to the facts set forth, that they may appreciate the wisdom of the early Christian Fathers, and of our Reformers, in adopting, as their sole rule of faith, the written word, which is fixed and certain; and from experience learn the danger of wandering into the regions of tradition, which, from its very nature, is uncertain.

The work entrusted to our reformers and martyrs was not to destroy, but, under the direction and guidance of Divine Providence, to exhume and bring to light the hidden truths which had been so long buried under the accumulated rubbish of human tradition. The principle on which they separated from the Roman church was, not that they had discovered any new views of Scripture doctrine, but that they desired to return to the primitive confession; to the views held by the apostles, as handed down to us by their writings.

The great object of our reformers was, as Bishop Jewel observed, "to approach, as much as they possibly could, to the church of the apostles and ancient Catholic bishops and fathers;"[1] and, as another testified, "to depart no further from the church of Rome than she had departed from the primitive church."[2] And so anxious and careful were they that preachers should not put forward their particular fancies, and thus fall into the other extreme, that the Upper House of Convocation, in the year 1571, directed that they "should in the first place be careful not to teach anything in their sermons, to be religiously held and believed by the people, except that which is agreeable to the doctrine of the Old and New Testaments, and which has been deduced from the same by the Catholic fathers and ancient bishops."[3] And on the re-establishment of the Protestant religion in this country, on the accession of Queen Elizabeth, the first Act of her reign (cap. i., sec. 36) was to declare that no person having authority under the Crown "to reform or correct errors, heresies, abuses, or enormities, by virtue of that Act, should in any wise have authority or power to order, determine, or adjudge any matter or cause to be heresy, but only such as theretofore had been determined, ordered, or adjudged to be heresy by the authority of the canonical Scriptures, or by the first four General Councils, or any of them, or by any other general council."

We will state in a few words what these first four General Councils taught.

Previous to the year 325, it appears that the church had not (authoritatively) drawn up a creed in a precise form of

---

[1] Jewel's Apology, p. 124. London, 1685.
[2] Neal's "History of the Puritans," vol. i. p. 38. London, 1837.
[3] Sparrow's Collection, p. 238. London, 1671.

words. What is called the "Apostles' Creed" is admitted by all Christians; but it is clear that the apostles themselves did not draw up that precise form, though it contains the doctrine they taught. Neither Clement (A.D. 68—107), Ignatius (A.D. 107), Polycarp (A.D. 108—169), nor Justin Martyr (163), have left any form of creed in their writings. We find in the writings of Irenæus (A.D. 178—202) the first form of creed, which he called the unalterable canon or rule of faith, and which, he says, in the first chapter of the first book "*Against heresies,*" every man received in baptism. He prefaces this creed with these words:—" The church, though it be dispersed over all the world from one end of the earth to the other, received from the apostles and their disciples the—

"Belief in one God, the Father Almighty, Maker of heaven and earth, the sea, and all things in them: and in one Christ Jesus, the Son of God, who was incarnate for our salvation: and in the Holy Ghost, who preached by the prophets the dispensations of God, and the advent and the being born of a Virgin, the passion, and resurrection from the dead, and bodily ascension into heaven in the flesh, of his beloved Son Jesus Christ our Lord, and his coming again from heaven, in the glory of the Father, to gather together in one all things, and raise the flesh of all mankind: that according to the will of the invisible Father, every knee should bow, both of things in heaven and things in the earth, and things under the earth to Jesus Christ our Lord and God; and that every tongue should confess to him, and that he may exercise just judgment upon all, consigning to everlasting fire all spiritual wickedness, both of the angels who transgressed and became apostates, with all ungodly, lawless, and blasphemous men; and grant life unto all them that are just and holy, that have kept his commandments, and persevere in his love, some from the beginning of their lives, others after repentance, on whom he confers immortality, and invests them with everlasting life."[1]

It is to this declaration of faith that Irenæus especially refers when he mentions the "Tradition of the Apostles," which he states they first gave by word of mouth, and afterwards handed down to us in their writings.

Tertullian (A.D. 195—218) also gives a form, which he prefaces with the words:—"There is one rule of faith only, which admits of no change or alteration." His form is as follows:—

"Believe in one God Almighty, the Maker of the world: and in Jesus Christ his Son, who was born of the Virgin Mary, crucified under Pontius Pilate, the third day arose again from the dead, was received into heaven, and sitteth at the right hand of the Father, and shall come again to judge the quick and the dead by the resurrection of the flesh."[2] * * *

We find the next form in the works of Origen (A.D. 216—253), in the "Dialogues against the Marcionites,"[3] where we read that—"The things that are manifestly handed down by the apostles' preaching are these:—

"First, there is one God, the Maker and Creator of all things, and one that is from him, God the Word, who is of one substance with him, and co-eternal: who in the last times (or last ages) took human nature upon him of the (Virgin) Mary, and was crucified, and raised again from the dead: I believe, also, the Holy Ghost, who exists from eternity."

---

[1] Iren. Adv. Hæres. cap. x. p. 50. Benedictine Edit. Paris, 1710.
[2] Regula quidem fidei una omnino est, etc. Tert. De Virginibus velandis, cap. i. vol. iii. p. 2. Edit. Halæ Magdeb. 1770. Tertullian gives another form to the same tenor or effect as the above. "De Præscriptionibus Hæreticorum," cap. 13, tom. ii. p. 17. Same edition. "Regula est autem fidei," etc. And he repeats the same, with no material variation, in his book "Adversus Praxen," chap. ii. vol. ii. p. 191.
[3] Origen, Cont. Marc. Dial. i. p. 815, tom. ii. Edit Latin. Basil, 1571. Westenius, who first published these dialogues in Greek, ascribes them to Origen; but Huet, to one Maximus, of the time of Constantine.

We have also handed down to us a form given by Gregory, bishop of Neo-Cæsarea (A.D. 255—270); and by Lucian, a presbyter of Antioch, both of which, as to doctrine, agree with the above.

But we must not pass over the form held by the church of Jerusalem, of which Cyril was bishop. It is believed to be one of the most ancient summaries of faith extant at this day. The introductory part is found in the liturgy ascribed, though without any certainty, to St. James, alleged to have been the first bishop:—

"I believe in one God the Father Almighty, Maker of heaven and earth, and of all things visible and invisible: and in one Lord Jesus Christ, the only begotten Son of God, begotten of the Father before all ages, the true God, by whom all things were made; who was incarnate, and made man, crucified and buried; and who rose again from the dead the third day, and ascended into heaven and sitteth on the right hand of the Father, and shall come to judge the quick and the dead; of whose kingdom there shall be no end: and in the Holy Ghost the Comforter, who spake by the prophets; in one baptism of repentance; in the remission of sins; and in one Catholic church; and in the resurrection of the flesh; and in life everlasting."[1]

We now come to the first form of creed formally adopted by the church, known as the "Nicene Creed," but which should more properly be called "the Nicene-Constantinopolitan Creed," which is as follows:—

"I believe in one God, the Father Almighty, Maker *of heaven and earth, and* of all things visible and invisible: and in one Lord Jesus Christ, the only begotten Son of God, *begotten of his Father before all worlds*, God of God, Light of Light, very God of very God, begotten not made, being of one substance with the Father; by whom all things were made:

[1] Cyril, Hier. Arch. Catechesis vi. p. 86. Paris, 1720.

who for us men and for our salvation came down *from heaven, and was incarnate by the Holy Ghost of the Virgin Mary*, and was made man, *and was crucified also for us under Pontius Pilate:* he suffered *and was buried,* and the third day he rose again *according to the Scriptures,* and ascended into heaven, *and sitteth on the right hand of the Father,* and shall come again *with glory* to judge both the quick and the dead, *whose kingdom shall have no end:* and *I believe* in the Holy Ghost, *the Lord and Giver of life, who proceedeth from the Father* [*and the Son*], *who with the Father and the Son together is worshipped and glorified, who spake by the prophets: and I believe one Catholic and apostolic church: I acknowledge one baptism for the remission of sins: and I look for the resurrection of the dead; and the life of the world to come.*"[1]

This creed was the joint production of those two councils, held respectively in the years 325 and 381. Those parts in italics were added by the second council. The words in brackets [ ] *filioque*,[2] "and the Son," were added by the Latin church some time after, in opposition to the Greeks, who opposed any change in the creed.

In A.D. 431, an attempt was made to alter this creed; but the Third General Council, that of Ephesus, opposed the proposition, and declared "that it should not be lawful for any one to profess, to write, or to compose any other form of faith than that defined by the holy Fathers, who, with the Holy Ghost, had assembled at Nice." And this council proceeded to declare respecting all "such as shall presume either to compose or to provide or to offer any other form of faith to those wishing to be converted to the acknowledgment of the truth, whether from paganism or from Judaism, or from any other form of heresy, that they,

---

[1] Mansi's Edit. of Councils, tom. ii. p. 665. Florentiæ, 1759.
[2] According to Baronius, this addition was first made at the Council of Toledo, A.D. 447. See Landon's "Manual of Councils," p. 579. London, 1846.

be they bishops or clergymen, should be deposed, the bishops from their episcopacy, and the clergy from their clerical office; but if laymen, they should be subjected to anathema." [1]

And again, the General Council of Chalcedon (A.D. 451), confirmed the decision of the three previous general councils; and when the creed was rehearsed, it is recorded in all the histories of this council that the assembled bishops exclaimed:—

"No person makes any other exposition of faith. We neither attempt nor dare to do so. For the Fathers have taught, and in their writings are preserved, those thing which have been set forth by them [namely, in the said creed], and other than these we cannot speak. These principles which have been set forth are sufficient; it is not lawful to make any other exposition." [2]

And so also the assembled divines at the third session of the Trent Council (not contemplating what was to follow) declared that this same creed was the—

"Summary in which all who profess the faith of Christ necessarily agree, and that firm and only foundation against which the gates of hell shall never prevail; and that it was to be recited in those words in which it was read in all the churches."

We now can appreciate the wisdom and moderation of the reformers, at the time of Elizabeth, when they declared

[1] "His igitur prælectis, statuit sancta synodus, alteram fidem nemini licere proferre, aut conscribere aut componere, præter definitam a sanctis patribus, qui in Nicæa cum Spiritu Sancto congregati fuerunt. Qui vero ausi fuerint aut componere fidem alteram, aut proferre, vel offerre converti volentibus ad agnitionem veritatis, sive ex Gentilitate, sive ex Judaismo, sive ex qualicumque hæresi: hos quidem, si sunt episcopi aut clerici, alienos esse episcopos ab episcopatu, et clericos a clericatu, decrevit, si vero laici fuerint, anathemati subjici." See Mansi's Edition of Councils as above, tom. iv. col. 1362. Florent, 1759.

[2] Ibid. tom. vi. col. 630.

that nothing should be deemed heresy but such things as had been so declared by the authority of Scripture and the first four general councils.

The church of Rome, acknowledging this Nicene-Constantinopolitan creed, in its entirety, as part of her rule of faith, has within her the truths handed down to us by the apostles in their writings, but those truths lie hidden under the accumulated rubbish of her traditions.

1. She admits the Bible to be the word of God; but she alleges that word to be imperfect, inasmuch as she declares that we can only in part learn from it our salvation; and she has, therefore, added to it certain apocryphal books and traditions.

2. She admits that God is to be adored with a supreme worship, for the Bible is explicit on this point; but she divides the honour with him by giving an inferior quality of worship—a religious worship, nevertheless—to the Virgin Mary and supposed saints; for which she can show no other authority than her traditions.

3. And for this purpose, while she admits that God is the Judge of the "quick and the dead," because the Bible tells her so, she has taken upon herself to forestall God's judgment, by dogmatically declaring, before the day of resurrection and judgment, who are actually beatified spirits in heaven! An assumption founded on a modern innovation.

4. She admits Christ as a Mediator between God and man, because she cannot set aside the plain words of Scripture; but she teaches, on her own authority, that he is not the only Mediator. She includes those canonized saints in that holy and exclusive office of our Redeemer; and, for that purpose, awards to them certain attributes of the Deity

—namely, omniscience and omnipresence; otherwise how could they hear the "mental and verbal" prayers of the living offered up at different places at the same time?

5. She admits the atonement of Christ offered up on the cross, but which was, according to St. Paul, the one sacrifice offered up "once for all." It was essential to St. Paul's doctrine that this sacrifice should not be repeated, otherwise Christ would have often suffered (Heb. ix. 26); but the church of Rome professes to offer up the same Christ daily, under the hands of her priests: thus converting that which ought to be a commemoration of the sacrifice on Calvary, to be a daily propitiatory sacrifice for the living and the dead. This she does by a perversion of the whole gospel scheme of the ONE Atonement and Redemption.

6. She admits that God is a Spirit, and is to be worshipped in spirit, for the Bible is also plain on this point; but she also declares that he is to be worshipped under the form of a consecrated piece of bread, made by men's hands—an invention of priests to increase their dignity and consequence, but degrading to the Deity.

7. She admits that God can and does pardon sin, and teaches that his clemency is reserved for the contrite; while it is left to the church, by her priests, through the (so-called) sacrament of penance, to make up what is wanting in the penitent who brings only an imperfect repentance; and thus she would save those whom God rejects: a modern invention which has not even the advantage of tradition to support it. She takes upon herself to anticipate the judgment of God by absolution of the penitent from his sin, in this life.

8. She admits that God is a dispenser of graces and mercies; but she pretends to have a share in this power by

having at her disposal an "ecclesiastical treasure" of supposed accumulated merits of departed saints—a modern invention to make money.

9. And, for this purpose, while she admits that the merits of Christ are infinite, she also declares, contrary to the doctrine of Scripture, that the justified not only can be saved by their works, or rather thereby increase their right to acceptance before God, but that they can do more than is sufficient for their own salvation: which surplus can be applied for the benefit of others who have come short of the required standard.

10. She admits that God can pardon the punishment due to the sin committed; but she takes it upon herself to anticipate that pardon, by remitting the punishments due to sin in this life, as well as even the punishment supposed to be inflicted on the departed who have not sufficiently atoned for their sins in this life; and this is supposed to be accomplished by Indulgences, a process never mentioned in Scripture.

11. And, for this latter object, while she admits the existence of heaven and hell, the Bible clearly pointing them out to us, she has invented a third place, which she calls purgatory—a place of temporal torment after this life—a fable invented to work on the fears and credulity of the people. She assumes the power of delivering souls out of purgatory, by which she enhances the power of her priests, and replenishes her coffers.

12. She will allow confession of sin to God, because the Bible sanctions it; but she declares it absolutely necessary to our salvation that we should confess to one of her priests, at least once a year: a piece of priestcraft, the value of which is well appreciated.

13. She admits that Christ instituted two sacraments, baptism and the supper of the Lord, but to them she has added five others; but practically she denies us the benefit of all these by declaring that such benefit shall depend on the intention of the officiating priest: a modern invention, the object of which it is difficult to comprehend.

Such, then, are a few of the leading truths admitted by all classes of Christians, put in contrast with the errors which the church of Rome has superadded. "How has the pure gold become dross" in her hands! The reformers did nothing more than bring us back to that faith "once delivered to the saints," which had long been hid—buried under the novelties and innovations of successive ages, the inventions of a corrupt priesthood. The reformers "came not to destroy," but to uphold the doctrine of the apostles, which the church of Rome had practically rendered of none effect by her traditions.

A popular preacher has graphically represented the work of the reformation by an illustrative incident recorded in the travels of Lord Lindsay in Egypt:—

"He [Lord Lindsay] states, that in the course of his wanderings amid the pyramids of that patriarchal and interesting land, he stumbled on a mummy, proved by its hieroglyphics to be at least 2000 years of age. In examining the mummy, after it was unwrapped, he found in one of its closed hands a tuberous or bulbous root. He was interested in the question how long vegetable life could last: and he therefore took that tuberous root from the mummy's hand, planted it in a sunny soil, allowed the rains and dews of heaven to descend upon it, and in the course of a few weeks, to his astonishment and joy, that root burst forth and bloomed into a beauteous flower. It seemed to me that we have in this an answer to the question, Where was Protestantism before the Reformation? It was closed in the iron grasp of the Roman apostasy, and all that the Reformers did was to unclench that terrible hand, and extricate the seed of truth. Sowers started up in all lands, and planted it in England, in Scotland, and in Germany; and now the living seeds, through the blessing of God, have spread forth and grown up in all countries, and the vast number of churches scattered throughout the land are its blossoms."

The utmost Rome can claim for her innovations is custom, and for some few of them antiquity. We cannot more appropriately close our remarks than by recording the opinion of a venerable bishop of the church of Christ, and a martyr of the third century, Cyprian, bishop of Carthage, on these two claims. He wrote :—

"Custom, without truth, is but the antiquity of error; and there is a short way for religious and simple minds to find out what is truth. For if we return to the beginning and original of divine tradition, human error ceases. Thither let us return, to our Lord's original, the evangelical beginning, the apostolical tradition, and hence let the reason of our acts arise; from hence order and the beginning arose.

"If, therefore, Christ alone is to be the Head, we ought not to regard what another, before us, thought fit to be done, but what Christ, who is above all, did. For we ought not to follow the customs of man, but the TRUTH OF GOD; since God himself speaks thus by the Prophet Isaiah, 'In vain do they worship me, teaching for doctrines the commandments of men.' Which very words our Lord again repeats in the Gospel: 'Ye reject the commandment of God that ye may keep your own tradition.'"[1]

And once more. Tertullian, of the second century, and the earliest of the Latin Fathers, said :—

"No one is able to raise any prescription against the truth—

---

[1] Cyprian, Epist. lxiii ad Cæcelium Fratrum, p. 155, et lxxiv. ad Pompeium, p. 215. Edit. Oxon, 1682.

not space of time, nor the patronage of persons, nor the privilege of countries. From these things, indeed, custom, having gotten a beginning, by ignorance or simplicity, and being grown strong by succession, pleads against the truth. But our Lord Christ calls himself the Truth, not custom. Nor does novelty so much confute heresy as does truth. Whatsoever is against truth, that will be heresy—even old custom."[1]

[1] "..Hoc exigere veritatem, cui nemo præscribere potest, non spatium temporum, non patrocinia personarum, non privilegium regionum. Ex his enim fere consuetudo initium ab aliquâ ignorantiâ vel simpliciate sortita, in usum per successionem corroboratur, et ita adversus veritatem vindicatur. Sed dominus noster Christus veritatem se, non consuetudinem, cognominavit. Si semper Christus, et prior omnibus: æque veritas sempiterna et antiqua res. Viderint ergo quibus novum est quod sibi vetus est. Hæreseis non tam novitas quam veritas revincit. Quodcunque adversus veritatem sapit, hoc erit hæresis, etiam vetus consuetudo." Tertullian de Virginibus velandis. cap. i. *in init.* pp. 1, 2, vol. iii. Halæ Magd. 1770.

APPENDICES.

APPENDIX A.

EXTRACT FROM THE TREATISE OF BERTRAM[1] OF CORBY.

Quod in Ecclesia ore fidelium sumitur corpus et sanguis Christi, quærit vestræ magnitudinis excellentia, in mysterio fiat, an in veritate. Id est: Utrum aliquid secreti contineat, quod oculis fidei solummodo pateat! An, sine cujuscunque velatione mysterii, hoc aspectus, intueatur corporis exterius, quod mentis visus inspiciat interius, ut totum, quod agitur in manifestationis luce clarescat; et utrum ipsum corpus sit, quod de Maria natum est et passum, mortuum et sepultum, quodque resurgens et cœlos ascendens ad dextram Patris consideat.

The Excellency of your Highness asks me whether the body and blood of Christ, which, in the church, is received by the mouth of the faithful, is produced, only in a mystery or in reality. In other words, you ask me whether it contains somewhat secret, which is manifest to the eye of faith exclusively; or whether, without the veil of any mystery, the corporeal eye beholds that externally which the mental eye beholds internally, so that to the broad light of day the whole transaction is clear and open; whether, in short, it be the identical body, which was born from Mary and suffered, and died and was buried, and which, rising again, and ascending to heaven, sits at the right hand of the Father.

[1] Bertram. Presbyt. de Corp. et Sanguin. Domin., pp. 180, 222. Edit. Colon. 1551, or p. v.—lxxxix. Oxon. 1838. This work was addressed to Charles the Bald; but the Cologne Editors erroneously state that it was to Charlemagne. Bertram relies throughout on the great Fathers of the Church, Ambrose, bishop of Milan, and Augustine, bishop of Hippo. He flourished in the 9th century.

Harum duarum quæstionum primam inspiciamus: et, ne dubietatis ambage detineamur, definiamus, quid sit figura, quid veritas; ut, certum aliquid contuentes, noverimus quo rationis iter contendere debeamus.

Figura est adumbratio quædam, quibusdam velaminibus quod intendit ostendens. Verbi gratia, verbum volentes dicere, panem nuncupamus. Sicut, in oratione dominica, panem quotidianum dari nobis expostulamus: vel cum Christus in Evangelio loquitur, dicens, 'Ego sum panis vivus, de cœlo descendi:' vel cum seipsum 'vitem,' discipulos autem palmites, appellat, 'Ego sum' dicens 'vitis vera vos palmites;' hæc enim omnia aliud dicunt, et aliud innuunt.

Veritas, vero, est rei manifestæ demonstratio, nullis umbrarum imaginibus obvelatæ, sed puris et apertis (utque planius eloquamur) naturalibus significationibus insinuatæ: utpote cum dicitur, Christus natus de Virgine, passus, crucifixus, mortuus, et sepultus. Nihil enim hic figuris obvelantibus adumbratur; verum rei veritas, naturalium significationibus verborum,

Of these two questions, let us begin by inspecting the first; and, lest we should be detained by the windings of dubiety, let us set out with explicitly defining what is figure, and what is reality.

Figure, then, is a certain adumbration, showing its import under certain coverings. For example, wishing to mention the Word, we name bread. Thus, for instance, when, in the Lord's Prayer, we beg for our daily bread; or when Christ, in the Gospel, says 'I am the living bread which descended from heaven;' or when he calls himself the 'vine,' and his disciples the 'branches:' all these expressions say one thing, but mean another.

Reality, on the contrary, is the demonstration of a thing manifest, veiled in no images of shadows, but expressed in plain, and open, and natural significance; as when we say that Christ was born of the Virgin, that he suffered, that he was crucified, that he died, and that he was buried. For nothing is here shadowed out under the veil of figures; but the reality of the matter is

ostenditur: neque aliud hic, licet intelligi, quàm dicitur.

At, in superioribus, non ita; nam, substantialiter, nec panis Christus, nec vitis Christus nec palmites apostoli. Quapropter, hic figura; superiori vero veritas in narratione monstratur; id est, nuda et aperta significatio.

Nunc redeamus ad illa, quorum causa dicta sunt ista; videlicet, corpus et sanguinem Christi.

Si enim nulla sub figura mysterium illud peragitur, jam mysterium non rite vocitatur: quum mysterium dici non potest, in quo nihil est abditum, nihil a corporalibus sensibus remotum, nihil aliquo velamine contectum. At ille panis, quod per sacerdotis ministerium Christi corpus efficitur, aliud interiùs [? exteriùs] humanis sensibus ostendit, et aliud interiùs fidelium mentibus clamat.—Vinum quoque, quod sacerdotali consecratione Christi sanguinis efficitur sacramentum, aliud

shown forth in the plain signification of natural words; nor can we here understand anything beyond what is absolutely spoken.

In the former instances, however, it was not so; for, substantially, Christ is neither bread, nor a vine, nor yet are the apostles branches. Wherefore, here, there is figure; but, there, reality is displayed in the statement; that is, the meaning is open and manifest.

Let us now return to those matters, for the sake of which these definitions have been laid down: I mean the " body and blood of Christ."

If that mystery be not celebrated under a figure, it cannot rightly be called a mystery; because the name of mystery cannot justly be applied to that in which there is nothing hidden, nothing remote from the bodily senses, nothing hidden by a veil. But that bread which, through the ministration of the priest, is made the body of Christ, shows one thing internally [? externally] to the human senses, and speaks another way to the minds of the faithful.—The wine also which,

superficie tenus ostendit, aliud interius continet.—Hæc ita esse, dum nemo potest abnegare, claret, quia panis ille vinumque figurate Christi corpus et sanguinis existet.—Nam, si, secundum quosdam, figurate nihil hic accipiatur, sed totum in veritate conspiciatur; nihil hic fides operatur: quum nihil spirituale geritur; sed, quicquid illud est, totum secundum corpus accipitur. —Secundum speciem namque creaturæ formamque rerum visibilium, utrumque hoc, id est, panis et vinum, nihil habent in se permutatum. Et, si nihil permutationis pertulerunt, nihil aliud existunt quàm quod priùs fuere.—

Jam nunc secundæ quæstionis propositum est inspiciendum, et videndum; utrum ipsum corpus, quod de Maria natum est et passum, mortuum et sepultum, quodque ad dexteram Patris consideat, sit quod ore fidelium per sacramentorum mysterium in ecclesia quotidie sumitur.—

through sacerdotal consecration, is made the sacrament of the blood of Christ, shows one thing superficially, but contains another thing internally. —Since, then, no person can deny that such is the case, it is manifest that that bread and wine are the body and blood of Christ figuratively.—For if, as some pretend, nothing is here received figuratively, but the whole is discerned in reality, then there is no room for the operation of faith; inasmuch as nothing spiritual is transacted, but the whole is received according to the body.—According to the appearance of the creature, and the form of things visible, neither the bread nor the wine experience in themselves any transmutation. Therefore, if they have experienced no transmutation, they are nothing else but what they were before.

Let us now pass to the second question, and let us consider whether the identical body, which was born from Mary, and suffered, and died, and was buried, and which now sits at the right hand of the Father, is that which in the church is daily received by the mouth of the faithful,

APPENDIX A. 291

Secundum creaturarum substantiam, quod fuerunt ante consecrationem, hoc et postea consistunt. Panis et vinum priùs extitere: in qua etiam specie, jam consecrata, permanere videntur.—Nihil igitur hic corporaliter; sed spiritualiter sentiendum. Corpus Christi est, sed non corporaliter: et sanguis Christi est, sed non corporaliter.—Corpus, quod sumpsit de Maria Virgine, quod passum, quod sepultum est, quod resurrexit, corpus utique verum fuit; idem, quod visibile atque palpabile manebat; at vero corpus, quod mysterium Dei dicitur, non est corporale, sed spirituale.—Differunt, autem, caro spiritualis quæ fidelium ore sumiter, et sanguis spiritualis qui quotidie credentibus potandus exhibitur, a carne quæ crucifixa est, et a sanguine qui militis effusus est lancea. Non idem igitur sunt.—

In orationibus, quæ post mysterium sanguinis et corporis Christi dicuntur, et a populo

through the mystery of the sacraments.—

According to the substance of the creatures, what they were before consecration, that also they are after it; previous to consecration they were bread and wine; and in that same appearance, when consecrated, they are seen still to remain.—Nothing is here transacted corporeally; but it must be spiritually apprehended. It is the body of Christ—but not corporeally: it is the blood of Christ—yet not corporeally.—The body, which Christ received from the Virgin Mary, which suffered, which was buried, which rose again, was a real body; the same which remained visible and palpable; but the body, which is called the mystery of God, is not corporeal, but spiritual.—Spiritual flesh which is received by the mouth of the faithful, and spiritual blood which is daily given to be drunk by the faithful, differ from the flesh which was crucified and from the blood which was shed by the lance of the soldier. Therefore they are not the same.—

In the prayers, which are recited after the mysteries of the blood and body of Christ,

responditur *Amen*, sic sacerdotis voce dicetur :—

Pignus æternæ vitæ capientes, humiliter imploramus, ut, quod imagine contingimus sacramenti, manifesta sacramenti, manifesta participatione sumamus.

Et pignus enim et imago alterius rei sunt : id est, non ad se, sed ad aliud, aspiciunt.—Pignus enim illius rei est, pro qua donatur; imago illius, cujus similitudinem ostendit.—Qua de re et corpus Christi et sanguis est, quod Ecclesia celebrat; sed tamquam pignus, tamquam imago.—

Videmus, itaque, multa differentia separari, mysterium sanguinis et corporis Christi quod nunc a fidelibus sumitur in Ecclesia, et illud quod natum est de Virgine Maria, quod passum, quod sepultum, quod resurrexit, quod cœlos ascendit, quod ad dexteram Patris sedet.

and to which the people respond *Amen*, the priest uses the following language :—

"Receiving the pledge of eternal life, we humbly beseech Thee, that whatsoever in the sacrament we touch in the image we may receive the same by manifest participation."

Now, a pledge and an image, are a pledge and an image of some other thing; that is, they have respect, not to themselves, but to something else. For a pledge is a pledge of the thing for which it is given, and an image is an image of that whereof it shows forth the similitude.— Therefore, also, that which the church celebrates is the body and blood of Christ; but still, as a pledge; but still, as an image.—

We see, then, that the mystery of the blood and body of Christ, which is now received in the church by the faithful, is separated by a mighty difference from that which was born of the Virgin Mary, which suffered, which was buried, which rose again, which ascended to heaven, which sits at the right hand of the Father.

APPENDIX B.

BULL OF POPE PIUS IV.

"TOUCHING THE FORM OF THE OATH OF THE PROFESSION OF FAITH."

" PIUS, Bishop, Servant of the Servants of God, for the perpetual memory hereof.

The office of Apostolic servitude enjoined on us requires, that those matters, which Almighty God has vouchsafed divinely to inspire into the minds of the holy Fathers, assembled in His name for the provident guidance of his Church, we should hasten unhesitatingly to execute, unto His praise and glory. Whereas, therefore, according to the resolution of the Council of Trent, all who may happen henceforward to be placed over cathedral and superior churches, or who may have to take care respecting their dignities, canonries, and any other ecclesiastical benefices soever having the care of souls, are bound to make a public profession of the orthodox faith, and to promise and swear that they will continue in obedience to the Church of Rome; we, willing that the same thing be observed likewise by all persons soever, who shall have the charge of monasteries, convents, houses, and any other places soever, of all regular orders soever, and besides, to the end that the profession of one and the same faith be uniformly exhibited by all, and that one only, and a certain form of it, made known unto all, We, [willing] that a want of our solicitude should by no means be felt by any one in this particular, by strictly prescribing the tenor of those presents, We, by virtue of Our Apostolic authority, command, that the form itself be published, and be received and observed everywhere by those whom it concerns, in consequence of the decrees of the Council itself, as well as the other particulars aforesaid, and that the aforesaid profession be made solemnly according to this, and no other form, under the penalties enacted by the Council itself against all contravening, under the following terms :—

" I, N., believe and profess, with a firm faith, all and every one of the things which are contained in the symbol of faith which is used in the Holy Roman Church, namely :—

" I. I believe in one God, the Father Almighty, Maker of Heaven and Earth, &c.—[*The Nicene Creed.*]

" 2. I most firmly admit and embrace Apostolical and Ecclesiastical Traditions, and all other constitutions and observances, of the same Church.

" 3. I also admit the Sacred Scriptures according to the sense which the Holy Mother Church has held, and does hold, to whom it belongs to judge of the true sense and interpretation of the Holy Scriptures; nor will I ever take or interpret them otherwise than according to the unanimous consent of the Fathers.

" 4. I profess, also, that there are truly and properly Seven Sacraments of the New Law, instituted by Jesus Christ our Lord, and for the salvation of mankind, though all are not necessary for every one ; namely, Baptism, Confirmation, Eucharist, Penance, Extreme Unction, Orders, and Matrimony; and that they confer grace; and of these, Baptism, Confirmation, and Orders, cannot be reiterated without sacrilege.

" 5. I receive and admit the Ceremonies of the Catholic Church, received and approved in the solemn administration of all the above said Sacraments.

" 6. I receive and embrace all and every one of the things which have been defined in the holy Council of Trent, concerning Original Sin and Justification.

" 7. I profess, likewise, that in the Mass is offered to the true God, proper and propitiatory sacrifice for the living and the dead; and that in the most holy Sacrifice of the Eucharist there is really, truly, and substantially, the body and blood, together with the soul and divinity, of our Lord Jesus Christ; and there is made a conversion of the whole substance of the bread into the body, and of the whole substance of the wine into the blood, which conversion the Church calls Transubstantiation.

"8. I confess, also, that under either kind alone, whole and entire, Christ and a true sacrament are received.

"9. I constantly hold that there is a Purgatory, and that the souls detained there are helped by the suffrages of the faithful.

"10. Likewise, that the Saints reigning together with Christ are to be honoured and invocated with Christ; that they offer prayers to God for us, and that their relics are to be venerated.

"11. I most firmly assert, that the Images of Christ and of the Mother of God ever Virgin, and also of the other Saints, are to be had and retained, and that due honour and veneration are to be given them.

"12. I also affirm, that the power of Indulgences was left by Christ in the Church, and that the use of them is most wholesome to Christian people.

"13. I acknowledge the Holy Catholic and Apostolical and Roman Church THE MOTHER AND MISTRESS OF ALL CHURCHES, AND I PROMISE AND SWEAR TRUE OBEDIENCE TO THE ROMAN BISHOP, the successor of St. Peter the Prince of the Apostles and the Vicar of Jesus Christ.

"14. I also profess and undoubtedly receive, all other things delivered, defined, and declared by the Sacred Canon, and General Councils, and particularly by the Council of Trent; and likewise, I also condemn, reject, and anathematize all things contrary thereto, and all heresies whatsoever, condemned, rejected, and anathematized by the Church.

"15. This true Catholic Faith, OUT OF WHICH NO ONE CAN BE SAVED, which I now freely profess, and truly hold, I, N., promise, vow, and swear, most constantly to hold and profess the same, whole and entire, with God's assistance, to the end of my life; *and to procure as far as lies in my power, that the same shall be held, taught, and preached by all who are under me, or are entrusted to my care by virtue of my office. So help me God, and these Holy Gospels of God."*

The foregoing is the translation given by Charles Butler, Esq., an eminent Roman Catholic layman, in his work of "The Roman Catholic Church," London, 1825, except those parts in *italics*, which he has thought proper to omit; and we, therefore, give this last clause, 15, from the original:

"15. Hanc veram Catholicam fidem, extra quam nemo salvus esse potest, quam in præsenti sponte profiteor, et veraciter teneo, eandem integram, et inviolatam, usque ad extremum vitæ spiritum constantissime (Deo adjuvante) retinere et confiteri, atque a meis subditis, vel illis quorum cura ad me in munere meo spectabit, teneri, doceri et prædicari, quantum in me erit curaturum, ego idem N. spondeo, voveo, ac juro, Sic me Deus adjuvet, et hæc sancta Dei evangelia."

Concil. Trid. apud Bullas, p. 381, *et seq.*, *Romæ*, 1564.

THE END.

www.ingramcontent.com/pod-product-compliance
Lightning Source LLC
Chambersburg PA
CBHW030016240426
43672CB00007B/970